The Gartner Group
Glossary of
Information Technology
Acronyms and Terms

About Gartner Group and InfoEdge

Gartner Group, Inc., is the world's leading independent advisor to business professionals making information technology (IT) decisions. The company provides research, analysis and advice on strategies for users, purchasers and vendors of IT products and services. Concise, actionable advice saves you time, money and resources while increasing your success.

With more than 430 analysts in 75 locations worldwide, Gartner Group provides its more than 7,400 client organizations and over 28,000 clients around the world with timely, strategic advice on the application, management, measurement, market research and direction of IT, and training on IT.

InfoEdge was established in January 1993 and is based in Stamford, Connecticut. Through a unique licensing arrangement, InfoEdge has the right to market and distribute selected Gartner Group Executive Summary Reports, conference audiotapes and multimedia CD-ROMs. InfoEdge publishes, markets and distributes its products worldwide using the latest in telemarketing and direct mail techniques. InfoEdge is dedicated to giving information technology managers "the EDGE on information technology" by providing the tools necessary to navigate through critical IT issues today . . . and tomorrow.

The Gartner Group Glossary of Information Technology Acronyms and Terms

Editors:
Ned Frey, Lucy Hedrick, George Hoza,
Gisela Moriarty, Ed Younker

October 1997 editon

Order code #5404
ISBN 1-891234-00-5

Book design by Gay Christie

Published by:
InfoEdge, Inc. • Two Stamford Landing • Stamford • Connecticut 06902-7649 • U.S.A.

Introduction

This Glossary is a comprehensive collection of information technology (IT) acronyms and terms. The definitions and illustrations were written by Gartner Group analysts. The book is updated every two years so new terms can be included and the obsolete discarded.

Due to the proliferation of acronyms in speech as well as written communications, the definitions in this Glossary are attached to the acronyms. Therefore, under ATM, the reader will find "asyncronous transfer mode" and its definition, whereas under "asynchronous transfer mode," the reader will find the cross reference "See ATM."

Entries are arranged alphabetically, and spaces are ignored, along with hyphens and slashes. Numbers and symbols can be found at the beginning of the book. The editors have chosen to reflect correct capitalization, using lower case unless terms are product names, associations or industry standards.

The Gartner Group Glossary of Information Technology Acronyms and Terms

Contents

Numbers

10Base-T
An Institute of Electrical and Electronics Engineers (IEEE) standard enabling transport of 10 megabits per second (Mbps) Ethernet local-area network (LAN) traffic over unshielded twisted-pair wiring.

24x7 (24 hours a day, seven days a week) or 24x365 (24 hours a day, 365 days a year)
Continuous availability: 24 hours a day, seven days a week. A continuously available system exhibits two characteristics: high availability and continuous operations. High availability means that the service tolerates unscheduled outages. Continuous operations means that the service does not require scheduled downtime.

3GL (third-generation language)
A high-level programming language such as FORTRAN, COBOL, BASIC, Pascal and C, intermediate to machine language.

3270
The generic term for IBM's synchronous, interactive terminal environment.

3380
An IBM direct-access storage device (DASD) family first introduced in 1980.

3390
An IBM family of DASD device first introduced in 1989.

3420
A family of IBM half-inch open-reel tape drives introduced in 1970, offering densities of up to 6,250 bits per inch.

3480
An IBM cartridge tape subsystem first introduced in 1984.

3745
An IBM front-end processor (FEP) that offers significant performance and availability improvements over the 3725 FEP. The 3745 was introduced in 1988.

3880
A family of IBM DASD controllers introduced in 1980, supporting a wide range of devices (3340, 3344, 3350, 3370, 3375 and 3380).

3990
An IBM DASD controller family introduced in 1987, supporting a wide range of devices (3380, 3390, 9340 and RAMAC).

4GL (fourth-generation language)
A high-level language suitable for end-user or programmer data access and capable of reasonably complex data manipulation. It includes two categories of software development tools: application generators for production applications, and information generators for decision-support applications. 4GLs are relatively nonprocedural and easier to use than 3GLs (e.g., COBOL, FORTRAN and C), but are less powerful and more wasteful of computer resources. Gartner Group uses a three-part classification for 4GLs:

- A procedural language integrated with a database management system. Examples include Ideal (Computer Associates) and Natural (Software AG).
- An information generator. Examples include FOCUS (Information Builders), Nomad 2 (Must Software) and Ramis (Computer Associates).
- A code generator or nonprocedural tool. Examples include SQL*Forms (Oracle) and Telon (Computer Associates). These tools are also called lower-CASE tools.

4381
An IBM midrange processor family introduced in 1984.

80x86
A family of Intel microprocessors used in IBM and IBM-compatible PCs and workstations.

9370
A family of midrange S/370 processors introduced in 1986 for the low end of the S/370 product line.

AA (automated attendant)
A device that is connected to a private branch exchange (PBX). Automated attendants are connected to voice mail systems. When a call comes in, this device answers it.

AAEC (American Association of Electronic Commerce)

AAL (ATM adaptation layer)
The "glue" that connects traditional packet and frame structures and multimedia data types with short, fixed-length asynchronous transfer mode (ATM) cells.

AAL2
ATM adaptation layer 2 for compressed video.

AB (Allen-Bradley)

ABC (activity-based costing)
An improved approach to understanding where and why costs are incurred within an organization. It provides the information for activity-based management, which focuses on the decisions and actions needed to reduce costs and increase revenue. ABC differs from traditional cost accounting in explicitly recognizing that not all cost objects place an equal demand on support resources.

ABI (application binary interface)
A set of specifications provided by AT&T that enable vendors that have chosen the same microprocessor to build object-code-compatible systems. The most prominent examples of ABIs are those for Scalable Processor Architecture (SPARC), the Motorola 88000 and the Intel 80x86. Systems built to the 80x86 ABI will not be object-code compatible with those built to the SPARC ABI or the 88000 ABI; ABIs enable compatibility only among products built on the same microprocessor architectures.

ABR (available bit rate)
An asynchronous transfer mode (ATM) service category, defined by the ATM forum and conceptually similar to a frame relay network, in which a minimal cell rate (MCR) will be guaranteed and bursts can be supported if the network resources allow it.

ACA (Application Control Architecture — Digital Equipment)

access line
The connection to the customer's local telephone company for origination of local and long-distance calls. It also represents the connection between the serving toll center and the serving office of the interexchange carrier used

---

for access to public switched network services. Also known as local loop or trunk.

access method
That part of a computer's operating system responsible for formatting of data sets and their direction to specific storage devices. Examples from the mainframe world include Virtual Storage Access Method (VSAM) and Indexed Sequential Access Method (ISAM). In a network, it is the technique by which the network distributes the right to transmit among its participating stations.

access point (See AP)

access to 3270 Data Stream
A facility that enables user-written programs to become "users" of terminal-based applications on an IBM mainframe. Common use would be in accessing applications under Customer Information Control System (CICS), Information Management System (IMS) and others.

ACD (automatic call distributor)
A specialized phone system that handles many incoming calls used, for example for order taking, help desks or dispatching service technicians. An ACD performs the following functions: It recognizes and answers an incoming call. It will look in its database for instructions on what to do with that call. Based on these instructions, it will send the call to a recording or to a voice response unit (VRU). It will then send the call to an agent as soon as that operator has completed his or her previous call, or after the caller has heard the prerecorded message.

ACE (Advanced Computing Environment)
A consortium founded in April 1991 — made up of vendors using or intending to use MIPS

Computer Systems' reduced instruction set computer (RISC) processor architecture or Intel's 80x86 microprocessor — whose goal was to establish at least source code compatibility between Santa Cruz Operation (SCO) and System V Release 4 (SVR4) Unix systems on either RISC or Intel products, as well as source compatibility of Windows NT systems on RISC or Intel systems. The primary founding members were Digital Equipment, Compaq Computer, MIPS Computer Systems, SCO and Microsoft.

ACF (Advanced Communications Function)
The generic name for a family of IBM licensed programs consisting mainly of VTAM, TCAM, NCP and SSP programs that use the principles of Systems Network Architecture (SNA) and include the distribution of function and resource sharing.

ACF2 (Access Control Facility 2 — Computer Associates — also called CA-ACF2)

ACF/NCP (See NCP)

ACF/VTAM (Advanced Communications Function/Virtual Terminal Access Method)
Part of the IBM family of Systems Network Architecture (SNA) communications products; provides support for LU 6.2, the logical unit for IBM's Advanced Program-to-Program Communications (APPC).

ACH (automated clearinghouse)

ACID (atomicity, consistency, isolation, durability)
Four well-established tests for verifying the integrity of business transactions in a data-processing environment.

ACM (Association for Computing Machinery)

ACMS (Application Control and Management System)
Digital Equipment's transaction processing (TP) monitor.

ACR (architecture conformance review)
Designed to achieve an alignment between information technology strategy and a major external force — vendors. It is a periodic, formal review of the enterprise's objectives and enterprise information architecture (EIA). It is intended to provide vendors with a clear direction regarding the enterprise's technology requirements during the next five years — requirements that will dictate acquisitions and determine vendor participation. More importantly, the ACR provides the enterprise with vendors' estimates of which products they will offer to conform to selected standards and when those products will be available during the next five years. Thus, the ACR, with the EIA, provides the structure to build and maintain a clear and comprehensive vision, and the means to manage (along with vendors in a positive working relationship) the implementation of that vision from a product perspective.

ACS (Affiliated Computer Systems)

active data dictionary
A facility for storing dynamically accessible and modifiable information relating to midrange-system data definitions and descriptions.

ActiveX
An application programming interface (API) that enhances Microsoft's Object Linking and Embedding (OLE) protocol. Often compared to Java, ActiveX facilitates various Internet applications, and therefore extends and enhances the functionality of Microsoft's Internet Explorer browser. Like Java, ActiveX enables the development of interactive content. When an ActiveX-aware browser encounters a Web page that includes an unfamiliar feature, it automatically installs the appropriate applications so the feature can be used. For ActiveX to be effective, Web pages must conform to standards established by Microsoft. While not a direct replacement for Java, ActiveX will allow Microsoft and other Windows software to gain some of the portability of Java applets.

activity-based costing (See ABC)

actuator
The mechanism that positions the disk read-write head over the selected track.

AD (applications development)

adaptive control
A control strategy that automatically changes the type or influence of control parameters to improve overall control system performance.

Adaptive Differential Pulse Code Modulation (See ADPCM)

ADE (applications development environment)

ADF (Application Development Facility — IBM)

Adjunct Switch Application Interface (See ASAI)

Adobe Type Manager (See ATM)

ADPCM (Adaptive Differential Pulse Code Modulation)

A speech-coding method that calculates the difference between two consecutive speech samples in standard pulse code modulation (PCM) coded telecommunications voice signals. This calculation is encoded using an adaptive filter and, as a result, is transmitted at a rate lower than the standard 64 kilobits per second (Kbps) technique. Typically, ADPCM allows an analog voice conversation to be carried within a 32-kilobit digital channel; three or four bits are used to describe each sample, which represents the difference between two adjacent samples. Sampling is done 8,000 times a second. In short, ADPCM, which many voice processing makers use, allows encoding of voice signals in half the space PCM allows.

ADSI (analog display services interface)

ADSL (Asymmetric Digital Subscriber Line)

ADSL is Bellcore's term for one-way T1 to the home over single twisted-pair wiring already existing in homes. ADSL is designed to carry video to the home and is one-way video with control signals returning from the home at 16 kilobits per second (Kbps). ADSL uses adaptive digital filtering, which adjusts to compensate for noise and other problems on the line. ADSL is expected to cause an explosion in potential applications including video-on-demand.

ADSM (ADSTAR Distributed Storage Manager)

An IBM software product that enables a user to manage storage, data access and backup across multivendor enterprisewide networks. ADSM supports five different server platforms and 10 different client platforms. Server platforms supported are IBM's VM, MVS, AIX, OS/400 and OS/2. Clients supported are DOS, OS/2, Macintosh, SunOS, Novell NetWare, AIX, Microsoft Windows, HP-UX, Digital Equipment Ultrix and SCO Unix.

ADSTAR Distributed Storage Manager (See ADSM)

ADSL

Asymmetrical Digital Subscriber Line Technology

Advanced Communications Function (See ACF)

Advanced Communications Function/ Virtual Terminal Access Method (See ACF/ VTAM)

Advanced Computing Environment (See ACE)

Advanced Function Printing (See AFP)

Advanced Function Printing Data Stream (See AFPDS)

Advanced Interactive Executive (See AIX)

Advanced Peer-to-Peer Networking (See APPN)

Advanced Peer-to-Peer Networking Topology and Accounting Management (See APPNTAM)

Advanced Program-to-Program Communication (See APPC)

advanced ship notice (See ASN)

advanced technology
A technology that is still immature but promises to deliver significant value, or that has some technical maturity but still has relatively few users. Among current examples: artificial intelligence, agents, speech and handwriting recognition, virtual reality and 3-D visualization, smart cards, real-time collaboration, enhanced user authentication, data mining, and knowledge management.

AFP (Advanced Function Printing)
An IBM all-points-addressable enterprisewide print architecture. IBM has delivered AFP platforms for AS/400 and OS/2 environments, which has enabled IS organizations to build enterprisewide AFP architectures for distributed printing.

AFP (AppleTalk Filing Protocol)

agent technology
Software that acts as an intermediary for a person by performing some activity. Agents can "learn" an individual's preferences and are intended to act in the person's best interest. For example, an agent for a purchasing manager could learn the corporate specifications.

AHP (analytical hierarchy process)
A process that uses hierarchical decomposition to deal with complex information in multicriteria decision making, such as information technology vendor and product evaluation. It consists of three steps: 1) developing the hierarchy of attributes germane to the selection of the IT vendor, 2) identifying the relative importance of the attributes, and 3) scoring the alternatives' relative performance on each element of the hierarchy. Developed by Thomas Saaty while he was teaching at the University of Pennsylvania's Wharton School of Business, the AHP is recognized as the leading theory in multicriteria decision making.

AI (artificial intelligence)
Computer systems that attempt to resolve problems by "reasoning," similar to the process used by the human mind. Commercially applicable topics include problem-solving techniques, learning, reasoning, speech, language comprehension, vision and robotics.

AIA (Applications Integration Architecture)
A set of Digital Equipment architecture and product development programs intended to provide a common application programming interface (API) across the VAX/VMS and Ultrix operating systems.

AIIM (Association for Information and Image Management)
A Maryland-based organization dedicated to promoting development of systems that store, retrieve and manage document images.

AIM
A proprietary benchmark designed and administered by AIM Technology, Santa Clara, Calif. AIM measures the performance of multiuser Unix systems. AIM is routinely quoted by system vendors and often required in requests for proposals.

AIR (architecture implementation review)
Designed to enable an alignment between information technology strategy and implementation, this review, which involves both information systems managers and end users, assures that tactical initiatives such as product acquisitions support the enterprise information architecture and, therefore, the business and technology objectives. The AIR can be a periodic, formal review or it can be ongoing (for example, each time the enterprise distributes a request for proposal for information technology equipment).

AIX (Advanced Interactive Executive)
The Unix operating system delivered by IBM for its mainframe, workstation and PC hardware.

ALE (Advanced Linking and Embedding)
SAP AG's proprietary middleware.

ALE (Application Link Enabling)

ALL-IN-1
Digital Equipment's VAX/VMS-based second-generation integrated office information system.

Alpha
Digital Equipment's proprietary VAX replacement architecture, based on 64-bit addressing

ALUW

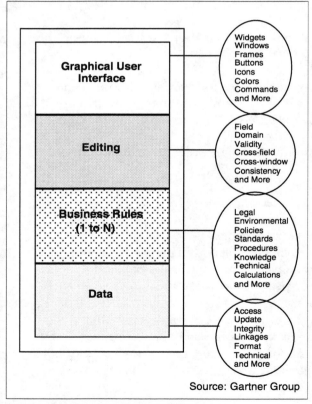

Source: Gartner Group

Application Logical Unit of Work

and reduced instruction set computer (RISC) processing techniques.

ALUW (application logical unit of work)
A design container that developers define for allocation across client/server environments. It is useful in designing enterprise client/server applications of a scope and complexity beyond traditional applications.

AMD (Advanced Micro Devices)

American National Standards Institute (See ANSI)

American Standard Code for Information Interchange (See ASCII)

AMIS (Audio Messaging Interchange Specification)
An enhanced key system feature for voice/call processing that enables enterprise locations to transfer and forward voice messages between systems.

AMPS (advanced mobile phone services)

analog
Information presented in the form of a continuously varying signal.

analytical hierarchy process (See AHP)

ANI (automatic number identification)

A series of digits, in either analog or digital form, which tells a user the originating number of the incoming phone call. They may arrive as touch-tone digits inside the call, on the same circuit or on a separate circuit. Specialized equipment is required to decipher the digits of the incoming call. ANI is touted as one of Integrated Services Digital Network's (ISDN's) most compelling advantages. However, it is also an advantage of Signaling System 7 (SS7). In the United States, there are various types of ANI. A long-distance phone company can provide ANI, which may arrive over the D channel of an ISDN primary rate interface (PRI) circuit or via a dedicated single line before the first ring. In contrast, the signaling for caller ID, as delivered

AM

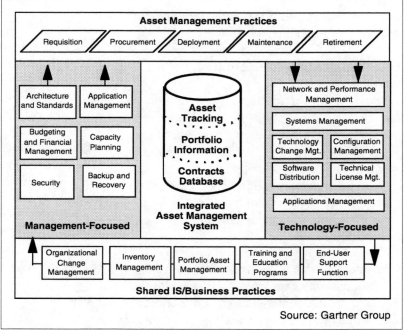

Integrated Asset Management Practices

by a local phone company, is delivered between the first and second rings.

ANSI (American National Standards Institute)

In the United States, ANSI serves as a quasi-national standards organization. It provides "area charters" for groups that establish standards in specific fields. These groups include the Institute of Electrical and Electronics Engineers (IEEE) and the Electronic Industries Association (EIA). ANSI is unique among the world's standards groups as a nongovernmental body granted the sole vote for the United States in the International Standards Organization (ISO). This status is part of the reason ANSI bends over backward to limit its role to that of facilitator, or catalyst, in the production of standards.

ANSI X3B11

The evolving standards for smaller-format optical storage subsystems.

AOCE (Apple Open Collaboration Environment)

Provides a top-level application programming interface (API) for applications developers and a service provider interface for various back-end providers within the Macintosh operating system. With Vendor Independent Messaging (VIM) in its architecture, it offers pure AOCE for Macintosh-only development, and a VIM interface for portability among Macintosh, Windows and DOS.

AOR (architecture objectives review)

As part of enterprise information management, is focused on achieving an alignment between business and information technology strategies.

This alignment was explored in some detail throughout the 1980s. In fact, more than 45 different methods are now being used throughout the industry.

AP (access point)

The basic building block of a roaming wireless local-area network (LAN) infrastructure. APs attach to a wired backbone and provide wireless connectivity to all devices within range of the AP. As devices move out of the range of one AP, they move into the range of another.

API (application programming interface)

A set of calling conventions that defines how a service is invoked through software. An interface that enables programs written by users or third parties to communicate with certain vendor-supplied program products. The facility enables users and third parties to add functions to vendor-supplied software. APIs, not products, are strategic. They are the important component of any software product. There are no "strategic" software products, only strategic interfaces. IBM's Systems Application Architecture (SAA), for example, is not a product grouping, but a collection of APIs.

APPC (Advanced Program-to-Program Communications)

The programming interface to LU 6.2, IBM's protocol for peer relationship program-to-program communications under Systems Network Architecture (SNA). Also known as LU 6.2. APPC is the Systems Application Architecture (SAA) interface for cooperative processing.

Apple Open Collaboration Environment (See AOCE)

applet

A small program that runs within an application. Applets are commonly used to make otherwise static World Wide Web pages more interactive. Some examples are: animated graphics, games, configurable bar charts, and scrolling messages. Applets can help companies develop strong and positive identities through corporate Web sites. Applets also play an important role in network computers (NCs). They increase an NC's independence from the server because they do not have to communicate with the operating system (resident on the server) to function once the applet has been received by the NC. Applets are an ingredient in a functioning NC installation, and therefore contribute to saving companies significant money in their desktop computing strategies.

AppleTalk Local-Area Network Connect

Connection from the midrange system to Macintoshes via AppleTalk protocols.

application

A specific use for the computer such as for accounts payable or payroll. The term is sometimes used in place of "application program," "software" or "program," which are used to process data for the user. Examples of programs and software include both prepackaged productivity software such as spreadsheets (e.g., Microsoft Excel and Lotus 1-2-3) word processors (e.g., Corel's WordPerfect and Microsoft Word), or customized larger packages designed for multiple users (e.g., Lotus Notes, E-mail and general-ledger software).

application binary interface (See ABI)

application generator

A tool or toolset that is more sophisticated than simple query/report facilities, and that enables reasonably complex interactive or batch applications to be created at a higher level more easily than the compiler languages mentioned under "traditional processing." Code that is generated should be compiled rather than interpreted for better performance.

application layer

The top of the seven-layer Open Systems Interconnection (OSI) model, generally regarded as offering an interface to, and largely defined by, the network user. It is the end-user layer in IBM's Systems Network Architecture (SNA).

application logical unit of work (See ALUW)

application programming interface (See API)

application-specific integrated circuit (See ASIC)

Application System (See AS)

Application System/400 (See AS/400)

Applications Integration Architecture (See AIA)

applications outsourcing

An outsourcing arrangement for a wide variety of application services including new development, legacy systems maintenance, offshore programming, management of packaged applications, year 2000 services, transitioning service retooling, and re-skilling and staff augmentation. While this form of outsourcing generally involves a transfer of staff, the use of the term has recently broadened to include arrangements where this is not the case, as in re-skilling or staff augmentation. It does not include systems integration activities.

APPN (Advanced Peer-to-Peer Networking)
IBM's APPN is an extension of Systems Network Architecture (SNA) Low-Entry Networking (LEN; also known as Physical Unit 2.1), which provides dynamic multipath routing among nodes.

APPNTAM (Advanced Peer-to-Peer Networking Topology and Accounting Management)
An IBM product designed to discover nodes and links in an APPN network and build a topology map in Resource Object Data Manager, IBM's object-oriented database used to store management information. APPNTAM provides functions such as:

- Dynamic status updates
- Graphical display of APPN topology
- Control of ports and links
- Centralized collection of Advanced Program-to-Program Communications (APPC) session and conversation accounting information.

Thus, the control of ports and links, as well as the collection of APPC session and conversation accounting information, can be automated using the NetView automation facilities.

AQL (acceptable quality level)

architecture
A framework and set of guidelines to build new systems. IT architecture is a series of principles, guidelines or rules used by an organization to direct the process of acquiring, building, modifying and interfacing IT resources throughout the organization. These resources can include equipment, software, communications, development methodologies, modeling tools and organizational structures.

architecture conformance review (See ACR)

architecture implementation review (See AIR)

architecture objectives review (See AOR)

ARD (application requirements definition)

Architecture

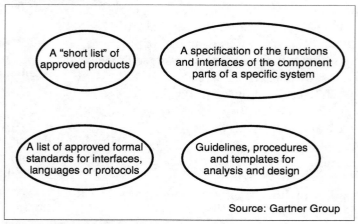

What is IT Architecture?

artificial intelligence (See AI)

AS (Application System)
IBM's second-tier fourth-generation language/
decision support system (4GL/DSS) program
product.

AS/400 (Application System/400)
IBM's midrange system that replaced the IBM
System/36 and System/38 product families.

**ASAI (Adjunct Switch Application Inter-
face)**
An AT&T product that provides a detailed set of
technical specifications for having an outside
computer control an AT&T private branch exchange (PBX).

**ASCII (American Standard Code for
Information Interchange)**
A standard table of seven-bit designations for
digital representation of uppercase and lower-
case Roman letters, numbers and special control
characters in teletype, computer and word processor systems. ASCII is used for alphanumeric
communication by everyone except IBM, whose
own similar code is called EBCDIC. Since most
computer systems use a full byte to send an
ASCII character, many hardware and software
companies have made their own nonstandard
and mutually incompatible extensions of the
official ASCII 128-character set to a 256-char-
acter set.

ASI (Asset Software International)

**ASIC (application-specific integrated
circuit)**
A chip on which the pattern of connections has
been set up exclusively for a specific function.

ASN (advanced ship notice)
An electronic data interchange (EDI) transaction that identifies the contents of a container
that is en route from a supplier to a customer. It
is also known as UCC transaction set 856.

ASO (automated systems operations)
Often referred to as "lights-out operations."
This is a combination of hardware and software
that allows a computer installation to run unattended — that is, without the need for a human
operator to be physically located at the site of the
installation.

ASP (average selling price)

asset management
A system of practices intended to address
shortcomings, inefficiencies, waste and un-
avoidable failures in managing technology
and information technology equipment. It involves five major areas: 1) requisition, 2)
procurement, 3) deployment, 4) maintenance
5) retirement strategies. At its core is an integrated data repository that contains:
1) Asset tracking — technical information
about the equipment or software; 2) Portfolio
information — acquisition and financial details; and 3) a Contracts database — summa-
rizing key software and maintenance contracts terms and conditions.

**Association for Information and Image
Management (See AIIM)**

associativity
The ability to link computer-aided design (CAD)
data and models together in a manner that allows
design changes to be reflected automatically.

Unidirectional or downstream associativity permits model changes to automatically change downstream data such as drafting, analysis or computer-aided manufacturing (CAM) data. Bidirectional associativity allows downstream changes, such as in drawings, to change the model.

Asymmetric Digital Subscriber Line (See ADSL)

asynchronous
Characterized by not having a constant time interval between successive bits, characters or events. Transmission generally uses one start and one stop bit for character element synchronization (often called start-stop transmission).

asynchronous transfer mode (See ATM)

AT&T (American Telephone & Telegraph)

AT&T GIS (AT&T Global Information Solutions — now NCR)

ATG (advanced technology group)

ATL (automated tape library)

ATM adaptation layer (See AAL)

ATM (Adobe Type Manager)
A program that enables the user to view type of any size with the highest resolution the user's monitor can provide.

ATM (asynchronous transfer mode)
A wide-area network (WAN) technology, a transfer mode for switching and transmission that efficiently and flexibly organizes information into cells; it is asynchronous in the sense that the recurrence of cells depends on the required or instantaneous bit rate. Thus, empty cells do not go by when data is waiting. ATM's powerful flexibility lies in its ability to provide a high-capacity, low-latency switching fabric for all types of information, including data, video, image and voice, that is protocol-, speed- and distance-independent. ATM supports fixed-length cells 53 bytes in length and virtual data circuits between 45 megabits per second (Mbps) and 622 Mbps. Using statistical multiplexing, cells from many different sources are multiplexed onto a single physical circuit. The fixed-length fields in the cell, which include routing information used by the network, ensure that faster processing speeds are enabled using simple hardware circuits. The greatest benefit of ATM is its ability to provide support for a wide range of communications services while providing transport independence from those services. An example is ATM's time independence; there is no relationship between the application clock and the network clock. Ironically, first implementations of ATM will augment local-area network (LAN) transport (and then the WAN it was designed for).

ATM (automated teller machine)
A public banking machine that is usually hooked up to a central computer through leased local lines and a multiplexed data network.

atomicity, consistency, isolation, durability (See ACID)

Audio Messaging Interchange Specification (See AMIS)

AUI (autonomous unit interface)
Most commonly used in reference to the 15-pin D-type connector and cables used to connect single- and multiple-channel equipment to an Ethernet transceiver.

authentication service
A mechanism, analogous to the use of passwords on time-sharing systems, for the secure authentication of the identity of network clients by servers and vice versa, without presuming the operating system integrity of either (e.g., Kerberos).

automated attendant (See AA)

automated systems operations (See ASO)

automated tape library (See ATL)

automated teller machine (See ATM)

automatic call distribution (See ACD)

automatic hardware failure detection and reconfiguration
Performs fault detection and isolation and reconfigures the system, dynamically invoking redundant components without the need to bring the system down.

automatic number identification (See ANI)

automatic restart — "warm" recovery
Resumption of operation after a system failure with minimal loss of work or processes (as opposed to a cold restart, which requires a complete reload of the system with no processes surviving).

autonomous unit interface (See AUI)

autovectorizing
Software used in technical document control systems to convert certain bit-mapped data to geometrical values.

AV (audio-visual)

available bit rate (See ABR)

available to promise
The uncommitted portion of a company's inventory or planned production. This figure is frequently calculated from the master production schedule and is maintained as a tool for order promising.

avatar
Computer representation of users in a computer-generated 3-D world, used primarily in chat and entertainment Web sites. Potential business applications include customer support, training or sales, where avatars in an enterprise's Web site help out potential customers through text or audio links.

average inventory
In an inventory system, this is the sum of one-half the lot sizes plus the reserve stock in formula calculations.

B

B1

Mandatory labeled security protection. A class of computer system security defined by the U.S. Department of Defense. In a military context, B1 systems offer a higher degree of security than C2 systems by enforcing the concept of information sensitivity classifications (e.g., unclassified, confidential, secret, top secret) with corresponding user clearance requirements. B1 security has little or no relevance to commercial applications.

backbone

A high-speed line or series of lines that forms the fastest (measured in bandwidth) path through a network.

backbone network

A high-speed transmission facility, or an arrangement of such facilities, designed to interconnect lower-speed distribution channels or clusters of dispersed user devices.

backward scheduling

A technique where the schedule is computed starting with the due date for the order and working backward to determine the required start date. This can generate negative times, thereby identifying where time must be made up.

bandwidth

1. The range of frequencies that can be passed through a channel. A channel carrying digital information has a data rate proportional to its bandwidth.

2. The signal-to-noise ratio (SNR) of a modulated signal is tested within a range of frequencies on either side of the carrier frequency. This range is also called a bandwidth. In the case of videodiscs, it is often 15 kilohertz (KHz) on either side, or a bandwidth in measuring SNR often returns a different SNR, with SNR degrading as bandwidth increases.

3. The amount of information that can be effectively handled by a given device at a given time. Typically measured in bits per second, the bandwidth of a fast modem can be up to 25,000 bits per second (bps). This is fine for pages of text but is much more of an issue when dealing with complicated graphical images or full-motion, full-screen video at more than 10 million bps.

Bandwidth On Demand Interoperability Group (See BONDING)

BASIC (Beginner's All-purpose Symbolic Instruction Code)

A high-level algebraic programming language, developed at Dartmouth College in the 1960s and widely taught to beginning programmers. It is simple to use but lacks speed.

Basic Input/Output System (See BIOS)

Basic Rate Interface (See BRI)

BASISplus
Information Decisions' content-based retrieval/document management product.

battery backup
Provision of sufficient battery backup to enable the nonvolatile storage of data, and graceful system shutdown, in the event of a power interruption.

baud rate
A measure of the speed at which computers send data from one device to another, with higher numbers representing faster transmissions. One baud is one bit of data per second.

BBS (bulletin board service)
In a Web-based electronic-commerce environment, BBS support allows broadcast and secure communications with trading partners and other parties. BBS can be tailored for groups, discrete accounts and individuals, and can be used for private and public messaging, ordering, inquiries, and acknowledgments, as well as public bidding forums and announcements.

BBS (bulletin board system)
An information systems communications initiative for sharing information and experience via a dial-up message center.

BCOCA (Bar Code Object Content Architecture)

BDLS (bidirectional loop switching)
The ability of fiber rings to be recovered in either of two directions, typically by using two pairs of fiber in the ring.

BEA (Bureau of Economic Analysis)

BEA (BEA Systems)

Beginner's All-purpose Symbolic Instruction Code (See BASIC)

Bell Communications Research (See Bellcore)

Benchmarking

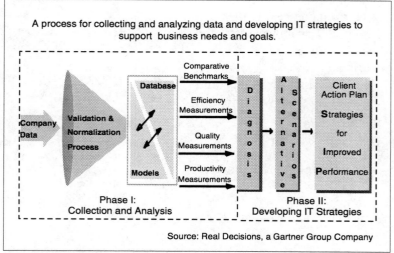

Real Decisions' IT Benchmarking Methodology

Bellcore (Bell Communications Research)
A jointly owned, financed and centrally staffed organization of the seven regional holding companies (RHCs). Among other activities, it performs testing and coordination for the procurement of much of the RHC equipment.

Bell operating company (See BOC)

benchmarking
The comparison between vendor performance and designated benchmark organizations or indexes. An index is a publicly available indicator for a factor that is associated with a pricing element.

• Internal benchmarking is the continuous process of measuring a company's products, services and practices to determine whether the best possible job is performed with the resources at hand. This can include comparing similar functions of different operating units in an organization or comparing the operations of a specific division from one year to the next.

• External benchmarking is the continuous process of measuring a company's products, services and practices and comparing them with those of another company. This can include comparisons with industry peers, functional leaders or best-in-class performers.

Berkeley 4.2Bsd
The Unix version developed by the University of California at Berkeley, which dominated technical computing applications until it was merged with AT&T's System V Unix operating system through an agreement between AT&T and Sun Microsystems. The merger was completed in System V release 4 (SVR4).

best practice
An innovative process or concept that moves a company to a position of improved competitive advantage. While there are many ways to find best practices, networking with other enterprises that have a common interest, similar environments and a commitment to sharing their experiences to develop best practices is most productive.

BI (business intelligence)
1. The class of applications and tools by which end users without a high degree of computer literacy may access, analyze and act on information. BI applications evolve from

Best Practice

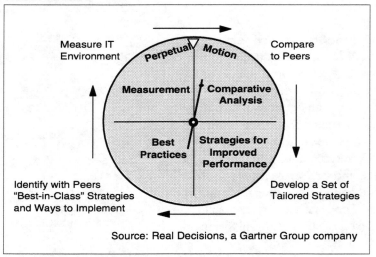

Source: Real Decisions, a Gartner Group company

Continuous Improvement Life Cycle Model

spreadsheets, executive information systems, text management systems using content-based retrieval methods, and decision support systems.

2. A user-centered process of exploring data, data relationships and trends, thereby helping to improve overall decision making. This involves an interactive process of accessing data (ideally stored in a data warehouse) and analyzing it, thereby deriving insights, drawing conclusions and communicating findings with the purpose of effecting positive change within an enterprise. There are four major product segments that constitute BI:

- Interactive query tools
- Reporting tools
- Decision support systems
- Executive information systems

bidirectional loop switching (See BDLS)

bill of material
A listing of all the subassemblies, parts and raw materials that go into a parent assembly showing the quantity of each required to make an assembly. There are a variety of formats for bills of material, including single-level, indenteds, modular (planning), transient, matrix and costed.

bill-of-material processor
Refers to the computer applications supplied by many manufacturers for maintaining, updating and retrieving bill-of-material information on direct-access files.

binary large object (See BLOB)

Binary Synchronous Communications (See BSC)

BIOS (Basic Input/Output System)
Contains the buffers required to send information from a program to the hardware/desktop receiving the information.

B-ISDN (Broadband Integrated Services Digital Network)
A high-speed (greater than ISDN primary rate), asynchronous, time division multiplexed transmission facility, or an arrangement of such facilities, designed to provide a wide range of audio, video and data applications in the same network.

bit
Abbreviation for binary digit, the minimum unit of binary information as stored in a computer system. A bit can have only two states, on or off, which are commonly called ones (1) and zeros (0).

bit-mapped
Generally refers to the ability of a device (e.g., monitor or printer) to read and display a vast number of picture elements, or pixels. Has an impact on quality in imaging and graphics; compare to character-oriented.

Bitbus
A serial, low-speed network developed by Intel Corp. in 1983 for sensor and factory-level controlling devices.

bits per inch (See bpi)

bits per second (See bps)

BLOB (binary large object)
A generic term used to describe the handling and storage of long strings of data by database management systems. Typically associated with image and video.

BMC (BMC Software)

BOC (Bell operating company)
One of 23 Bell telephone companies whose primary business is providing local telephone service to customers. These companies were spun off from AT&T as a result of divestiture, and were reorganized into seven Bell regional holding companies (RHCs). (There are now five.) BOCs are allowed to market, but not manufacture, telephone equipment. BOCs handle intra-LATA (local access and transport area) traffic, and are also referred to as local exchange carriers (LECs). The BOCs under their respective RHCs are:

- Ameritech — Illinois Bell, Indiana Bell, Michigan Bell, Ohio Bell and Wisconsin Bell.
- Bell Atlantic — Bell of Pennsylvania, Diamond State Telephone, Chesapeake and Potomac Company, Chesapeake and Potomac of Maryland, Chesapeake and Potomac of Virginia, and Chesapeake and Potomac of West Virginia. Merged with NYNEX — New York Telephone and New England Telephone.
- BellSouth — Southern Bell and Southeastern Bell.
- FBC Communications — Southwestern Bell — Southwestern Bell Telephone — merged with Pacific Telesis Group — Alascom, Pacific Telephone and Nevada Bell.

- US West — Northwestern Bell, Mountain Bell and Pacific Northwest Bell. Telecommunications services in Hawaii are provided by Hawaiian Telephone, a subsidiary of GTE.

BONDING (Bandwidth On Demand Interoperability Group)
A network group created to develop common control and synchronization standards to manage high speed data on the public network. Equipment from vendors is intended to interoperate over existing Switched 56 and Integrated Services Digital Network (ISDN) services. Initial versions of the standard described four modes of inverse multiplexer (I-Mux) interoperability, enabling inverse multiplexers from different manufacturers to subdivide a wideband signal into multiple 56- or 64-kilobit per second (Kbps) channels, pass these individual channels over a switched digital network, and recombine them into a single high-speed signal at the receiving end.

BPA (business process automation)
The automation of complex business processes and functions beyond conventional data manipulation and record-keeping activities, usually through the use of advanced technologies. It focuses on "run the business" as opposed to "count the business" types of automation efforts and often deals with event-driven, mission-critical, core processes. BPA usually supports an organization's knowledge workers in satisfying the needs of its many constituencies.

bpi (bits per inch)
A measurement used to calculate the number of bits stored in a linear inch of a track on a disk, tape or other recording surface.

BPM (business process management)
Outsourcing of an entire business process, such as logistics, sales support, billing and processing, and customer service, to a vendor. Also called business process outsourcing.

BPO (business process outsourcing)

BPR (business process re-engineering)
The fundamental analysis and radical redesign of business practices and management systems, job definitions, organizational systems, and beliefs and behaviors to achieve dramatic performance improvements. BPR uses objective, quantitative methods and tools to analyze, redesign and implement innovative business transformation processes and their supporting organization structures, performance standards, information and delivery systems, and management decision-making processes to achieve dramatic improvements in financial performance, product/service quality and customer satisfaction. Information technology is a key enabler for business process re-engineering.

BPR analytical techniques
Mathematical, graphical, logical and managerial algorithms for describing and modeling business processes, information systems and/or management decision-making systems.

BPR methodology
An integrated set of management policies, project management procedures, and modeling, analysis, design and testing techniques for analyzing existing business processes and systems; designing new processes and systems; testing, simulating and prototyping new designs prior to implementation; and managing the implementation process.

BPR tools
Combinations of techniques and software products that allow electronic capture, analysis, testing, simulation, reconfiguration, and persistent memory of business and systems models

bps (bits per second)
A measurement used to calculate the speed of data transfer in a communications system.

BR (business routing)
A Gartner Group category of call routing used for sales or service functions. The general objective is to determine, as transparently as possible, the caller's needs, business value and relationship, and ultimately to automate the call's routing to a resource. The process is usually driven by multiple databases, with each factor considered becoming a decision or value point.

BRA (Basic Rate Access — Canada and Europe; known as BRI in United States.)

BRI (Basic Rate Interface — United States, known as BRA in Canada and Europe)
The Integrated Services Digital Network (ISDN) Basic Rate Interface consists of two 64-kilobit per second (Kbps) data or voice channels, which are designated as B (bearer) channels. The interface also has a 16-Kbps signaling or packet data channel designated as the D (delta) channel. The interface is, therefore, often referred to as 2B+D.

bridge
A relatively simple device that passes data from one local-area network (LAN) segment to another without changing it. The separate LAN segments that are bridged use the same protocol.

broadband

A general term for communications at speeds above 1.5 megabits per second (Mbps) and usually at or above T3. The term has an analog heritage where it referred to bandwidths greater than 20 kilohertz (KHz). Broadband implies an analog circuit providing greater bandwidth than a voice-grade telephone line, i.e., operating at a bandwidth of 20 KHz or higher. Broadband channels are used for many communications applications, including high-speed voice and data communications, radio and television broadcasting and some local-area networks (LANs).

Broadband Integrated Services Digital Network (See B-ISDN)

browser

A software application used to locate and display World Wide Web pages. Most browsers can display graphics as well as text, and can present multimedia information including sound and video. Popular examples of Web browsers are Netscape Navigator and Microsoft Internet Explorer.

BRP (business recovery planning)

Mathematical, graphical, logical and managerial algorithms for describing and modeling business processes, information systems or management decision-making systems.

BRS Search

Content-based retrieval product from BRS Software Products, McLean, Va.

BSC (Binary Synchronous Communications)

A half-duplex, character-oriented data communications protocol originated by IBM in 1964. It includes control characters and procedures for controlling the establishment of a valid connection and the transfer of data. Also called bisync. Although still in widespread use, it has largely been replaced by IBM's more efficient protocol, Synchronous Data Link Control (SDLC), which is under Systems Network Architecture (SNA).

BU (business unit)

bug

A problem with software or hardware that causes unexpected results. The problem is often a result of inputs not anticipated by the developer. Minor bugs can cause small problems that do not affect usage, but major bugs can not only affect software and hardware usage, but could also have unintended effects on connected devices or integrated software and cause corruption of data files.

bulletin board service (See BBS)

bulletin board system (See BBS)

bundling

Packaging multiple features and products together for a single price.

buoyancy effect

The explosion in the number of applications and application providers caused by the increase in the ease of applications development that arises from the increasing robustness and standardization of base platforms and middleware.

bus

1) In data communications, a network topology in which stations are arranged along a linear medium (e.g., a length of cable).

2) In computer architecture, a path over which information travels internally among various components of a system.

business continuity
A comprehensive plan consisting of procedures and facilities designed to keep the critical processes of a business running without interruption.

business intelligence (See BI)

business process automation (See BPA)

business process management (See BPM)

business process re-engineering (See BPR)

business recovery planning (See BRP)

business routing (See BR)

BWA (buy where appropriate)

bypass
Any of several configurations of alternative transmission arrangements whose purpose is to avoid the local telephone company switched network. "Service" bypass involves using the telephone company's own (cheaper) facilities, while "facilities" bypass involves privately owned fiber or radio transmission.

byte
Shortened form of binary table, a byte is a group of eight bits handled as a logical unit. A bite is equivalent to a single character such as a letter, a dollar sign or a decimal point.

C

C

The programming language created by Dennis Ritchie of the former Bell Laboratories in 1972, when he and Ken Thompson worked on the Unix operating system design. It was based on Thompson's B language and has found widespread use on personal computers.

C++

An extension to the C language defined by Bjarne Stroustrop at Bell Laboratories in 1986. As a superset of C (another language, developed at Bell Laboratories by Dennis Ritchie in 1972), it provides additional features for data abstraction and object-oriented programming. C++ can be used to develop programs for almost all computers.

CA (certificate authority)

CA (Computer Associates International)

C&S (calendaring and scheduling)

cable modem

The fastest of the current Internet connection technologies. Cable modems are devices that enable very high-speed data access via a cable TV network. Fast cable modems can transfer a megabyte (Mbyte) of information in less than one second vs. 4.6 minutes/Mbyte for a 28.8-kilobit per second (Kbps) telephone modem, about one minute/megabyte for a 128-Kbps Integrated Services Digital Network (ISDN) modem, and six seconds/Mbyte for a T1 line.

CAD (computer-aided design)

CAD systems are high-speed workstations or personal computers that use specialized software and input devices such as graphic tablets and scanners for specialized use in architectural, electrical and mechanical design. With few exceptions, CAD systems rely extensively on graphics.

CADAM (Computer Graphics Augmented Design and Manufacturing System)

A licensed program by IBM consisting of three-dimensional construction, modification, analysis and display (geometrical representation), including hidden-line removal, parts selection, partial interference checking and other support capabilities.

CADD (computer-aided drafting and design)

Interactive graphic programs that automate the methodologies of drafting and design layouts. A few programs are successful enough that it is difficult to justify designing the layouts manually; application examples include integrated circuits and printed circuit boards.

CAE (computer-aided engineering)
An area of automated manufacturing and design technology for building end products that had its roots in finite element methods, but today it includes all types of performance systems, e.g., heat transfer, structural, electromagnetic, aeronautics and acoustic analysis. Major improvements have been in the architecture, mechanical, electronic and electrical-engineering disciplines.

CAGR (compound annual growth rate)

call center
A group or department where employees receive and make high volumes of telephone calls. Call centers can have internal customers (e.g., help desks) or external customers (e.g., customer service and support centers). The call center uses a variety of technologies to improve the management and servicing of the call. Typically, a large percentage of customer interactions happen through the call center, making them a critical component of providing good customer service.

caller ID
A telephone service that provides the telephone number of the incoming call. Caller ID systems can be integrated with customer databases to streamline a call center process. This integration can make all relevant customer information (e.g., name, location, list of products and previous issues) immediately available to the person who is receiving the call. This can reduce the amount

of time that both the customer and the customer support representative spend on the telephone, and enhance the level of service that the customer support representative can provide.

CALS (Continuous Acquisition and Life-Cycle Support, originally Computer-Aided Acquisition and Logistics Systems)
A joint project of industry and the U.S. Department of Defense to exchange technical-support information in digital form. Now dubbed "Commerce at Light Speed," it has become a set of peacetime programs for integrating electronic commerce (EC) initiatives, intended to enhance the development of pro forma and de facto standards (particularly for graphics exchanges) and to drive new methods for concurrent manufacturing in the automotive, aerospace, electronics and heavy-equipment industries. CALS is a useful way for manufacturing enterprises to combine a number of productivity-enhancing initiatives under one umbrella.

CAM (computer-aided manufacturing)
The manufacturing of goods controlled and automated via computer and robot. Frequently used in conjunction with computer-aided design (CAD).

CANDA (computer-assisted new drug application)

CAP (Carrierless Access Protocol)

CAP (carrierless amplitude phase)

CAP (competitive access provider)
A U.S. provider of bypass services.

capacity requirements planning (See CRP)

CAPE (concurrent art-to-product environment)

CAPE represents the third wave of design. It requires a wide variety of synergistic applications to work together, including visualization, rapid prototyping, analysis, materials selection, machining and cost estimation. Key to CAPE are application frameworks, data management and product geometry exchanges, so that any person who is involved in product design and approval can participate in the process.

CAPE application-specific elements

Technological components that are necessary for a specific application area. Application-specific elements are grouped into three vertical application markets — mechanical design, process plant design and electronics design — which account for the majority of industrial design activity.

CAPE base elements

The seven generic elements that represent the technological foundation and underpinning of the CAPE systems architecture including hardware independence, software architecture, framework incorporation, application integration, data exchange, data management and enterprise pricing policies.

Carrier Sense Multiple Access with Collision Detection (See CSMA/CD)

cartridge

In optical technology, an enclosure, generally of plastic, in which an optical medium is kept for protection; also called a "cassette." Some vendors captivate their media in the cartridges (this mode is called "spin in"), providing a window for the light beams; others remove the medium from the cartridge inside the drive.

cascade control

A control strategy that uses the output of one controller as the setpoint for another.

CAPE

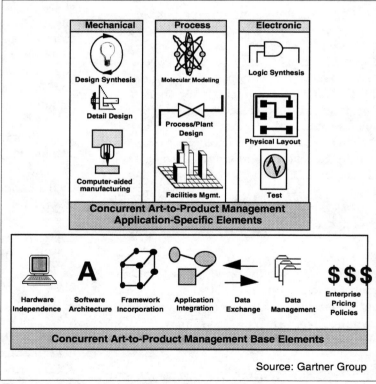

Elements of Concurrent Art-to-Product Environment

CASE (computer-aided software engineering)

An umbrella term for a collection of tools and techniques that are said by their distributors to promise revolutionary gains in analyst and programmer productivity. The two prominent delivered technologies are application generators and PC-based workstations that provide graphics-oriented automation of the front end of the development process.

CASE analysis and design tools

Graphical, interactive tools for the analysis and design phases of application software development.

CASE tools for client/server applications

Software development tools (higher-level than remote procedure call compilers) specifically oriented toward the design and implementation of client/server applications.

case-based reasoning (See CBR)

Cash Concentration and Disbursement plus addendum (See CCD+)

CATV (community antenna television)

The original name for cable TV, which used a single antenna at the highest location in the community.

CBDS (Connectionless Broadband Data Service)

A European metropolitan-area networking term similar in many respects to Switched Multimegabit Data Service.

CBR (case-based reasoning)

An artificial-intelligence problem-solving technique that catalogs experience into "cases" and correlates the current problem to an experience. CBR is used in many areas, including pattern recognition, diagnosis, trouble-shooting and planning. These systems are easy to maintain in comparison to rule-based expert systems.

CBR (constant bit rate)

An asynchronous transfer mode (ATM) service category, defined by the ATM Forum, that guarantees a constant bandwidth with low delay, jitter and cell loss. Circuit emulation is a typical application.

CBR (content-based retrieval)

Search methodology for retrieving information based on words or phrases in the text.

CBSI (Complete Business Solutions, Inc.)

CBT (computer-based training)

CC (control code)

A multibit code reserved for controlling hardware, such as printers.

CCD (Cash Concentration and Disbursement)

CCD+ (Cash Concentration and Disbursement plus addendum)

One of the primary message formats for enterprise-initiated payments to traverse the U.S. national banks' clearinghouse system. The format is limited to a single addendum record (one invoice, one payment), and many banks can process it.

CCD (charge coupled device)

A semiconductor device capable of both photodetection and memory, which converts light to electronic impulses. One- and two-dimensional CCD arrays are used in scanners to perform the first stage in converting an image into digital data. They are particularly attractive because they can step the signals from each detector across the array in response to a clock signal, permitting each scan line to be read through a single electrical connection.

CCITT
Abbreviation of the French name for the International Telegraph and Telephone Consultative Committee (Comite Consultatif International Telegraphique et Telephonique). In March 1993, the name was changed to the International Telecommunications Union Telecommunications Standards Sector (ITU-TSS) or just ITU. The ITU is a specialized Agency of the United Nations based in Geneva and coordinates and fosters cooperation in the use of international telecommunications systems.

CCITT Group III (Also now called ITU Group III)
The original standard for compression and decompression for facsimile.

CCITT Group IV (Also now called ITU Group IV)
The optimized standard for black-and-white office documents. Neither Group III nor Group IV handles color. Both are required to reduce bandwidth and storage demand.

cc:Mail Import/Export — Lotus Development
The file format used by cc:Mail is held as proprietary to cc:Mail. In order to read or write such a file, the import/export utility provided by cc:Mail must be used. Putting the actual file format behind this utility permits cc:Mail to make changes to the actual structure of the file without disturbing existing programs. The import utility creates the message header, or envelope, by writing field tags and data to the file in the cc:Mail structured data format. The export utility extracts the data by parsing the data structure.

CCN (common control node)

CCS (computer-communications services)

CD (compact disc)
The trademarked name for the laser-read digital audio disc, 12 centimeters in diameter, developed jointly by Philips and Sony.

CD-R (compact disc-recordable)
A standard and technology that enables users to write on and read from a compact disc. This new technology is compatible with existing CDs and CD players.

CD-ROM (compact disc read-only memory)
A version of the standard compact disc intended to store general-purpose digital data; provides 650-megabyte (Mbyte) user capacity at 10-13 corrected bit error rate compared to 635-Mbyte at 10-9 for the standard CD. CD-ROMs can be used for a wide variety of data storage such as music, video, graphics and other multimedia. They are also often used by software companies to deliver programs such as word-processing or spreadsheet applications since they hold significantly more data than a typical floppy disk (2.8 Mbytes).

CDA (compound document architecture)

CDA (Compound Document Architecture)
Digital Equipment's proprietary method for describing and interchanging data, which may include rich text, synthetic graphics, scanned images, voice, relational and spreadsheet-like tables, and full-motion video.

CDD/Plus (Command Data Dictionary/Plus)
Digital Equipment's active, distributed data dictionary system that provides a single logical repository for data definitions and descriptions.

CDDI (Copper Distributed Data Interface)
Standard for running the Fiber Distributed Data Interface (FDDI) on unshielded twisted-pair wiring.

CDE (Common Desktop Environment — COSE)
The first user interface specification (based on Motif) from the Common Open Software Environment group, a consortium of major vendors dedicated to standardizing Unix.

CDE (Cooperative Development Environment — Oracle)

CDIF (CASE Data Interchange Facility)
An effort by vendors, users and researchers organized solely to outline standards to address information-bridging challenges. The focus for CDIF is to define a standard whereby any one tool only provides one import and export interface to enable the effective exchange of information with any other CDIF-compliant tool.

CDLA (Computer Dealers and Lessors Association)
A trade association of North American-based computer dealers and lessors. The principal purpose of the organization is to promote professional integrity among its members. It also promotes alternate instruments for computer financing.

CDMA (code division multiple access)
A user access technique based on the simultaneous transmission and reception of several messages, each of which has a coded identity to distinguish it from the other messages.

CDPD (cellular digital packet data)
Transmission of digital data over a cellular network; with it, data moves at 19.2 kilobits per second (Kbps) over ever-changing unused intervals in the voice channels.

CDR (call detail recording)

CDR (clinical data repository)

CDS (cell directory service)
A core Distributed Computing Environment (DCE) server component provided for applications to locate resources. It functions primarily as a naming service, which provides a mapping between a logical name and a physical address.

CDW (corporate data warehouse)

CE (concurrent engineering)
A collaborative, team-based approach for designing products that combines multiple departments and disciplines into a project team.

CE (customer engineer)

CE (Windows CE)
A lightweight, micro-kernel-based operating system targeted at non-PC devices, licensed by

Microsoft for use in pocket-sized devices called HPCs (handheld PCs), and expected to appear in new-form-factor information appliances in the arenas of commercial enterprise and consumer electronics.

CEC (central electronics complex)

The term generically used to refer to the central processing unit (CPU), and includes the power unit, service units, console and other units, but not any peripherals. Within a sysplex or coupled complex it is any serial-numbered processor (which may be made up of multiple engines). Within a parallel sysplex complex, it is a single parallel processor that can house multiple engines. (Today this is an uncommon configuration.)

cell

A block of fixed length identified by a label at Layer 1 of the Open Systems Interconnection (OSI) reference model. It is the fundamental building block of asynchronous transfer mode (ATM) and Broadband Integrated Services Digital Network (B-ISDN). The agreement on 48-byte plus 5-byte header sizes was a major international breakthrough for ATM.

cell controller

A supervisory computer used to sequence and coordinate multiple machines and operations.

cell directory service (See CDS)

cell relay

A transmission mode that utilizes fixed-length cells as the bearer mechanism, as with asynchronous transfer mode (ATM), which uses 48 bytes of payload plus five overhead bytes as the standard cell size.

cellular digital packet data (See CDPD)

center of excellence

A central clearinghouse for knowledge capital that is used across all business transformation projects.

central electronics complex (See CEC)

central office (See CO)

central processing unit (See CPU)

centralized dispatching

Organization of the dispatching function into one central location. This often involves the use of data collection devices for communication between the centralized dispatching function, which usually reports to the production control department, and the shop manufacturing departments.

Centrex

A telephone company service offering that uses a central-office switch to provide premises switching capability similar to that of a private branch exchange (PBX). It can be located in a central office or on a large customer's premises.

CEO (chief executive officer)

CF (coupling facility)

CFCC (coupling facility control code)

CFI (Computer-Aided Design Framework Initiative)

A nonprofit organization formed to develop framework standards to facilitate the integration of CAD tools, particularly in the electronics design arena.

CFO (chief financial officer)

CGA (Color Graphics Adapter)
The first color video adapter, introduced by IBM in 1981. It displays four colors simultaneously.

CGI (Common Gateway Interface)
A data-passing specification used when a Web server must send or receive data from an application such as a database. A CGI script passes the request from the Web server to a database, gets the output, and returns it to the Web client.

CGS (Cap Gemini Sogeti)

channel service unit (See CSU)

character-oriented
Generally refers to a type of information display in which the information is limited to that which may be displayed in a fixed array of rows with a fixed number of positions per row. Character-oriented displays have very poor graphics capabilities. The most popular character-oriented terminals are IBM's 3270 family and Digital Equipment's VT family.

charge coupled device (See CCD)

chief information officer (See CIO)

CHIN (community health information network)
An encompassing term to describe any community-based network open to (and perhaps required for) all healthcare organizations.

chip
And integrated circuit that is the foundation of computer processing and data storage. Chips are used in everything from watches and calculators to personal computers and high-performance computers.

CHRP (Common Hardware Reference Platform)

CI (Computer Interconnect)
The local-area network (LAN) used in a VAXcluster.

CICS (Customer Information Control System)
An IBM subsystem (transaction-processing monitor) for implementing transaction-processing (TP) applications. CICS is IBM's strategic general-purpose subsystem for implementing TP applications. CICS invokes customer-written application programs in response to transactions entered at teleprocessing terminals and provides the services needed by those applications to retrieve and update data in files and respond to the terminal that invoked them.

CIDR (classless interdomain routing)
This is the successor to current class-oriented domains for Internet routing and allows for better allocations of Internet addresses.

CIF (common intermediate format)

CIFS (Common Internet File System)

CIL (Component Integration Labs)

CIM (Common Information Model)
Within the Web-based Enterprise Management (WBEM) proposal, the new name applied to Hypermedia Management Schema (HMMS) by the Desktop Management Task Force. (See also HMMS)

CIM (computer-integrated manufacturing)

The integration of manufacturing operations by integrating human systems, information systems and manufacturing systems. The goal of such systems is to combine electronically the systems and functions necessary to manufacture products more effectively.

CIM Series/400

Introduced by IBM in October 1990 as the first series of products that meet IBM's CIM architecture. It was designed with the AS/400 midrange computer as the core engine and includes software designed to tie together engineering, business and controls systems by linking PS/2s, AS/400s and RS/6000s.

CIO (chief information officer)

The person responsible for planning, choosing, buying and installing a company's computer and information-processing operation. Originally called data-processing managers, then management information system (MIS) directors, CIOs develop the information technology (IT) vision for the company. They oversee the development of corporate standards, technology architecture, technology evaluation and transfer; sponsor the business technology planning process; manage client relations; align IT with the business; and develop IT financial management systems. They also oversee plans to reinvest in the IT infrastructure, as well as in business and technology professionals. They are responsible for leading the development of an IT governance framework that will define the working relationships and sharing of IT components among various IT groups within the corporation.

CIR (committed information rate)

In a frame relay network, the minimum speed maintained between nodes.

CISC (complex instruction set computer)

A computer in which individual instructions may perform many operations and take many cycles to execute, in contrast with reduced instruction set computer (RISC). Examples include IBM System/370, Digital Equipment VAX, Motorola 68020 and Intel 80386.

CIT (Computer Integrated Telephony)

Computer Integrated Telephony is Digital Equipment's program that provides a framework for integrating voice and data in an applications environment. The telephone and terminal on the desktop are synchronized so that the arriving call appears on the terminal's screen and the data can be efficiently exchanged within an organization. CIT supports inbound and outbound telecommunications applications. For inbound calls, the application will recognize the caller's originating phone number through automatic number identification, or the dialed number through Dialed Number Identification Service (DNIS). It will then match the information to database records and automatically deliver the call and the data to a call center or agent. In an outbound application, dialing can be automated, thus increasing the number of connected calls.

CL/1

A client/server database access product developed by Network Innovations, a subsidiary of Apple Computer.

CLA (Corporate License Agreement — Novell)

A licensing agreement option under Novell's "Customer Connections" program. It offers an alternative for midsize organizations that have made an upfront purchase of $25,000 but cannot qualify for Novell's Master License Agreement (MLA).

class

A specification that defines the operations and the data attributes for a set of objects.

classless interdomain routing (See CIDR)

CLEC (competitive LEC)

Provides competition in the local telephone services market. Two types of CLECs will likely emerge: the local-services reseller or aggregator that buys local services in volume at wholesale prices and resells them to the market, and "hybrid" resellers, carriers that will build portions of the local network band and buy the remaining service components.

CLI (call-level interface)

CLI (Compression Labs Inc.)

client

A system or a program that requests the activity of one or more other systems or programs, called servers, to accomplish specific tasks. In a client/server environment, the workstation is usually the client.

client library (See CTLIB)

client/server

The splitting of an application into tasks performed on separate computers, one of which is a programmable workstation (e.g., a PC). The client does its own processing, while the server typically stores information and software. The

Client/Server

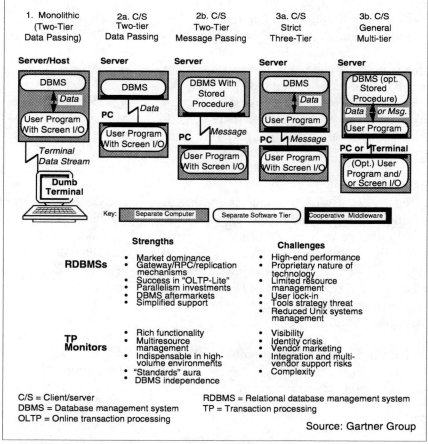

Online Transaction Processing Client/Server

two sides are connected via a local-area network (LAN) or a wide-area network (WAN).

Client/Server Interface (See C/SI)

closed-loop MRP (closed-loop material requirements planning)

A system built around MRP that also includes production planning, master production schedule, and capacity requirements planning. Once the planning phase is complete and the plans have been accepted as realistic and attainable, the execution functions come into play. These include the shop floor control functions of input/output measurement, detailed scheduling and dispatching, as well as anticipated delay reports from both the shop and vendors, purchasing follow-up and control, and other functions. The term "closed loop" implies that not only is each of these elements included in the overall system, but also that there is feedback from the execution functions so the planning can be kept valid at all times.

clustering

The capability to define resources on one or more interconnected midrange systems as transparently available to users and applications from within the specified group of loosely coupled midrange systems in a local- or metropolitan-area network. Examples include Digital Equipment VAXclusters and the Lotus Transparent Computing Facility.

CM (configuration management)

A function that enables impact/dependency analysis of application components.

CMC (common messaging calls)

A set of calls developed by XAPIA (the X.400 API Association) for use on top of any existing messaging system. Programmers developing applications using these calls may request services of whatever messaging system is accepting the call. The number of calls is limited to the most popular messaging and directory lookup functions. CMC is similar to simple Messaging Application Programming Interface (MAPI) in its breadth of services, but provides greater portability of applications.

CMIP (Common Management Information Protocol)

The Open Systems Interconnection (OSI) protocol for the exchange of network management information.

CMIS (Common Management Information Standard)

An Open Systems Interconnection (OSI) standard that defines the network monitoring and control function.

CMOS (complementary metal-oxide semiconductor)

A semiconductor technology that uses less power and generates less heat (enabling higher circuit density), but is typically slower than bipolar technologies.

CMS (Conversational Monitor System)

A single-user interactive operating system that was implemented for and together with the Virtual Machine (VM) environment. Its prime function has historically been software development. An emerging use within the departmental arena is to house production applications. The CMS file system is oriented toward small files rather than large, however, and CMS is not generally suitable for mission-critical applications.

CNC (computer numerical control)

CNE (Certified NetWare Engineer)

CNOS (corporate network operating system)
An evolved, service-rich network operating system (NOS) that provides the service underpinnings for local-area network- (LAN-) based middleware. Enterprise-satisfying NOS solutions fall along two lines. Infrastructure NOSs will continue to develop the directory, network management and wide-area network (WAN) support services to build the horizontal infrastructure. Application support NOSs will tightly integrate with desktop operating systems, providing the best base for advanced workgroup and collaborative applications, in a fashion that can be termed "shrink-wrapped client/server."

CO (central office)
The telephone company's centralized switching facility, where subscriber loops terminate. The CO handles a specific geographic area, identified by the first three digits (NXX) of the local telephone number.

CO (Contract Option — Lotus)

COBOL (Common Business Oriented Language)
A language compiler compliant, at the high level of required modules, with the American National Standards Institute X3.23-1985 standard.

CODASYL (Conference on Data Systems Languages)

code division multiple access (See CDMA)

codec (coder/decoder)

COL (Component Object Library)
Microsoft's distributed OLE/COM uses a non-CORBA object request broker (the Component Object Library) running on a proprietary Distributed Computing Environment-like underpinning (Object RPC).

COLD (computer output to laserdisc)
Microfiche replacement system. COLD systems offer economies as a replacement medium when rapid or frequent access to archived documents is necessary. Typically, a 12-inch optical-disc platter holds approximately 1.4 million 8.5-by-11-inch pages of information, equal to 7,000 fiche masters.

Color Graphics Adapter (See CGA)

COLS (commercial online service)
A company that provides its subscribers with access to a data base, via a modem and telephone line, for a fee.

COM (Component Object Model — Microsoft)
A robust component architecture in Microsoft's desktop operating system.

COM (computer output to microfilm or microfiche)
A system in which digital data is converted into an image on dry processed microfilm.

communications
1. The transfer of information including data, voice, video and multimedia.
2. Compression and decompression software and hardware.

COM-R (computer output to microfiche replacement)

Command Data Dictionary/Plus (See CDD/Plus)

commercial online service (See COLS)

commercial parallel processing (See CPP)

committed information rate (See CIR)

Common Desktop Environment (See CDE)

Common Gateway Interface (See CGI)

Common Information Model (See CIM)

Common Management Information Protocol (See CMIP)

Common Management Information Standard (See CMIS)

common messaging call (See CMC)

Common Object Request Broker Architecture (See CORBA)

Common Open Software Environment (See COSE)

Common Programming Interface (See CPI)

Common Programming Interface for Communications (See CPI-C)

Common User Access (See CUA)

Communications Oriented Production Information and Control System (See COPICS)

community antenna television (See CATV)

community health information network (See CHIN)

compact disc (See CD)

competitive access provider (See CAP)

competitive local-exchange carrier (See CLEC)

complementary metal-oxide semiconductor (See CMOS)

complex instruction set computer (See CISC)

compliance unit (See CU)

Component Object Library (See COL)

Component Object Model (See COM)

compound document
Any document containing more than one data type, typically rich text, synthetic graphics and raster images.

compound document architecture (See CDA)

compression
In the specific context of digital image representation, compression refers to the process of compacting the data based on the presence of large white or black areas in common business documents, printed pages and engineering drawings. The International Telecommunications Union Telecommunications Standards Sector digital facsimile standards contain standard one- and two-dimensional compression/decompression algorithms.

Computer-Aided Acquisition and Logistics Systems (See CALS)

computer-aided design (See CAD)

Computer-Aided Design Framework Initiative (See CFI)

computer-aided drafting and design (See CADD)

computer-aided engineering (See CAE)

computer-aided manufacturing (See CAM)

computer-aided software engineering (See CASE)

Computer Dealers and Lessors Association (See CDLA)

Computer Graphics Augmented Design and Manufacturing System (See CADAM)

Computer Integrated Telephony (See CIT)

computer output to laserdisc (See COLD)

computer output to microfilm or microfiche (See COM)

Computer Supported Telephony Architecture (See CSTA)

computer-telephony integration (See CTI)

concentrator
A device that merges many low-speed asynchronous channels into one or more high-speed synchronous channels to achieve economies of data transmission.

concurrent art-to-product environment (See CAPE)

concurrent backup — databases
A system-level facility to allow a database to be backed up to another disk or to magnetic tape while the database is still open for application access.

concurrent backup — files
A system-level facility to allow disk files to be backed up to another disk or to magnetic tape while the files are still open for application access.

concurrent database restore
A system-level facility to allow a database or portion thereof to be restored while the database is still open for application access.

concurrent engineering (See CE)

concurrent use
A way to measure the usage of software licenses. Software can typically be licensed in one of the following manners:

- Individual – software cannot be shared with other users.
- Site – a group of users can use the software, often limited to some maximum amount.
- Concurrent users – usage is limited to a maximum number of users at any one time.

The software vendor typically sets the guidelines on the type of software license, and measurement is sometimes facilitated by the vendor or by the user. When the software usage is measured by the user, the vendor could require a user to supply detailed reports or could rely on the user's pledge. Organizations have the opportunity to save money or avoid liability by accurately measuring the number of users.

configuration management (See CM)

Connect via System/370 Channel as SNA Device
A hardware connection to a System/370 channel emulating a Systems Network Architecture (SNA) device (e.g., 3174) to accommodate high-speed and bulk data transfers where communication and Token Ring Network (TRN) connections are not appropriate.

connectionless
The interconnection model in which communication takes place without first establishing a connection.

Connectionless Broadband Data Service (See CBDS)

consolidated service desk (See CSD)

consolidation effect
The reduction in the number of vendors that can afford to supply all of the hardware, operating systems and middleware necessary to compete effectively.

constant bit rate (See CBR)

constraint management
The ability to define model topology in the form of geometric constraints such as parallelism or tangency.

consulting
1) Management consulting — Tier 1 (executive): assistance regarding setting or execution of corporate business strategy or vision; Tier 2 (business): assistance regarding business processes (re-engineering) or change management.
2) IS consulting — includes systems architecture design or development and IS organizational planning.
3) Application or technical consulting — includes application project management and development, technology assessment, and product tuning.

contact database
Software that holds names and addresses and is used for appointments for the purposes of keeping track of sales and prospects.

content-based retrieval (See CBR)

Continuous Acquisition and Life-Cycle Support (See CALS)

continuous improvement
A manufacturing methodology used to improve overall quality by continuously increasing precision in part specification.

continuous operations
Those characteristics of a data-processing system that reduce or eliminate the need for planned downtime, such as scheduled maintenance. One element of 24x7 operation.

continuous process improvement (See CPI)

continuous production
A production system in which the productive units are organized and sequenced according to the steps to produce the product. The routing of the jobs is fixed, and setups are seldom changed.

continuous quality improvement (See CQI)

control code (See CC)

Conversational Monitor System (See CMS)

conversion
The process of preparing, capturing and indexing paper files to digital files.

Convert Macintosh WP
A translation facility that enables documents created at the Macintosh by third-party de facto standard word-processing packages (e.g., MacWrite, Microsoft Word) to be sent to the midrange system for viewing and modification using the midrange system vendor's standard word processor. Minor inconsistencies due to incompatible document format definitions are expected and acceptable.

cookie
A permanent code placed in a file on a client computer's hard disk by a server that the client has visited. The code uniquely identifies, or "registers," that user and can be accessed for number of marketing and site-tracking purposes.

Cooperation
NCR's third-generation office information system and end-user computing initiative.

cooperative processing
The splitting of an application into tasks performed on separate computers. Physical connectivity can occur via a direct channel connection, a local-area network (LAN) node, a peer-to-peer communication link or a master/slave link. The application software can exist in a distributed processing environment, but this is not a requirement.

coordination mechanics
A term coined by Coordination Technology's founder, Anatole Holt. It generally refers to a class of workflow that is heuristic in nature; i.e., a higher form of workflow concentrating on human behavior.

COPICS (Communications Oriented Production Information and Control System)
IBM's mainframe material requirements planning product. Several versions are now supported, including COPICS-D (defense) and a version using IBM's DB2.

Copper Distributed Data Interface (See CDDI)

CORBA (Common Object Request Broker Architecture)
A 300-vendor Object Management Group interoperability standard for object-oriented applications communicating over heterogeneous networks.

Corporate License Agreement (See CLA)

corporate network operating system (See CNOS)

corporate trade exchange (See CTX)

corporate trade payment (See CTP)

COSE (Common Open Software Environment)
Interoperability and portability across Unix platforms.

cost center
The smallest segment of an organization for which costs are collected. The criteria in defining cost centers are that the cost be significant and the area of responsibility be clearly defined. A cost center may not be identical to a work center. Normally, it would encompass more than one work center.

costed bill of material
A form of bill of material that, besides providing the normal information such as components, quantity of each, and effectivity data, also extends the quantity of every component in the bill by the cost of the components.

CP (central processor)

CPE (customer premises equipment)
Any apparatus —including telephone handsets, private branch exchange (PBX) switching equipment, key and hybrid telephone systems, and add-on devices — that is physically located on a customer's property, as opposed to being housed in the telephone company's central office or elsewhere in the network.

CPG (consumer packaged goods)

CPI (continuous process improvement)
A methodology for improving production, driven by formal metrics and measurement programs, including methodology upgrades.

CPI (Common Programming Interface — part of IBM's SAA)

CPI-C (Common Programming Interface for Communications)
A superset of IBM communications verbs containing bits of Advanced Program-to-Program Communications/Virtual Machine (APPC/VM), Transparent Services Access Facility (TSAF) and Server/Requester Programming Interface (SRPI). It provides a high-level interface to APPC.

CPM (critical path method)
The series of activities and tasks in a project that do not have built-in slack time. Any task in the critical path that takes longer than expected lengthens the total time of the project.
CPP (commercial parallel processing)
The use of parallel-processing systems for complex commercial-type applications.

cps (characters per second)

CPU (central processing unit)
The component of a computer system that controls the interpretation and execution of instructions. The CPU of a PC consists of a single microprocessor, while the CPU of a more powerful mainframe consists of multiple processing devices, and in some cases, hundreds of them.

CQI (continuous quality improvement)
A program to continually improve the quality-, cost-, time-, information- and touch-based factors of the goals and processes a corporation has determined are right for it.

CRC (cyclic redundancy check)
An error-detection system using a key generated by a cyclic algorithm.

critical-path method (See CPM)

critical ratio
A dispatching rule that calculates a priority index number by dividing the time to due date remaining by the expected elapsed time to finish the job. Typically ratios of less than 1.0 are behind, ratios greater than 1.0 are ahead, and a ratio of 1.0 is on schedule.

critical success factor (See CSF)

Cross System Product (See CSP)

CRP (capacity requirements planning)
The functions of establishing, measuring and adjusting limits or levels of capacity that are consistent with a production plan. The term "capacity requirements planning" in this context is the process of determining how much labor and machine resources are required to accomplish the tasks of production. Open shop orders, and planned orders in the material requirements planning (MRP) system, are input to CRP, which "translates" these orders into hours of work by work center and by time period.

CRTC (Canadian Radio-television and Telecommunications Commission)

CRUD (create, retrieve, update, delete)
Guidelines for defining how different people or communities within an organization deal with data elements owned by the organization.

C/S (See client/server)

CSA (Calendaring and Scheduling API)

CSA (client services applications)

CSC (Computer Sciences Corp.)

CSD (consolidated service desk)
An organizational structure that contains the people and skills (physically or virtually), tools (i.e., systems and network management platforms, and utilities), and procedures that deliver service and support to customers. It provides base functions for problem tracking, escalation, notification and resolution, and tightly integrates with asset and change management. It is guided by a service-level agreement (SLA).

CSF (critical success factor)
A methodology, management tool or design technique that enables the effective development and deployment of a project or process.

CSI (Computer Security Institute)

C/SI (Client/Server Interface)

An interface published by Sybase and delivered with release 4.0 of its SQL Server product. Open Client, which resides on the client, is an application programming interface (API) that allows applications or third-party products to access SQL Server or Open Server. Open Server is a set of protocols that allows communications with other servers, and can provide gateways to critical data that is not managed by the native SQL server.

CSMA/CD (Carrier Sense Multiple Access with Collision Detection)

A local-area network (LAN) access technique in which multiple stations connected to the same channel can sense transmission activity on that channel and defer the initiation of transmission while the channel is active. Sometimes called contention access.

CSP (Cross System Product)

IBM's strategic fourth-generation language (4GL). It presents self-contained development and execution environments that IBM has posted among all System/370 and System/390 environments, as well as the 8100 and PC. Enhancements have included library management, structured programming constructs and limited relational support.

CSTA (Computer Supported Telephony Architecture)

A European Computer Manufacturers Association standard for linking computers to telephone systems.

CSU (channel service unit)

A device found on digital links that transfers data faster than a modem (in a range from 56 kilobits per second to 1.5 megabits per second) but does not permit dial-up functions. It also performs certain line-conditioning and equalization functions, and responds to loop-back commands sent from a central office. A CSU is the link between digital lines from the central office and devices such as channel banks or data communications devices.

CTG (Computer Task Group)

CTI (computer-telephony integration)

The intelligent linking of computers with switches, enabling coordinated voice and data transfers to the desktop.

CTLIB (Client Library)

Sybase's application programming interface (API) set required for users to exploit the System 10 version of its SQL Server database management system.

CTO (chief technology officer)

The CTO has overall responsibility for managing the physical and personnel technology infrastructure including technology deployment, network and systems management, integration testing, and developing technical operations personnel. CTOs also manage client relations to ensure that service objective expectations are developed and managed in the operations areas.

CTP (corporate trade payment)

An electronic-commerce standard format that was established in the early 1980s using bank-developed transaction sets. It supported up to 9,999 addenda records, but used a fixed format and was retired in 1996. It was a member of a class of formats designed to transit a bank's clearinghouse networks and offer varying amounts of payment information associated with the transfer of funds. Client enterprises can choose between having funds transfer information travel with the payment data or having the payment data travel separately, typically through a value-added network (VAN). In the latter approach, data and value must be matched and reconciled by a client's applications.

CTS (corporate technology strategy)

CTX (corporate trade exchange)
An electronic-commerce standard format that allows for inclusion of 9,999 "addenda" records in addition to the primary financial records (i.e., amount being moved, bank routing number and checking-account number). It supports up to 80 bytes of ANSI data in each addendum. The banking system does not perform any edit checks on the addenda information.

CU (compliance unit)
A logical partition of applications and data to be upgraded together.

CUA (Common User Access — part of SAA)
IBM's attempt to set a common graphical user interface (GUI) standard. CUA specifies con-ventions for the dialog between a user and the computer, but has not caught on as a broadly accepted market standard.

cumulative lead time
The longest length of time involved to accomplish the activity in question. For any item planned through material requirements planning, it is found by reviewing each bill-of-material path below the item, and whichever path adds up to the greatest number defines cumulative material lead time.

Customer Information Control System (See CICS)

customer premises equipment (See CPE)

customized network management
Tools to allow assignment of levels of network management functions and capabilities to selected nodes throughout the network. With this, the degree of centralization vs. decentralization of network management can be varied depending on the environment.

CWC (Clear With Computers)

cyclic redundancy check (See CRC)

D

DA (data administrator)
An information systems (IS) employee who can help gather information about the operational data and assist in designing the data model that will be used for the data warehouse database management system (DBMS).

DACS (digital access and cross-connect system)

DAE (Distributed Automation Edition)
An IBM software solution for writing factory-floor applications independent of the distributed data, local-area network (LAN) protocol or terminal type.

DAL (Data Access Language)
From Apple Computer, a database interface — itself a superset of Structured Query Language (SQL) — that enables access to Macintoshes or non-Apple computers.

DAL (dedicated access line)

DAP (Directory Access Protocol)
A protocol for interworking among X.500 Directory Service Agents.

DARPA (Defense Advanced Research Projects Agency)

DASD (direct-access storage device)
Generic nomenclature for a storage peripheral that can respond directly to random requests for information; usually denotes a disk drive.

DASS (Digital Access Signaling System)
The original British Telecom (BT) Integrated Services Distributed Network (ISDN) signaling developed for single-line and multiline Integrated Digital Access (IDA) but used in the BT ISDN pilot service for single-line IDA only.

DAP

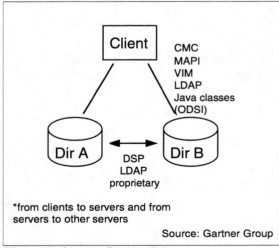

Directory Access Protocols*

DAT (digital audiotape)
A magnetic tape that stores audio data converted to digital form.

data
Unprocessed facts and figures that are processed into usable information. Data such as cash receipts mean little until processed into information such as an open receivable balance.

Data Access Language (See DAL)

data administrator (See DA)

database
An electronic filing system organized by fields, records and files. A field is a single piece of information; a record is one complete set of fields; and a file is a collection of records. To access information from a database, you need a database management system (DBMS), a collection of programs that enables you to enter, organize, and select data in a database. Increasingly, the term database is used to mean DBMS.Database-2 (See DB2)

database administrator (See DBA)

Database/Data Communication (See DB/DC)

Database Library (See DBLIB)

database management system (See DBMS)

Database Manager
IBM's relational database management system offered as part of OS/2 Extended Edition.

database partitioning
The practice of separating a database into portions that may reside on more than one disk volume or more than one system.

data circuit terminating equipment (See DCTE)

data communications equipment (See DCE)

data definition language (See DDL)

data dictionary
A repository of information about data, such as its meaning, relationships to other data, origin, usage and format. The dictionary assists company management, database administrators, systems analysts and application programmers in effectively planning, controlling and evaluating the collection, storage and use of data. A data dictionary manages data categories such as alias, data elements, data records, data structure, data stores, data models, data flows, data relationships, processes, functions, dynamics, size, frequency, resource consumption and other user-defined attributes.

Data Encryption Standard (See DES)

data exchange interface (See DXI)

Data Extract (See DXT)

Data Facility Data Set Services (See DFDSS)

Data Facility Product (See DFP)

Data Facility Sort (See DFSORT)

Data Facility Storage Management Sub-system (See DFSMS)

data integrity
Accuracy, validity and consistency of data (according to a set of rules for changing the database).

Data Interpretation System (See DIS)

Data Language/1 (See DL/1)

Data Link Switching (See DLS)

data management/middleware
Manages the efficient storage, retrieval, security and integrity of any kind of information.

data manipulation language (See DML)

data mart
A decentralized subset of data found in the data warehouse that is designed to support the unique business unit requirements of a specific decision support system. Data marts focus on the specific requirements of a particular application and maintain data and a data model to meet this need. A single data mart, as compared with a data warehouse, is less complex since it focuses on a business issue that needs to be solved.

data mining
The process of discovering meaningful new correlations, patterns and trends by sifting through large amounts of data stored in repositories, using pattern rec-ognition technologies as well as statistical and mathematical techniques. This process can be performed by human analysts, intelligent agents or other machine learning techniques.

data over voice (See DOV)

Data Packet Network (See DPN)

data service unit (See DSU)

data terminal equipment (See DTE)

data warehouse
A process and architecture that requires robust planning for aggregating, sorting and cleaning data from multiple sources so that it can be stored in a database for later access. The goal of the process is to provide flexibility to support

Data Mining

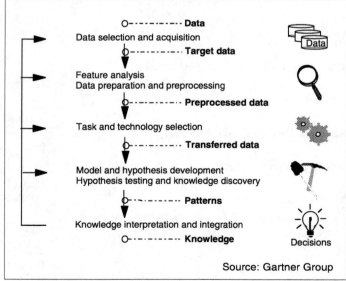

The Data Mining Process

existing and future applications that help organizations to analyze results. Ultimately, a data warehouse supports decision making.

Dataphone Digital Service (See DDS)

DB/DC (Database/Data Communication)
This acronym refers to IBM's collection of transaction managers and database managers, e.g., Customer Information Control System (CICS), Information Management System (IMS), Database-2 (DB2) and SQL/DS.

DB/file distribution management
Selective distribution of all or part of a central database to selected remote midrange systems. A facility for predefining the selection criteria and time for distribution should be included.

DB2
IBM's relational database management offering, originally built for Multiple Virtual Storage (MVS) systems. It uses Structured Query Language (SQL) as its data manipulation and definition language. IBM has also released versions of DB2 for OS/2 and AIX/6000. DB2 is IBM's strategic product for general-purpose information storage, including database management. It is a reasonably complete implementation of the relational technology. DB2 was a reconceptualization of IMS, and a revolutionary change from it. The most strategic component or aspect of DB2 is its interface — namely, SQL. In fact, DB2 is properly viewed as an SQL engine.

DBA (database administrator)
The person responsible for managing data, namely dataset placement, database performance, and data recovery and integrity at a physical level.

DBLIB (Database Library)
The native application programming interface (API) for Sybase's SQL Server. It began as a custom Sybase call interface. Other vendors, however, implemented DBLIB for a wide variety of client tools and even for other middleware, such as Micro Design's Database Gateway. Sybase has since produced an enhanced version, CTLIB.

DBMS (database management system)
A software package that enables end users or application programmers to share data. DBMSs

Data Warehouse

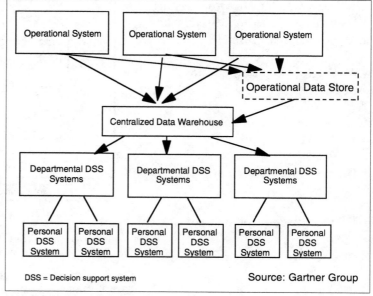

Data Warehouse Example

are generally also responsible for data integrity, data access control, and automated rollback, restart and recovery. The DBMS has a complete software facility for building, maintaining and generating reports from a database. It has evolved along three generic forms:

1) Hierarchical DBMS — records are organized in a pyramid-like structure, with each record linked to a parent.
2) Network DBMS — records can have many parents, with embedded pointers indicating the physical location of all related records in a file.
3) Relational DBMS — records are conceptually held in tables, similar in concept to a spreadsheet. Relationships between the data entities are kept separate from the data itself. Data manipulation create new tables, called views.

DBS (direct broadcast satellite)
A wireless technology for broadcasting by transmitting a compressed high-speed video signal via satellite.

DCA (Digital Communications Associates)

DCA (Document Content Architecture — IBM)

DCDB (disconnected client database)

DCDBMS (disconnected client DBMS)

DCE (data communications equipment)
A device that establishes, maintains and terminates a session on a network; typically, a modem that converts signals for transmission.

DCE (Distributed Computing Environment)
Open Software Foundation's (OSF's) partial solution to the problems of interconnectivity in a heterogeneous environment while addressing interoperability, standards and security. DCE consists of two service sets: fundamental services including naming, timing, threading, security and remote procedure calls (from Digital Equipment, Hewlett-Packard, MIT and Siemens-Nixdorf) and data-sharing services, including a distributed file system and PC support (from

DCE

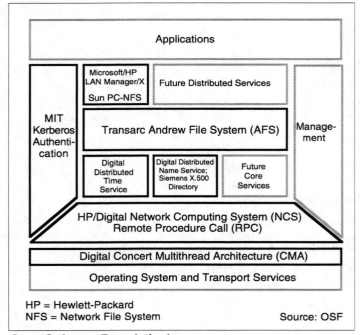

HP = Hewlett-Packard
NFS = Network File System
Source: OSF

Open Software Foundation's
Distributed Computing Environment Architecture

Microsoft, Sun Microsystems and Transarc).
DCE integrates remote procedure calls, presentation services, a naming directory, security, threads (sequential flows of control similar to tasks), time services (to synchronize clocks) and a distributed file system.

DCF (Document Composition Facility)

Program used in Professional Office System (PROFS) for creating text. Also known as SCRIPT/VS.

DCOM (Distributed Component Object Model)

DCS (distributed control system)

1) A process control system using computers dispersed throughout a manufacturing facility.
2) A series of computer-based devices that operate in conjunction with one another on a variety of applications.

DCT (digital cordless telephone)

DCT (discrete cosine transformation)

A video compression algorithm similar to Fast Fourier Transform but easier to compute.

DCTE (data circuit terminating equipment)

The equipment installed at the user's premises that provides all of the functions required to establish, maintain and terminate a connection. It also provides the signal conversion and coding between the data terminal equipment and the line.

DDA (Distributed Data Architecture)

Groupe Bull's scheme for data interoperability.

DDBMS (distributed database management system)

A DBMS that enables end users or application programmers to view a collection of physically separate databases as one logical single-system image. The concept that is most fundamental to the DDBMS is location transparency, meaning the user should not be conscious of the actual location of data.

DDE (Dynamic Data Exchange)

Microsoft specification for exchanging data between Windows applications.

DDI (Digital Document Interchange)

The Compound Document Architecture format for encoding revisable form text, graphics and image information.

DDL (data definition language)

A language for describing the data model for a user database, i.e., the names and access paths for the data and how they are interrelated. For some software products, DDL describes the logical, not the physical, data. Other products use it to describe both.

DDM (distributed data management)

A form of cooperative processing in which some portion of the database management system executes on two or more nodes.

DDS (digital data service)

A dedicated digital data transmission service that typically offers transmission speeds of up to 56 Kbps over interconnected, point-to-point digital private lines.

DDW (distributed data warehouse)

de facto standards
Specifications or styles that have not been approved by vendor-independent standards bodies, but have, nonetheless, become widely accepted by vendors and users.

debit/credit benchmark
A discredited performance measurement for online transaction processing (OLTP) throughput. The debit/credit transaction, sometimes called ET-1, simulates an automated teller machine (ATM) function. It has been replaced by TPC-A and TPC-B, defined by the Transaction Processing Performance Council (TPC).

decentralized
The description for an application that is distributed, but originates with the IS organization, has central applications development, and is centrally supported.

decision support system (See DSS)

DECnet
Digital Equipment family of network products based on Ethernet. Supports peer-to-peer processing.

DECnet end node
Interconnected support that enables a midrange system to act as an end node in a DECnet network.

DECOmni (DEC Open Manufacturing Network Interface)
Digital Equipment's version of the Open Systems Interconnection (OSI) Manufacturing Message Service protocol to be used for control-level device communications.

DECT (Digital European Cordless Telephone)
An interface specification for European digital mobile telephony. An access technology for "distance communications" with voice, data and video services, depending on the network accessed. DECT employs 10 carrier frequencies between 1.88 gigahertz (GHz) and 1.9 GHz. Time division multiple access (TDMA) is used to provide 24 time slots on each channel. DECT has 12 slots for transmission and 12 slots for receiving, and can provide 12 simultaneous calls. DECT's basic data rate is 32 kilobits per second (Kbps), but only 75 percent of the bits are used for voice or data. Slots may be combined to achieve flexible data rates from 25 Kbps to 500 Kbps. A maximum data rate of 10 megabits per second (Mbps) is possible. The major strength of DECT is its extremely high traffic-handling capacity. DECT is designed to handle 10,000 erlangs per square kilometer (10,000 erlangs represents at least 50,000 users per square kilometer).

DECtp
Digital Equipment's name for its entire online transaction processing (OLTP) marketing program.

DECwrite
Digital Equipment's compound document editor. It is based on the editor engine from Frame Technologies.

demand management
The function of recognizing and managing all the demands for products to ensure that the master scheduler is aware of them. It encompasses the activities of forecasting, order entry,

order promising, branch warehouse require-ments, interplant orders and service parts re-quirements.

dependent demand
Demand is considered dependent when it is directly related to or derived from the demand for other items or end products. Such demand is thus calculated and does not have to be forecast. A given inventory item may have both dependent and independent demand at any given time.

DES (Data Encryption Standard)
A security specification developed by IBM in 1977. Still in use today, it is available at no charge from many online bulletin boards and is based on a single key encryption algorithm. If user A wants to send an encrypted file to user B, user A would first encrypt it with a private key (sometimes referred to as a "secret" key). User B would then decrypt the file with an identical private key. The concern with this encryption-only technique is key management. Recipients must prearrange for possession of the appropri-ate key for decryption to take place.

design synthesis
The set of technological capabilities for model-ing, simulating and analyzing product designs. Also known as conceptual design or top-down design.

desktop management interface (See DMI)

desktop services
Acquisition, maintenance and ongoing manage-ment of PC hardware and software assets.

DFDSS (Data Facility Data Set Services)
A member of IBM's Data Facility family of software products. It provides copy, dump-re-store and direct access storage device (DASD) space management functions.

DFHSM (Data Facility Hierarchical Stor-age Manager)
A member of IBM's Data Facility family of software products. It provides automatic space and availability management among a hierarchy of storage.

DFP (Data Facility Product)
Originally called MVS/DFP, it was the MVS component that contained the access methods and handled catalog management. This facility was late renamed DFSMSdfp.

DFS (Distributed File System — Transarc)
A Distributed Computing Environment stan-dard that provides users with a common file system across different operating systems. Thus Windows users can connect to a Unix machine without knowing any Unix operating-system commands. When files are moved, DFS tracks the new location by storing its address in a database. DFS also eases backup difficulties by automating regular backup routines across each cell through a backup server.

DFSMS (Data Facility Storage Manage-ment Subsystem)
The conceptual repackaging of IBM's Data Fa-cility family of products and Resource Access Control Facility (RACF). It is intended to sim-plify the management and use of external stor-age resources by providing a device-indepen-dent means of requesting services by data set.

DFSMSdfp (DFSMS Data Facility Product) (See DFP)

DFSMShsm (DFSMS Hierarchical Storage Manager) (See HSM)

DFSORT (Data Facility Sort)
A member of IBM's Data Facility family of software products. It provides high-performance rearrangement of data.

DG (Data General)

DHCF (Distributed Host Command Facility)
A function that helps create or support the link between a terminal and an application.

DHCP (Dynamic Host Configuration Protocol)
An Internet Engineering Task Force (IETF) Transmission Control Protocol/Internet Protocol (TCP/IP) specification for allocating Internet Protocol (IP) addresses and other configuration information based on network adapter addresses. It enables address pooling and allocation and simplifies TCP/IP installation and administration.

DIA (Document Interchange Architecture — part of SAA)
Defined by IBM as a set of services performed by peer communications processes. DIA functioned as a set of communication programs — i.e., software that uses communication facilities such as Systems Network Architecture (SNA) — to carry out functions requested by users, which can be people, application programs or devices.

dial-up
The process of, or the equipment or facilities involved in, establishing a temporary connection via the switched network.

Dialed Number Identification Service (See DNIS)

DICOM (Digital Imaging and Communications in Medicine)

DID (direct inward dialing)
A system that allows an outside caller to reach an extension without operator assistance.

differentiation
The methods a vendor uses to distinguish a product from the competition by providing unique benefits to users or independent software vendors.

Digital Access Signaling System (See DASS)

digital audiotape (See DAT)

digital data service (See DDS)

Digital Document Interchange (See DDI)

Digital European Cordless Telephone (See DECT)

Digital Private Network Signaling System (See DPNSS)

Digital Signal Level 0-4 (See DS-0 through DS-4)

digital signal processor (See DSP)

Digital Standard Relational Interface (See DSRI)

digital switching
The process of establishing and maintaining a connection under stored program control where binary-encoded information is routed between an input and an output port. Generally, a "virtual" through circuit is derived from a series of time slots (time division multiplexing), which is more efficient than requiring dedicated circuits for the period of time that connections are set up.

Digital Table Interchange Format (See DTIF)

digital videodisc (See DVD)

digitizer
A purely graphical input device — i.e., a computer-aided design/computer-aided manufacturing (CAD/CAM) system digitizer used in computer-aided engineering (CAE) for converting locations into storable electronic impulses — with a surface on which a location or a point is selected and then automatically converted into a digital X-Y coordinate suitable for transmission to a computer.

direct-access storage device (See DASD)

direct broadcast satellite (See DBS)

direct digital control
The use of computers for machine and process control by direct interface to sensors, valves and other control devices.

direct inward dialing (See DID)

direct inward system access (See DISA)

direct memory access (See DMA)

Directory Access Protocol (See DAP)

directory services
Middleware that locates the correct and full network address for a mail addressee from a partial name or address. A directory service provides a naming service and extends the capabilities to include intelligent searching and location of resources in the directory structure.

directory system agent (See DSA)

dirty forms
Paper documents that are bent, folded or mutilated to some degree, making then difficult to scan and recognize.

DIS (Data Interpretation System)
A marketing-oriented decision support system (DSS) product co-marketed by IBM and Metaphor.

DIS (draft international standard)

DISA (Data Interchange Standards Association)

DISA (direct inward system access)
This feature allows an outside caller to dial directly into the company telephone system and access all the system's features and facilities. DISA is typically used for making long-distance calls from a remote location using the company's less-expensive long-distance lines.

disaster recovery planning (See DRP)

discrete cosine transformation (See DCT)

discretionary security controls
An operating-system security rating of C2 or higher based on U.S. Department of Defense trusted computer system evaluation criteria.

disk drive
A storage device attached to a computer that reads from, writes to and stores information on a floppy disk or hard disk.

disk mirroring
The duplication of disks and controllers so that two access paths exist in case a failure occurs on one of them.

Disk Operating System (See DOS)

Disk Operating System/Virtual Storage Extended (See DOS/VSE)

dispatching
The selecting and sequencing of available jobs to be run at individual workstations and the assignment of these jobs to workers.

Distributed Automation Edition (See DAE)

Distributed Computing Environment (See DCE)

distributed control system (See DCS)

Distributed Data Architecture (See DDA)

distributed data management (See DDM)

distributed database
A database whose objects (tables, views, columns and files) reside on more than one system in a network, and can be accessed or updated from any system in the network.

distributed database management system (See DDBMS)

distributed DB — read
Availability of a distributed, location-transparent database facility residing on multiple midrange system nodes whereby location of and access to information are transparently managed by the system rather than by applications at each node. Remote access is at least read-only.

distributed DB — read/update
Availability of a distributed, location-transparent database facility residing on multiple midrange system nodes whereby location of and access to information are transparently managed by the system rather than by the applications at each node. Remote access is for update as well as read.

Distributed File System (See DFS)

distributed function
A form of cooperative processing in which some of the application program logic executes on one node, possibly with a database, and the rest of the application resides on another node, possibly along with presentation services.

Distributed Host Command Facility (See DHCF)

distributed lock manager (See DLM)

Distributed Management Environment (See DME)

distributed memory parallel processors (See DMPP)

Distributed Naming Service (See DNS)

distributed naming/directory services
Directory facilities available transparently to all midrange systems in the network allowing cross-network resource location and access. Directories can be maintained centrally and independently of each midrange system operation. More than one copy of the main directory at multiple nodes could be used to improve directory access performance.

Distributed Object Computing Architecture (See DOCA)

Distributed Object Management Facility (See DOMF)

Distributed Office Support System (See DISOSS)

distributed OLTP monitor
An online transaction processing (OLTP) monitor implementation that enables deployment of the application across multiple systems with minimal application programmer involvement or foreknowledge.

distributed parallel processing (See DPP)

distributed presentation
A form of cooperative processing in which some of the presentation handling executes on one node and the rest of the presentation, along with the remainder of the application and the database, executes on another node.

distributed processing
A data-processing organizational concept under which computer resources of a company are installed at more than one location with appropriate communication links. Processing is performed at the user's location, generally on a minicomputer, and under the user's control and scheduling. This is in contrast to a large, centralized computer system which handles processing for all users. It is also the ability of an application to run on one or more nodes of a multiplatform network. The user need not be aware of the physical location of the data or the application software. The application can operate using cooperative processing, but this condition is not necessary.

Distributed Queue Dual Bus (See DQDB)

Distributed Relational Data Architecture (See DRDA)

Distributed Request (See DR)

distributed resource management (See DRM)

Distributed System Object Model (See DSOM)

distributed systems
Refers to computer systems in multiple locations throughout an organization working in a cooperative fashion, with the system at each

location serving the needs of that location but also able to receive information from, and supply information to, other systems within the network.

Distributed Systems License Option (See DSLO)

distributed systems management (See DSM)

Distributed Transaction Processing (See DTP)

Distributed Unit of Work (See DUOW)

distribution requirements planning (See DRP)

distribution service
Middleware that ensures a mail package is delivered to the specified addressee.

divestiture
The Justice Department's legal action against AT&T leading to the terms of the Modified Final Judgment. AT&T agreed to the 1982 Consent Decree, and in 1984 it relinquished ownership and control of its 22 wholly owned local Bell telephone operating companies.

DL/1 (Data Language/1)
The "language" in which the application programmer specifies requirements to Information Management System/Database Manager (IMS/DB). It also denotes the DOS version of IMS/DB. For some time now, DL/1 has been synonymous with IMS/DB, even for IBM.

DLL (down line load)

DLL (Dynamic Link Library)
Windows and OS/2 feature.

Distributed Systems

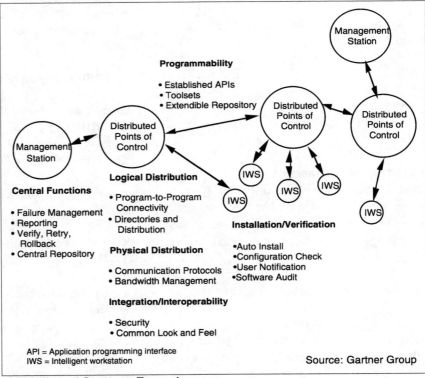

A Distributed Systems Example

DLM (distributed lock manager)
An architecture critical to maintaining locking consistency across multiple processing nodes and maintaining coherency between the multiple database buffer pools that exist on those different nodes.

DLS or DLSw (Data Link Switching)
An IBM-developed technique for carrying Systems Network Architecture (SNA) and NetBIOS over Transmission Control Protocol/Internet Protocol (TCP/IP). DLS "tunnels" or encapsulates SNA traffic utilizing the transport services of TCP/IP. Upon entry into a router-based intranet, SNA traffic is placed into TCP segments, which are then sent across the network as IP datagrams. Intermediate routers along the session path "see" only standard IP datagrams and addresses, with no need to recognize SNA information flowing through them. At the destination router, TCP/IP headers are stripped off, and the original SNA traffic is sent in "native" mode to an SNA network or destination device using SNA addresses. With DLS, the entire TCP session "looks like" a source-route bridged LLC2 connection to SNA products at either end. Other features of DLS support remote Synchronous Data Link Control (SDLC) connections without the need to send polling information across the Internet. (Besides SNA, DLS can also be used to send "nonroutable" NetBIOS traffic across TCP/IP sessions.)

DMA (direct memory access)
A means of handling data transfer between memory and a peripheral device that bypasses the central processing unit (CPU).

DMA (Document Management Alliance)

DMI (desktop management interface)
An industry standard specification for how management data and information about the attributes of a system get communicated from the system to a management tool locally or remotely.

DML (data manipulation language)
The language by which an application programmer invokes functions from a database management system (DBMS) product to access and manipulate data.

DMPP (distributed memory parallel processor)
Massively parallel processing machine without shared-memory capabilities; also known as "loosely coupled."

DMT (discrete multitone)

DMTF (Desktop Management Task Force)
A group of support providers and vendors of help desk tools who have joined together to review and propose standards for desktop-related products.

DNA (Digital Network Architecture — Digital Equipment)

DNIC (data network identification code)

DNIS (Dialed Number Identification Service)
DNIS is a feature of 800 and 900 lines. The long-distance carrier transmits the DNIS of the incoming call to identify the numbers the person is calling. Those DNIS digits may be received via in-band or out-of-band format, Integrated Services Digital Network (ISDN), or data channel.

DNS (Distributed Naming Service)
A DECnet service that enables a network resource to be named independently of its physical location. Using DNS, a database could be referred to as "Sales," regardless of where it was located or relocated.

DNS (Domain Naming System)
The online distributed database system that serves as the map between names and Internet addresses.

DOCA (Distributed Object Computing Architecture)
An application architecture on which System Software Associates (SSA) has largely based its BPCS 6.0 product for the enterprise resource planning (ERP) market. It has tools to enable interoperability.

Document Composition Facility (See DCF)

Document Interchange Architecture (See DIA)

document management
An application or middleware that performs data management tasks tailored for typical unstructured documents (including compound documents). It may also manage the flow of documents through their life cycles.

document representation standards
Internal data streams that can support the transport of text, data, graphics, image and, in the future, voice and video.

DOD (Department of Defense)

domain name
A unique identifier for an Internet site. Consists of at least two (but sometimes more) parts separated by periods (e.g., http://www.info-edge.com). Top-level domains for Web sites must be registered with the Web Internet Registry, and a yearly fee (currently $50) must be paid to maintain the registry.

Domain Naming System (See DNS)

DOMF (Distributed Object Management Facility)
Hewlett-Packard's (HP's) DOMF is based on the Common Object Request Broker Architecture (CORBA) standard from the Object Management Group (OMG). DOMF provides a location-transparent object-communication mechanism across heterogeneous networks by using the DCE standard. HP has been working with IBM to integrate HP's DOMF with IBM's System Object Model (SOM), which will provide users with scalability, profitability and interoperability of distributed applications across HP and IBM platforms.

DOMS (Distributed Object Management System — a k a HD-DOMS, from HyperDesk)

DOS (Disk Operating System)
The command-driven operating system that is standard for IBM PC and compatible computers and uses disks for data storage.

DOS/VSE (Disk Operating System/Virtual Storage Extended)
The low-end operating system for IBM's S/370 architecture computers. DOS/VSE typically

operates on smaller machines, especially in nonadvanced environments.

Double-Byte Character Set Support

Support for system and application use of double-byte character sets as required for Far Eastern national language support.

DOV (data over voice)

A technology that transmits data and voice simultaneously over twisted-pair copper wiring and is used primarily with local Centrex services or a special customer premises private branch exchange (PBX). Data rates for Centrex operation are 9.6 kilobits per second (Kbps) and 19.2 Kbps.

download

The process of bringing a file down to a computer through a network and typically from a server, or some other computing device. Download times can be greatly effected by the method of connection to the network.

download of DB2, IMS, VSAM data

A facility allowing the midrange system to initiate an information download DB2, Information Management System (IMS) or Virtual Storage Access Method (VSAM) data files on a System/370 mainframe to a data file or database on the midrange system for local access and processing.

downsizing

The process of moving computing work to smaller computers.

DPA (Document Printing Architecture)

International Standards Organization (ISO) standard 10175, which defines print objects, attributes and protocols for submitting print requests across heterogeneous systems. Designed to provide a distributed printing system with high levels of interoperability, robustness, reliability and stability.

dpi (dots per inch)

A measurement of resolution; e.g., the number of pixels per inch on a cathode ray tube display.

DPN (Data Packet Network)

Northern Telecom's public packet networking product. With DPN, large organizations have the option of expanding their private networks into public networks. This brings two primary benefits. First, external revenue can defray the cost of the organization's telecom infrastructure. Second, the provision of network services to key clients, suppliers and others can be a significant competitive advantage.

DPNSS (Digital Private Network Signaling System)

A standard which enables private branch exchanges (PBXs) from different vendors to be connected with E1 lines and pass calls transparently between each — as if the phones were extensions of the same PBX. This originated in Britain.

DPP (distributed parallel processing)

Distribution of a job to whichever processor or network is best equipped to handle the job at that time.

DQDB (Distributed Queue Dual Bus)

The Institute of Electrical and Electronics Engineers (IEEE) 802.6 standard for a metropolitan-area network (MAN). DQDB is a very high-speed (150 Mbps), distance-insensitive network that transports both voice and data. It uses a form of asynchronous time division multiplexing. By watching for empty cells on the buses, it avoids the need to pass tokens, as in Fiber Distributed Data Interface (FDDI). DQDB is the underlying media access control protocol developed for the IEEE 802.6 MAN standard. DQDB supports data rates of 45 Mbps to 155 megabits per second (Mbps) and isochronous circuits up to 1.44 Mbps. DQDB, which was designed for MAN usage, complements emerging asynchronous transfer mode (ATM) networks on the wide-area network (WAN) side, as 802. 6 uses the same format and cell size as ATM.

DR (Distributed Request)
One of the four functional elements of IBM's Systems Application Architecture Distributed Relational Database strategy that systematically executes a single Structured Query Language (SQL) statement accessing multiple databases.

DRAM (dynamic random-access memory)
Computer memory chip that requires electronic refresh cycles to preserve data stored for manipulation by logic chips.

DRDA (Distributed Relational Data Architecture)
IBM's architecture for enterprisewide data access, announced in July 1990. The architecture is designed to homogenize the way data is defined and accessed across IBM's different hardware/software platforms, as well as address multilingual coding standards. While explicitly concerned with relational data (hence, its name), DRDA also attempts to deliver distributed access to pre-relational data, an issue with which IBM continues to struggle.

DRM (distributed resource management)
An evolving discipline consisting of a set of software, hardware, network tools, procedures and policies for enabling distributed enterprise systems to operate effectively in production. DRM embraces solutions for the daily monitoring, resource planning, system administration, change management, operations, performance and other initiatives that are needed to maintain effective productivity in a distributed networked computing environment.

DRP (disaster recovery planning)
Operational procedures for ensuring recovery of hardware and communications assets and recovery of data.

DRP (distribution requirements planning)
The process of assessing from where products and services should be deployed, and determining the stock-keeping unit (SKU) and location level replenishment plan.

DRP (Distribution Resource Planning — J.D. Edwards & Co.)

DS-0 (Digital Signal Level 0)
A telephony term for a 64 kilobits per second (Kbps) standard telecommunications signal.

DS-1 (Digital Signal Level 1)
A telephony term describing the 1.544 megabits per seoncd (Mbps) digital signal, or T1 rate.

DS-1C (Digital Signal Level 1C)
A telephony term describing a 3.152 megabits per second (Mbps) digital signal.

DS-2 (Digital Signal Level 2)

A telephony term describing the 6.132-megabits per second (Mbps) digital signal carried on a T2 facility.

DS-3 (Digital Signal Level 3)

A telephony term describing the 44.7 megabits per second (Mbps) digital signal.

DS-4 (Digital Signal Level 4)

A telephony term describing the 274.2 megabits per second (Mbps) digital signal.

DSA (directory system agent)

The electronic-messaging component that receives requests for addresses, looks them up and returns the address.

DSA (Dynamic Server Architecture)

From Informix Software, DSA is a parallel, scalable architecture that supports large databases running on massively parallel, loosely coupled, symmetric multiprocessing (SMP) and uniprocessor computers. DSA is designed to be independent of platforms and transparent to applications.

DSC (digital selective calling)

DSC (DSC Communications Corp.)

DSLO (Distributed Systems License Option)

An IBM software license option that is available to IBM customers with a basic license for the software product that allows them to copy certain IBM-licensed material for the purpose of installing multiple systems.

DSM (distributed systems management)

A technology for managing the interconnected parts of a system. As managed items — i.e., components of applications, nodes, links or subsystems — become active, they must notify their manager of their status. DSM tools are capable of dealing with a limited number of distinct elements and require a strong directory.

DSOM (Distributed System Object Model)

IBM's distributed object technology, which originated on OS/2 and AIX and could be ported to other operating environments, including Windows. DSOM is a follow-up to System Object Model (SOM), an operating-system extension that provides object-oriented programming (OOP) mechanisms such as method dispatching and inheritance to OS/2. DSOM is a Common Object Request Broker Architecture (CORBA)-compliant system.

DSP (digital signal processor)

Specialized computer chip optimized for high data rates needed to process digitized wave forms.

DSRI (Digital Standard Relational Interface)

Digital Equipment's proprietary, low-level application programming interface (API) to Rdb.

DSS (decision support system)

System designed to support the information needs of tactical and strategic decision making, as opposed to systems responsible for running the business. A data-processing mode emphasizing user friendliness and ad hoc query, reporting and analysis capabilities. This mode is contrasted to online transaction processing (OLTP), which focuses on low-cost, fast-response, predictably structured applications.

DSSI (Digital Storage Systems Interconnect)

DSU (data service unit)
A device designed to connect data terminal equipment to a digital phone line to allow digital communications. A DSU is the digital equivalent of a modem.

DSU (disk storage unit)

DTE (data terminal equipment)
The part of a data station that serves as a data source, data sink or both, and provides for the data communication control function according to protocols.

DTIF (Digital Table Interchange Format)
The Compound Document Architecture-specified format used for the storage and interchange of documents that contain data tables, formulas and spreadsheets.

DTMF (dual-tone multifrequency)

DTP (desktop publishing)

dumb terminal
A terminal not performing local processing of entered information; serves only as an input/output device for an attached or network-linked processor.

DUOW (Distributed Unit of Work — part of DRDA)
Part of IBM's classification of distributed-database capabilities; a self-contained set of Structured Query Language (SQL) requests accessing data that may be situated at multiple physical locations. Each SQL request can access only one system. One of the four functional elements of IBM's Systems Application Architecture (SAA) Distributed Relational Data Architecture (DRDA) strategy that coordinates the systematic execution of multiple SQL statements accessing multiple databases.

DVD (digital videodisc)
An optical disk with the ability to store large quantities of video data.

DXI (Data Exchange Interface)
A first-generation, frame-oriented, external asynchronous transfer mode (ATM) interface standard supporting ATM adaptation layer 3/4 and 5, but not constant bit rate (CBR) traffic.

DXT (Data Extract)
An IBM-licensed program designed for use with user-written exits to support data extraction from a variety of Multiple Virtual Storage (MVS) files. Originally designed to support extraction of data from Information Management System/Database Manager (IMS/DB) and Virtual Storage Access Method (VSAM) into DB2 and SQL/DS, DXT now supports extraction from DB2 and SQL/DS and, with version 2.3, from third-party database management system (DBMS) products. Version 2.4 enables extraction from Digital Equipment VAX/VMS data sources.

dyadic
A multiprocessor design term that IBM introduced with the 3081. Multiple Virtual Storage (MVS) sees a dyadic processor as two processors running as one.

dynamic adaptive routing
Automatic selection and use of alternative communications paths among two or more midrange systems of the same supplier in the event of a congested, faulty or downed circuit within the preferred data path.

Dynamic Data Exchange (See DDE)

dynamic database restructuring
The ability to change the relational-database structure, table capacities and security without unloading and reloading the database.

dynamic hardware reconfiguration
The ability to add or delete midrange system hardware components and modify operating-system hardware configuration tables by operator control without turning power off and re-initializing the operating system.

Dynamic Host Configuration Protocol (See DHCP)

Dynamic Link Library (See DLL)

dynamic random-access memory (See DRAM)

Dynamic Server Architecture (See DSA)

E-mail (electronic mail)
Any communications service that permits the electronic transmission and storage of messages and attached or enclosed files.

E-mail/document transfer
The process of sending electronic mail and documents to users on midrange systems from the same supplier within the same logical network.

E.164
The next-generation public network address, E.164 is a 10-digit phone number with the freedom of choice in all digits that was implemented starting in 1997.

E1
The two megabits per second (Mbps) level in the European digital hierarchy, roughly equivalent to North American T1, which is 1.544 Mbps.

E3
The 34 megabits per second (Mbps) level in the European digital hierarchy, roughly equivalent to North American T3, which is 44.74 Mbps.

E-4GL (enterprise fourth-generation language)

E-AD (enterprise applications development)

EAM (enterprisewide asset management; also called equipment asset management)
A systemic approach to managing IT assets, including IS department staff, users, IT procurement teams, suppliers, facilities, hardware and software. Effective asset management must optimize the use and deployment of those assets, using a total-cost-of-ownership approach when making IT investment decisions. The goals of asset management should be: 1) to optimize the utilization of all assets, 2) to lower operating costs, and 3) to enable effective IT risk management.

EARS (Electronic Authoring and Routing System)
Digital Equipment workflow application built by Digital's field organization using ALL-IN-1 mail and FMS, the forms system native to ALL-IN-1.

EBCDIC (Extended Binary-Coded Decimal Interchange Code)
A coded character set consisting of eight-bit coded characters. EBCDIC is the usual code generated by synchronous IBM devices.

EC (electronic commerce)

Electronic commerce includes technologies and integrated applications to link enterprises, and multienterprise business strategies that are made possible by EC technologies and applications.

EC (engineering change)

A revision to a parts list, bill of material, engineering drawing or engineering part model authorized by the engineering department. Changes are usually identified by a control number and are made for safety, cost reduction or functionality reasons. To effectively implement engineering change, all affected functions should review and agree to the changes, e.g., the materials, quality assurance, assembly engineering and other departments. Also called ECO (engineering change order) or ECN (engineering change notice).

EC (European Community, now known as European Union)

ECC (error-correcting code)

The diagnostic code used to correct data storage errors and to isolate hardware failures. Based on a concept of simultaneous polynomial equations, the read-back process generates a "correction" profile over the incorrect data. All ECCs have a very small but finite failure rate; that is, some uncor-

rectable errors will either appear as correctable or appear as having no error at all. In either situation, bad data is passed as verified and valid.

ECL (emitter-coupled logic)

A type of bipolar (a category of chip design) transistor characterized by extremely fast switching speeds.

ECMA (European Computer Manufacturers Association)

economic life

The remaining period over which the property is expected to be economically usable with normal repairs and maintenance.

economic order quantity (See EOQ)

EC

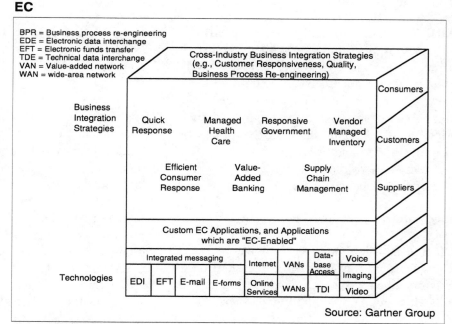

The Components of Electronic Commerce

ECR (efficient customer response)

ECS (enterprise client/server)

ECU (European Currency Unit, now known as "euro")

EDA (electronic design automation)
The use of a computer to design and simulate performance of electronic circuits on a chip. Similar to automatic test equipment, which tests primarily chips in electronic systems.

EDA/SQL (Enterprise Data Access/Structured Query Language)
A product by Information Builders, EDA provides a common interface between a wide range of Structured Query Language (SQL) programs and SQL databases. Queries on data from different types of databases can be queried simultaneously using EDA.

EDD (electronic document distribution)
Distribution of information without the use of paper. The goal is to enable viewers to actively interact with a document, directing the document to display information upon request. The complexity of this task is compounded by the addition of media unsupported by print (for example, sound and animation). EDD market problems are twofold: limiting technology and lack of acceptance by end users.

edge gateway (See EGW)

EDI (electronic data interchange)
The electronic transfer of pre-formatted business documents, such as purchase orders and bills of lading, between trading partners.

EDIF (Electronic Data Interchange Format)
A standard for defining the exchange of electronic data.

EDIFACT (Electronic Data Interchange for Administration, Commerce and Transportation)

EDM (enterprise desktop manager)
A software application used to manage the total desktop environment. It includes functions such as software distribution and installation; configuration management; change management; and hardware and software inventory.

EDM (EMC Data Manager)
Backup and recovery software for the relational database management system (RDBMS) environment developed by EMC. It is considered to be a high-end replacement for EMC's Epoch Systems.

EDMS (electronic document management system)
A system for managing electronic documents.

EDO (extended data output)
Extended data output memory is a fairly simple, pin-compatible derivative of standard fast-page mode asynchronous memory. EDO can improve memory performance by as much as 20 percent or 30 percent by shortening the page mode cycle of traditional memory. It can be used for dynamic random-access memory (DRAM) or video random-access memory (VRAM). It does not command a significant premium over standard page-mode DRAM.

EDS (electronic data streaming)

EDS (Electronic Data Systems)

EEC (European economic community)

EFT (electronic funds transfer)
The transfer of money between accounts or organizations electronically.

EGW (edge gateway)
The perimeter switching technology that offers users the interface to a variety of virtual public data services.

EHLLAPI (Extended High-Level Language Application Programming Interface)

EIA (Electronic Industries Association)

EIA (enterprise information architecture)
Enterprise-specific definition of rules defining the use of middleware in third-generation office systems. The EIA rules include both application programming interfaces (APIs) and protocols addressing both interoperability and portability of applications, whether acquired or developed internally. The EIA is a living specification requiring constant management and regular review for enhancement.

EIA/TIA (Electronic Industries Association/ Telecommunications Industry Association)

E-IDE (Enhanced Integrated Drive Electronics)
An interface that supports larger capacities than standard Integrated Drive Electronics (IDE) and allows for more peripherals to attach to the interface, providing some incremental flexibility and expandability.

EIM (enterprise information management)
EIM is an architecture management approach for resolving architectural differences within office information system (OIS) implementations. EIM is a tool for strategic planning comprising the enterprise information architecture (EIA) and a set of strategic IS management practices. By applying EIM to their enterprises, users have been able to migrate from the incompatible systems of the 1980s to the interoperable systems of the 1990s.

EIS (executive information system)
An application program specifically designed for use by the corporate executive. Presentation of material is often structured after the "board briefing book" concept. Detailed information on the summarized charts is often made available by using a concept known as "drilling." The EIS acts as a usable interface to a database of company information. It automates high-level analysis and reporting, and typically has a graphical and intuitive interface.

EISA (Extended Industry Standard Architecture)
Originally developed as an alternative 32-bit master bus to IBM's Micro Channel master bus for its PS/2 family of micro computers. Unlike the Micro Channel, one of the design goals of the EISA bus was to enable the use of add-on cards developed for IBM's PC and PC/AT computers.

EKA (enterprise knowledge architecture)
The table of contents, or "yellow pages," for information bases accessible through the information services of the intranet, including E-mail and Lotus notes. It enables a user to navigate to enterprise resources using a hyperlink to the

specific Web page, narrowing the search before launching a search inquiry.

Electronic Authoring and Routing System (See EARS)

electronic commerce (See EC)

electronic data interchange (See EDI)

Electronic Data Interchange Format (See EDIF)

electronic design automation (See EDA)

electronic document distribution (See EDD)

electronic funds transfer (See EFT)

electronic mail (See E-mail)

Electronic Mail Association (See EMA)

electronic marketplace (See EM)

electronic messaging
The sending and receiving of messages and, increasingly, data through a network. Like paper messaging, it is accomplished through a number of tasks, including composition, assembly, addressing, posting, sorting, routing and delivery.

Electronic Messaging Association (See EMA)

electronic software distribution (See ESD)

electronic switching system (See ESS)

electronic tandem network (See ETN)

ELS (enterprise library service)

EM (electronic marketplace)
A network service shared by multiple individuals and enterprises where information about products and services is shared electronically among enterprises, and where those products and services may be purchased without the aid of voice or paper-based exchanges. Examples of EMs would be the Internet, membership-based online services, bulletin boards, interconnected private networks and value-added third-party networks.

EM

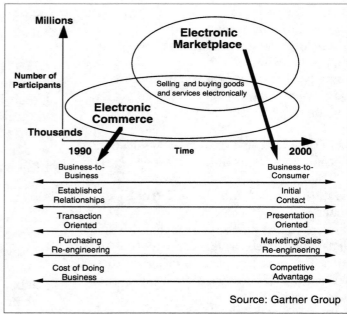

Electronic Commerce vs. Electronic Marketplaces

**EMA (Electronic Messaging Association—
formerly Electronic Mail Association)**

An Arlington, Va.-based electronic-mail industry organization, with 50 percent end-user membership. Has played a role in bringing together
various application programming interface (API)
factions to develop the Common Mail Call specification.

**EMA (Enterprise Management Architec-
ture — Digital Equipment)**

**Embedded Structured Query Language
(See ESQL)**

E-mail (electronic mail)

The transmission of messages (generally text or
graphics) over communications networks. Some
E-mail systems are limited to communications
between users on the same network, while others have gateways that allow users to send messages to their designated computer systems or
worldwide over the Internet.

EMC (EMC Corp.)

emitter-coupled logic (See ECL)

**EMS (Enterprise Messaging Server —
Microsoft)**

Former name for Microsoft Exchange, an enterprisewide messaging and mail system. Rolled
into Exchange, it and other planned products
will ship as a single system: a work-group-
focused, enterprise-scoped platform for stan-
dards-based messaging, groupware, work flow,
document management and "information exchange" through a single, multimedia mailbox.

EMS (Expanded Memory Specification)

EMU (enterprise messaging utility)

A stable infrastructure for electronic messaging.

EMU (European monetary union)

EN (end node)

A node that only sends and receives information
and cannot route and forward information to
another node.

encapsulation

The binding and the hiding of the underlying
implementation of an object's data and operations. The set of operations that is accessible is
the object's interface.

end node (See EN)

end user

1. The person, program or equipment that uses
   the computer network to obtain, process or
   exchange data.
2. An individual who interacts with a computing device through applications. Technical
   personnel are not considered to be users
   when they are programming or operating
   the computer.

end-user computing (See EUC)

engineering change (See EC)

**Enhanced Integrated Drive Electronics
(See E-IDE)**

**enhanced private shared communications
service (See EPSCS)**

Enterprise Data Access (See EDA)

**Enterprise Data Access/Structured Query
Language (See EDA/SQL)**

enterprise desktop manager (See EDM)

**enterprise information architecture (See
EIA)**

**enterprise information management (See
EIM)**

**enterprise knowledge architecture (See
EKA)**

Enterprise Messaging Server (See EMS)

enterprise messaging utility (See EMU)

enterprise resource planning (See ERP)

enterprise server platform (See ESP)

Enterprise Systems Architecture (See ESA)

**Enterprise Systems Connection (See
ESCON)**

**enterprisewide asset management (See
EAM)**

enterprisewide web (See EWW)

Entry Server Offering (See ESO)

EO (Enterprise Option — Lotus)

**E-OOA/OOD (enterprise object-oriented
analysis/object-oriented design)**

EOQ (economic order quantity)
The fixed order quantity that is the amount of
product to be purchased or manufactured at one
time to minimize the total cost involved. EOQ
includes the ordering costs (setup of machines,
writing order, checking receipts) and carrying
costs (cost of capital invested insurance, taxes,
space, obsolescence and spoilage).

EOS (electronic output strategies)

**EPSCS (enhanced private shared commu-
nications service)**
EPSCS is a service designed to provide customized private communications to customers.
Switching centers are located on telephone company premises and may be shared with other
EPSCS customers or other telephone company
services. Private-line channels between switching centers and a customer's premises are dedicated to specific customers.

equipment asset management (See EAM)

erasable optical storage device
An optical storage device on which data can
be rewritten, either after bulk erasure or spot
erasure.

ERP (enterprise resource planning)
A concept developed by Gartner Group describing the next generation of manufacturing business systems and manufacturing resource planning (MRP II) software. It includes the client/
server architecture, uses graphical user interfaces (GUIs) and can be crafted with open systems. Beyond the standard functionality that is
offered, other features are included, e.g., quality, process operations management and regula-

tory reporting. In addition, the base technology used in ERP will give users both software and hardware independence as well as an easy upgrade path. Key to ERP is the way in which users can tailor the application so it is intrinsically easy to use.

error-correcting code (See ECC)

ESA (Enterprise Systems Architecture)
ESA/370 is IBM's System/370 extended architecture for the 3090 and 4381 processors, and is supported by MVS/ESA (Multiple Virtual Storage/ESA). The major ESA feature is the support of data spaces in addition to the program-and-data address spaces of System/370.

ESCON (Enterprise Systems Connection)
A high-speed fiber-optic serial channel for IBM's ES/9000 processors announced in September 1990. ESCON was initially based in part on a fiber-optic link operating at a speed of 200 meagabits per second (Mbits) regardless of the driver light source, but has been driven much faster.

ESD (electronic software distribution)
A means of installing software by transmitting it over a network. ESD is designed to help users distribute programs and files in their environments. The development of client/server applications has made ESD a critical requirement. Without an effective means of automating the distribution and installation of software, most applications of client/server technology will not be viable.

ESDI (Enhanced Small Device Interface)

ESDS (electronic software delivery system)

ESF (Extended Super Frame)
AT&T's and Bell Communications Research's (different) framing standards that improve networking performance monitoring.

ESIOP (Environment-Specific Inter-ORB Protocol)

ESO (Entry Server Offering)
A large-system processor marketing program from IBM. It includes the hardware, a standard suite of IBM software, maintenance and services.

ESOP (employee stock ownership plan)

ESP (enterprise server platform)
An inherently distributable, multiply interoperable server engineered for use within the context of a larger information technology architecture. It transparently provides services to any authorized client. ESP is a collection of services that will enable enterprises to manage and leverage the benefits of personal, workgroup and enterprise information processing resources.

ESP (external services provider)
Firm that is a separate legal entity from the contracting company and that provides services such as consulting, software development (including systems integration) and outsourcing.

ESPRIT (European Strategic Program for Research and Development of Information Technology)
A research and development (R&D) program, funded by the European Community, that was

chartered to create a technology base for the development of products, processes and services for European companies in an effort to gain world information market share.

ESQL (Embedded Structured Query Language)
Statements inserted within a program during its preparation that will not change when the program is run.

ESS (electronic switching system)
A circuit switch environment that has supported delivery of services through telecommunications networks for most of this century. The architecture is now changing over to asynchronous transfer mode (ATM).

Ethernet
A baseband local-area network (LAN) developed by Xerox. It has a bus topology with carrier sense multiple access with collision detection (CSMA/CD) access control. Ethernet is not identical to Institute of Electrical and Electronics Engineers (IEEE) 802.3.

Ethernet LAN connect
Connection from the midrange system to Macintoshes via Ethernet protocols.

ETN (electronic tandem network)
A private telecommunications network in which calls are automatically switched over specific trunks.

ETSI (European Telecommunications Standards Institute)
The European counterpart to the American National Standards Institute (ANSI) chartered to help pave the way for telecommunications integration in the European Union.

EU (European Union)

EUC (end-user computing)
Computer operations or activities carried out by the end user, often incurring hidden costs.

ESP

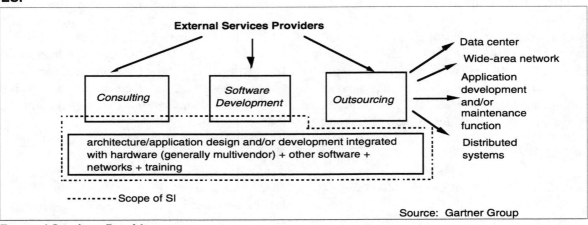

External Services Providers

European Strategic Program for Research and Development of Information Technology (See ESPRIT)

European Telecommunications Standards Institute (See ETSI)

EWW (enterprisewide web)
Internal implementations of Web-based system components and standards that support basic intraenterprise publishing, broadcasting and information-sharing capabilities.

executive information system (See EIS)

expert system
A software system that consists of two basic components: a knowledge base and an inference engine. The system mimics the reasoning process of an expert. A knowledge-based system is sometimes also referred to as an expert system.

explicit input
The definition of model dimensions using explicit numbers as opposed to variables.

explosion
An extension of a bill of material into the total of each of the components required to manufacture a given quantity of upper-level assembly or subassembly.

Extended Architecture (See XA)

Extended Binary-Coded Decimal Interchange Code (See EBCDIC)

extended data output (See EDO)

Extended Industry Standard Architecture (See EISA)

Extended Recovery Facility (See XRF)

Extended Super Frame (See ESF)

external services provider (See ESP)

extranet
The extension of the internal Web infrastructure to include business partners and other trusted organizations external to the implementing organization. Extranets allow these external groups access to protected applications and services supported by an existing intranet.

F

F-UNI (Frame User Network Interface)

facsimile (See fax)

fair market value (See FMV)

FAPs (formats and protocols)
Rules that specify format, timing and error checking between clients and servers.

FASB (Financial Accounting Standards Board)
A self-regulated organization of the accounting profession.

FASB 13 (Financial Accounting Standards Board Statement No. 13)
This statement specifies the classification, accounting and reporting of leases by lessees and lessors.

fault detection and isolation
Online diagnostics that detect and isolate faults in real time, prevent contamination into other areas, and attempt to retry operations.

fault tolerance
The ability to produce correct results, even in the presence of faults or errors through the use of redundancy in hardware or checking techniques.

fax (facsimile)
The process or equipment that sends and receives data or printed information over the telephone lines or radio via electronic signals. The information is then printed at the receiving end.

FC (Fiber Channel)

FC-AL (Fiber Channel-Arbitrated Loop)
A subset of the Fiber Channel Standard that was defined to support network storage. It is an inexpensive technology that supports up to 127 devices on a single loop. Only one pair of devices can talk at one time on the loop. Each port on the loop sees all messages and ignores those not intended for it.

FC-EL (Fiber Channel-Enhanced Loop)
An expanded version of FC-AL aimed at extending loop topologies to support additional applications.

FCC (Federal Communications Commission)
The U.S. federal agency responsible for regulating interstate telecommunications, as well as international telecommunications, aspects of cellular communications and broadcasting. The FCC was established by the Communications Act of 1934.

FCIF (Full Common Intermediate Format)

Part of the H.261 worldwide video code standard, which is designed to accommodate both the North American National TV System Committee (NTSC) and European PAL protocols, that is, the accommodation is accomplished by using the NTSC frame rate and the PAL resolution in a compromise called the Common Intermediate Format (CIF), of which there are two versions: Full CIF (FCIF) and Quarter CIF (QCIF). Full CIF pictures will be sharper in the future, but at the cost of additional processing power requirements.

FCLC (Fiber Channel Loop Community)

FCP (Foundation for Cooperative Processing)

FCS (Fiber Channel Standard)
A definition of fiber channel specifications undertaken by the American National Standards Institute (ANSI) Technical Committee (now known as X3T11) as the Fiber Channel Initiative of 1988. The developers wanted to provide an extremely flexible method of information transfer that can support both channel-style and network-style peripheral interconnections.

FCS (first customer shipment)

FDDI (Fiber Distributed Data Interface)
An American National Standards Institute (ANSI) standard for 100 megabits per second (Mbps) fiber-optic local-area networks (LANs). Incorporates token processing and supports circuit-switched voice and packetized data.

FDM (frequency division multiplexing)
The division of a transmission frequency range into narrower bands to create two or more channels, enabling each data source to have its own channel.

FDMA (frequency division multiple access)
A user access technique based on the division of the available bandwidth into smaller frequency slots.

FD:OCA (Formatted Data: Object Content Architecture)
An architecture, central to Distributed Relational Data Architecture (DRDA), that can exchange field-formatted information — that is, primarily Structured Query Language (SQL) data. It associates tags with data so that heterogeneous database management systems (DBMSs), initially within IBM but potentially beyond, can converse.

FE (field engineer)
An engineer who can be on-site.

fear, uncertainty and doubt (See FUD)

feature-based modeling
A modeling technique that allows the creation of manufacturing form features, e.g., through holes, ribs or slots, when defining mechanical component models.

feature-driven manufacturing
The ability to automatically create optimized process instructions and machine tool paths by utilizing mechanical component form features.

FEC (forward error correction)

Federal Communications Commission (See FCC)

**Federal Information Processing Standard
(See FIPS)**

FEP (front-end processor)
A communications processor that relieves a host computer of certain processing tasks, such as line control, message handling, code conversion, error control and application functions.

FEPI (front-end programming interface)

FFAPI (File Format Application Programming Interface)
The file format used only by Microsoft Mail is held as proprietary to Microsoft. In order to read or write such a file, the FFAPI utilities provided by Microsoft must be used. The utility creates the message header, or envelope, by writing field tags and data to the file in the Microsoft Mail structured data format. Another utility extracts the data by parsing the data structure.

FFS (fee for service)

FFT:DCA (Final Form Text: Document Content Architecture)
The data stream for passing documents in final form (i.e., unrevisable) under IBM's second-generation Document Content Architecture.

Fiber Distributed Data Interface (See FDDI)

Fiber Channel Standard (See FCS)

fiber optics
A high-bandwidth transmission technology that uses light to carry digital information. One fiber telephone cable carries hundreds of thousands of voice circuits. These cables, or light guides, replace conventional coaxial cables and wire pairs. Fiber transmission facilities occupy far less physical volume for an equivalent transmission capacity, which is a major advantage in crowded ducts. Optical fiber is also immune to electrical interference.

Fiber Channel-Arbitrated Loop (See FC-AL)

Fiber Channel-Enhanced Loop (See FC-EL)

field engineer (See FE)

file
A collection of bytes that together make data, information or programs. Examples include:

- Data file or table
- Spreadsheet
- Document
- Image
- Program
- Audio
- Video

file server
A computer containing files available to all users connected to a local-area network (LAN). In some LANs, a microcomputer is designated as the file server, while in others it is a computer with a large disk drive and specialized software. Some file servers also offer other resources such as gateways and protocol conversion.

File Transfer, Access and Management (See FTAM)

File Transfer Protocol (See FTP)

Final Form Text: Document Content Architecture (See FFT:DCA)

Financial Accounting Standards Board (See FASB)

Financial Accounting Standards Board Statement No. 13 (See FASB 13)

financial footprint

The amount of money paid, monthly or yearly, to a vendor to support a particular system or application. Because most hardware and software is easily upgradable, financial-footprint management involves managing a stream of recurring payments instead of physical assets.

finite loading

Conceptually, the term means putting no more work into a factory than the factory can be expected to execute. The term usually refers to a computer technique that involves automatic shop priority revision to level load operation by operation.

FIPS (Federal Information Processing Standard)

A set of standards produced by the National Institute of Standards and Technology setting forth protocols, encryption, interoperability, hardware, and other specifications for the federal government.

firewall

An application that acts as a boundary between networks to control access and improve the flow of network traffic. Firewalls have become critical applications as the use of the Internet has increased. A firewall can help to ensure that uninvited visitors do not have access to proprietary resources stored on a network.

FireWire

Also known as Institute of Electrical and Electronics Engineers (IEEE) 1394, this is a high-speed serial bus similar to the Universal Serial Bus (USB), but much faster and more expensive to implement. Its primary supporters are Apple Computer and consumer electronics firms such as Fuji, Sony, Hitachi and Nintendo. These firms will use FireWire as the input/output (I/O) bus for next-generation digital products: camcorders, VCRs, TVs, digital cameras and game players.

FireWire

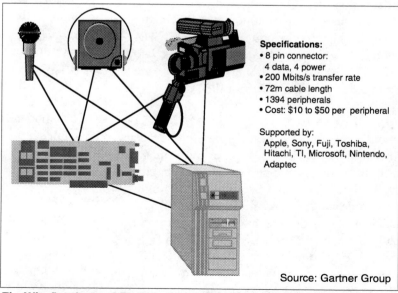

Specifications:
• 8 pin connector:
  4 data, 4 power
• 200 Mbits/s transfer rate
• 72m cable length
• 1394 peripherals
• Cost: $10 to $50 per peripheral

Supported by:
Apple, Sony, Fuji, Toshiba, Hitachi, TI, Microsoft, Nintendo, Adaptec

Source: Gartner Group

FireWire/Institute of Electrical and Electronics Engineers 1394

firm planned order

A planned order that can be frozen in quantity and time. The computer is not allowed to automatically change it; this is the responsibility of the planner in charge of the item that is being planned. This technique can aid planners working with material requirements planning (MRP) systems to respond to material and capacity problems by firming up selected planned orders. Additionally, firm planned orders are the normal method of stating the master production schedule.

firmware

A category of memory chips that hold their content without electrical power and include ROM, PROM, EPRON and EEPROM technologies. Firmware becomes "hard software" when holding program code.

first generation

The class of office information systems (OIS) products dominated by dedicated word processors, such as Digital Equipment's DECmate, IBM's DisplayWriter and Wang's OIS. The period began with the first word processors (late 1970s) and lasted until the introduction of the first integrated office systems (1983).

floppy disk

A reusable, portable storage tool. Floppy disks, sometimes called diskettes, were the primary method of software and data distribution beginning in the 1970s. They were originally eight inches wide and enclosed in a flexible envelope; a 5.25-inch version was later introduced, and finally a 3.5-inch floppy disk encased in rigid plastic has become the standard. CD-ROMs have become a popular alternative to floppy disks, especially for larger software and multi-media files, given their higher storage capacity. E-mail has also become an alternative to floppy disks as network transmission speeds have increased.

FLOPS (floating-point operations per second)

FM (frequency modulation)

Varying the number of cycles (frequency) of a carrier signal to enable the use of a single path for a number of channels.

FMV (fair market value)

The price for which equipment could be sold in an arm's-length transaction between unrelated parties.

FOCA (Font Object Content Architecture)

Focus

A fourth-generation language (4GL) from Information Builders. It belongs to a class of software called information generators. Focus boasts easy-to-use, English-language commands with online help and error correction. Focus features "talk" windows, which improve end-user productivity. It also provides integrated reporting, ad hoc queries, graphs, statistics, financial modeling and a spreadsheet for building decision support systems.

FODS (front office decision support)

form factor

The size and shape of a product. For example, most 5.25-inch Winchester drives have the same dimension so that they can fit interchangeably into computer cabinets. For the same reason, 5.25-inch optical drives are expected to have the same form factor as their predecessor Winchesters.

formal standards
Specifications or styles that are approved by vendor-independent standards bodies, such as the American National Standards Institute (ANSI), the International Standards Organization (ISO), the Institute of Electrical and Electronics Engineers (IEEE) and the National Institute for Standards and Technology (NIST).

formats and protocols (See FAPs)

Formatted Data:Object Content Architecture (See FD:OCA)

formatting
The preparation of a storage medium with guidance information, synchronization information, and a structure for keeping or collecting information for a directory; this collection of material placed on the disk before user data is written is called a "format," and frequently also includes room for error correction check sums and rewriting of bad or updated sectors.

FORTRAN (Formula Translator)
A programming language developed primarily for numeric computations and chiefly used in mathematics, science and engineering. It was introduced in the 1950s as the first high-level language (i.e., closer to natural language than to machine language).

FP (function point)
Function points measure the size of an application system based on the functional view of the system. The size is determined by counting the number of inputs, outputs, queries, internal files and external files in the system and adjusting that total for the functional complexity of the system. Function point analysis, originally developed at IBM, has as an advantage its focus on measuring software produced in terms of functionality delivered to the end user, rather than in terms of development deliverables, which have no direct bearing on the end user.

FPS (frames per second)

FR (frame relay)
An American National Standards Institute (ANSI) standard (T1S1) for an Integrated Services Digital Network (ISDN) packet-mode bearer service that defines a user-to-network interface. The two main benefits are bandwidth on demand and integrated access. The standard currently addresses data communications speeds up to 2 megabits per second (Mbps) over permanent virtual circuits. By reducing the network functions performed, frame relay takes advantage of more error-free physical facilities to improve throughput.

FRAD (frame relay assembler/ disassembler)
A communications device that formats outgoing data into the format required by a frame relay network. It is the frame relay counterpart to the X.25 packet assembler/disassembler.

frame relay (See FR)

frame relay assembler/disassembler (See FRAD)

framework
A style guide that defines the look, feel and interoperability of software applications.

frequency division multiple access (See FDMA)

frequency division multiplexing (See FDM)

frequency modulation (See FM)

front-end processor (See FEP)

frontware
Software that runs on a programmable workstation to provide better end-user interfaces for application programs running elsewhere.

FS (Future System)
FS was thought by some factions within IBM to be the successor architecture to S/370. It featured one-level addressing, an object orientation, interactive interfaces for operations and programmers, and high-level input/output (I/O).

FTAM (File Transfer, Access and Management)
The Open Systems Interconnection (OSI) standard for file transfer (i.e., the communication of an entire file between systems), file access (i.e., the ability to remotely access one or more records in a file) and management (e.g., the ability to create/delete or name/rename a file).

FTC (Federal Trade Commission)

FTE (full-time equivalent)

FTP (File Transfer Protocol)
A Transmission Control Protocol/Internet Protocol (TCP/IP) standard used to log onto a network, list directories and copy files. That is, it provides authentication of the user and lets users transfer files, list directories, delete and rename files on the foreign host, and perform wild-card transfers.

FTTC (fiber to the curb)

FUD (fear, uncertainty and doubt)
A marketing tactic that can be used by major computer system vendors.

Full Common Intermediate Format (See FCIF)

full duplex
Pertaining to the capability to transmit in two directions simultaneously.

function point (See FP)

Future System (See FS)

G

gateway
1. A computer that sits between different networks or applications. The gateway converts information, data or other communications from one protocol or format to another. A router may perform some of the functions of a gateway. An Internet gateway can transfer communications between a corporate network and the Internet. Because organizations often use protocols on their local-area networks (LANs) that differ from those of the Internet, a gateway will often act as a protocol converter so that users can send and receive communications over the Internet.
2. A physical or logical network station that interconnects two otherwise incompatible networks, network nodes, subnetworks or devices. Gateways perform protocol conversion operations across a wide spectrum of communications functions or layers. A product or feature that uses proprietary techniques to link heterogeneous systems.

Gbyte (gigabyte)
One billion bytes.

Gbit (gigabit)
One billion bits.

GDDM (Graphical Data Display Manager)
A format manager that handles both graphics and alphanumerics on display devices and printers. Its major component is a set of functions for drawing pictures and handling text. The GDDM application programming interface (API) is the basis for the Systems Application Architecture (SAA) Presentation Manager (PM).

GDMO (Guidelines for the Definition of Managed Objects)
An International Standards Organization (ISO) common object modeling technology standard, part of the Open Systems Interconnection (OSI) Common Management Information Protocol (CMIP). A quasi-object database that "abstracts" objects but does not embed procedures (i.e., the objects have persistence and class, but not inheritance). It is endorsed by the Network Management Forum (NMF) of independent vendors and users.

GDP (gross domestic product)

GDS (Global Directory Service)
The part of the Distributed Computing Environment (DCE) directory services, based on Siemens Nixdorf's X.500 directory, that provides a pointer to resources between cells.

Gearbox
An industrialized personal computer developed by IBM that is configured much like a programmable logic controller.

GEIS (GE Information Services)

GEMMS (Global Enterprise Manufacturing Management System)
A manufacturing product for the process industries from Datalogix, with a niche-oriented process-manufacturing application.

GEMS (Global Enterprise Management of Storage)
A Legato NetWorker product that establishes a Web-server-based global control zone, which enables the administration of multiple NetWorker servers (data zones) as a single image.

General Inter-ORB Protocol (See GIOP)

geostationary
An orbit that permits a satellite to appear stationary relative to the Earth. It is a circular, 35,786-kilometer-high orbit in the plane of the equator. A satellite moving from west to east in this orbit has no apparent motion with respect to the surface of the Earth.

GFLOPS (giga-FLOPS)
One billion floating-point operations per second (if used with a specific amount, e.g., 50 GFLOPS).

GIF (Graphics Interchange Format)
An integrated Web component of Hypertext Markup Language (HTML) into which graphics files can be converted so that programs can read and write them.

gigabit (See Gbit)

gigabyte (See Gbyte)

giga-FLOPS (See GFLOPS)

GIOP (General Inter-ORB Protocol)
A protocol that defines a small set of messages and data formats. It enables a client-side object request broker (ORB) to forward object method invocations to another, server-side ORB and receive back replies and error messages.

GIOP

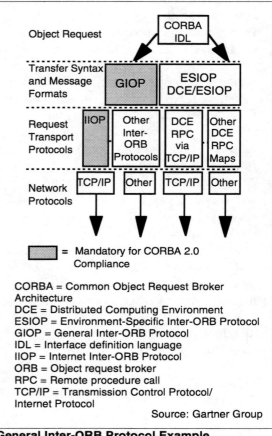

General Inter-ORB Protocol Example

GIPS (billion instructions per second)

GIS (geographic information system)

GL (graphics library)
A component of a graphical user interface (GUI)
that provides a high-level graphics programming interface.

Global Directory Service (See GDS)

**Global Enterprise Management of Storage
(See GEMS)**

**Global Enterprise Manufacturing Manage-
ment System (See GEMMS)**

Global Positioning System (See GPS)

**Global System for Mobile Communications
(See GSM)**

**GMLC (Graduated Monthly License
Charge)**
The traditional S/390 software pricing structure
offered by IBM.

**GOCA (Graphics Object Content Architec-
ture)**
IBM's Object Content Architecture format for
vector graphic objects. Describes complex pictures to interchange within or across environments.

**GOCA Extended (Graphics Object Content
Architecture Extended)**
An extension to GOCA that can describe complex pictures that contain advanced text, image
and graphics.

**GOSIP (Government Open Systems Inter-
connection Profile)**

governance
The process of defining the mechanisms for
accomplishing an organization's overall goals.
Governance determines how decisions are made,
executed and evaluated; it is the glue that holds
a distributed organization together.

GPC (general-purpose computer)

GPS (Global Positioning System)
An approach to calculating a location. A transceiver based in the vehicle detects signals from
multiple geostationary satellites to calculate the
vehicle's latitude and longitude. Those readings
can then be transmitted back to a dispatch center
using the satellite, cellular other two-way wireless service. The dispatch center can combine
the reading with mapping software to discern
the exact locations, which can then be used to
optimize routing and scheduling.

**Graduated Monthly License Charge (See
GMLC)**

granularity
The ability to increase a system's capacity and
performance through incremental processor expansion.

**Graphical Data Display Manager (See
GDDM)**

graphical shell
A graphical-user-interface-based "desktop manager" enabling the majority of end-user operations (e.g., running applications and manipulat-
ing files) to be performed in a "point and click"

manner without use of a traditional, character-oriented command language. Examples include Hewlett-Packard's Visual User Environment, IXI X.desktop, Visix Looking Glass and TeleSoft TeleUSE.

graphical user interface (See GUI)

Graphics Interchange Format (See GIF)

graphics library (See GL)

Graphics Object Content Architecture (See GOCA)

Graphics Object Content Architecture Extended (See GOCA Extended)

gray scale
A range of gray tones from black to white used to create an image.

group technology
An engineering and manufacturing philosophy which identifies the "sameness" of parts, equipment or processes. It provides for rapid retrieval of existing designs.

Groupe Speciale Mobile (See GSM)

groupware
Software that supports nonstructured, nondeterministic interpersonal processes and the objects with which people commonly work. Groupware was originally coined to describe a new class of applications designed to provide electronic support for groups of individuals working together toward a common goal. The term has been applied to applications ranging from unstructured electronic mail to rigorously structured workflow systems. Groupware is more useful as a concept when it is broken down into three major stages: communication, coordination and cooperation. In this light, groupware applications can be viewed in terms of the degree of structure in the group interaction and in the complexity of that structure, and the rigor with which the activity itself is monitored. This categorization of the groupware concept into stages provides meaningful differentiation and definition of the categories of applications it addresses.

GSM (Global System for Mobile Communications — formerly Groupe Speciale Mobile)
A pan-European digital mobile telephone network based on digital technology utilizing the 905-915 megahertz (MHz)/950-960 MHz reserved spectrum to provide the capability of roaming over 18 countries with competition both within and between countries. The digital GSM cellular system was implemented as the one compatible system across Europe, but calling a roaming station requires signaling on the digital terrestrial networks, which is not scheduled in some European networks until beyond the year 2000.

Guardian
Tandem's operating system, which resides in each processor of a multiprocessor complex and manages the system resources as a single image.

GUI (graphical user interface)
A generic user interface. GUIs include OpenLook, Motif and Apple Computer's Macintosh interface. A screen interface characterized by windows and icons that allows mouse input. A comprehensive GUI environment in-

cludes four components: a graphics library, a user interface toolkit, a user interface style guide and consistent applications. The graphics library provides a high-level graphics programming interface. The user interface toolkit, built on top of the graphics library, provides application programs with mechanisms for creating and managing the dialog elements of the windows, icons, menus, pointers and scroll bars (WIMPS) interface. The user interface style guide specifies how applications should employ the dialog elements to present a consistent, easy-to-use environment (i.e., "look and feel") to the user. Application program conformance with a single user interface style is the primary determinant of ease of learning and use, and thus, of application effectiveness and user productivity.

GUI applications development tools

Graphical, interactive tools for the nonprocedural development of application user interfaces compliant with the system's user interface style guide. Examples include Digital Equipment's Visual User Interface Tool and NeXT's Interface Builder.

Guidelines for the Definition of Managed Objects (See GDMO)

H

H.261
An International Telecommunications Union (ITU) standard for video compression (also known as px64). H.261 will be the worldwide standard and therefore must accommodate both the North American National Television System Committee (NTSC) and European PAL protocols.

H.320
An international standards specification for audioconferencing and videoconferencing that comprises many standards, including H.261 standard, the compression schema for video transmissions.

HACMP (High Availability Clustered Multiprocessing)
An IBM RS/6000 product originally designed to provide a high-availability configuration (by enabling automated failover from one RS/6000 to another). HACMP comprises:

- Cluster management software to restart an application or subsystem on an alternate RS/6000 processor after a failure of the primary processor.
- Distributed lock manager software to coordinate and synchronize process execution on multiple processors in a cluster.

- Configuration and topology software management tools to enable developers to build cluster-aware applications.

half duplex
Pertaining to the capability to transmit in two directions but not simultaneously.

hard disk
The fixed main storage area for computing devices. The hard disk is where the operating system and other software are permanently stored on a PC. Hard disks typically have a larger storage capacity and faster data retrieval capabilities than floppy disks.

hardware
Machinery and equipment associated with computing devices. A computer is composed of both hardware and software. The software provides the instructions, and the hardware performs the processing.

HBA (host bus adapter)

HCO (healthcare organization)

HDA (head disk assembly)
A sealed assembly containing magnetic disks, head and access arms. By reducing contamination, a sealed HDA enables the head to fly closer

to the disk surface, increasing the areal density that can be obtained.

HDCD (high-density CD)

HDD (hard disk drive)

HDLC (High-level Data Link Control)
A bit-oriented data link protocol developed by the International Standards Organization (ISO) and used in Open Systems Interconnection (OSI).

HDM (hardware device module)

HDS (Hitachi Data Systems)

head disk assembly (See HDA)

Health Level 7 (See HL7)

HEDIS (Health Plan Employer Data and Information Set)

helical-scan recording
In tape recording, when the tape is wrapped around a transport drum at an angle, track length is created that is nearly 10 times longer than the tape width. These diagonal tracks can increase track density and data transfer rates.

help desk
The first point of contact for all technical and end-user support issues, it includes Tier 1 and Tier 2 support levels. Tier 1 is the first point of contact. Tier 2 help desk analysts have more in-depth technical knowledge or specialized expertise.

help system
A consistent, system-supplied mechanism for system and application programs to offer online, context-sensitive help to end users.

Henderson Strategic Alignment Model
Developed by John Henderson of Boston University, this model provides a helpful framework for the CIO to understand the transition to a new management approach appropriate for the times. In this model, business strategy serves as a demarcation between current and future business platforms. The process of developing business strategy, including the requisite dialog between the IS organization and business units, leads to derivation of future business and IT architectures that will serve the enterprise.

hertz (See Hz)

Henderson Strategic Alignment Model

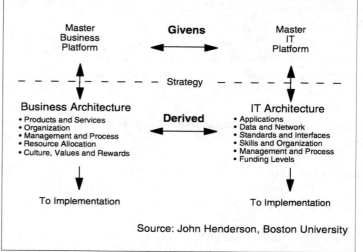

A Strategic Alignment Model

heterogeneous
A system composed of hardware, operating systems, middleware or applications from several different vendors.

HF (high frequency)

HFC (hybrid fiber co-ax)

hierarchical database
A database that is organized in a tree structure in which each record has one owner. Navigation to individual records takes place through predetermined access paths.

hierarchical storage management (See HSM)

Hierarchical Storage Manager (See HSM)

high availability
A high probability that a system at any given time will be operational for useful work and has the ability to recover quickly and with minimum disruption to the user in case of failure. Those characteristics of a data processing system that reduce or eliminate its vulnerability to unscheduled outages, such as power failures, code defects or hardware failures. One element of 24x7.

High Availability Cluster Multiprocessing (See HACMP)

High-level Data Link Control (See HDLC)

high-level language (See HLL)

High-Performance Parallel Interface (See HIPPI)

High-Performance Routing (See HPR)

High-Performance Space (See Hiperspace)

high-speed local-area network (See HS/LAN)

High-Speed Serial Interface (See HSSI)

high-speed subscriber data line (See HSDL)

highly parallel systems (See HPS)

HIMSS (Health Information Management and Systems Society)

Hiperspace (High-Performance Space)
Introduced with Enterprise Systems Architecture (ESA)/370, Hiperspace refers to an address space occupied only by data and to which access is controlled by hardware via special instructions.

HIPPI (High-Performance Parallel Interface)
An American National Standards Institute (ANSI) standard for high-speed channels used in I/O-intensive systems, including supercomputers.

HL7 (Health Level 7)
An application-level standard for community health information network (CHIN) initiatives, widely used in hospitals.

HLL (high-level language)
A procedural programming language that offers a higher level of abstraction than assembly language. Examples of HLLs include COBOL, FORTRAN, PL/I, C, Pascal and Ada. The term is interchangeable with "3GL."

HLLAPI (High-Level Language Application Programming Interface)

HMMP (Hypermedia Management Protocol)
This protocol is a part of the Web-Based Enterprise Management (WBEM) proposal. It operates over the Hypertext Transport Protocol (HTTP) standard, collecting and transporting device management data to populate a management database. Initially, HMMP will complement Simple Network Management Protocol (SNMP), not replace it, although that is the long-term objective.

HMMS (Hypermedia Management Schema)
A schema that was a part of the Web-Based Enterprise Management (WBEM) proposal. It describes what is to be contained in an object model, outlining a data model for representing the relationship between network elements, not just the elements themselves. The schema relies on basic object-oriented constructs, establishing classifications of managed elements in the network environment. The four classes are: system elements, application components, resource components and network components. HMMS has since been renamed Common Information Mode (CIM) by the Desktop Management Task Force (DMTF).

HMOM (Hypermedia Object Manager)
Included within the Web-Based Enterprise Management (WBEM) proposal, HMOM is an example of a specification designed to use the data model — as described by Hypermedia Management Schema (HMMS) — in developing a repository of object instances, each representing network elements. HMOM serves as a controller to management data (allowing network managers and management applications to observe and manipulate this data) through a series of management protocols and interfaces.

home page
The top-level page or entry point into a Web site.

host
Any computer connected to the Internet that has a domain name associated with it.

hot links and links
Areas on a Web page that when "clicked on" will transport the user to another Web page. These are analogous to hypertext.

HP (Hewlett-Packard)

HPC (high-performance computing)

HPCC (High Performance Computing and Communications — federal program)

HPR (High-Performance Routing)
IBM's technology to enable users to send Systems Network Architecture (SNA) traffic over frame and cell-based networks, making for more efficient communications. For example, the HPR version of Advanced Peer-to-Peer Networking (APPN) is generally superior to Transmission Control Protocol/Internet Protocol (TCP/IP), which uses reactive congestion control, while APPN is predictive, resulting in higher network utilization and throughput for APPN. Because it is newer, APPN can better take advantage of increasingly error-free, high-speed digital transmission facilities. TCP/IP's domain name service and limited (now insufficient) addressing

capacity are inferior in performance to APPN's topology database and use of logical unit names. APPN supports a prioritization/class-of-service mechanism for different types of network applications, while individual router vendors have been forced to add their own nonstandard prioritization capabilities to TCP/IP.

HPS (highly parallel systems)
Hardware configurations having from 10 to 99 central processing units (CPUs).

HP-UX
Hewlett-Packard's System V-based Unix implementation, with real-time extensions added.

HR (human resources)

HRM (human-resource management)

HRMS (human-resource management system — generic term)

HRMS (Human Resource Management System — PeopleSoft)

HSDL (high-speed subscriber data line)
A local phone line with full-duplex TI capabilities. As corporate intranets grow, bigger "pipes" are needed to maintain network performance. The use of inverse multiplexers that combine multiple E1 circuits will be the best way to deliver that bandwidth between the user site and the carrier's central office. But the use of HSDL technology, as an alternative to inverse multiplexing of E1 circuits, will be a "dark horse" alternative to inverse multiplexing. Unlike inverse multiplexing, HSDL would require new support systems and maintenance procedures.

HS LAN (high-speed local-area network)
A LAN operating at four megabits (Mbps) per second or more to facilitate rapid exchange of files and mail within a broader departmental or divisional environment.

HSM (hierarchical storage management)
A storage management technology that can be used to identify inactive data and move it to near-line storage, automate the retrieval process, and migrate the data back to the primary storage medium and provide access for the user.

HSM (Hierarchical Storage Manager — IBM, a k a DFSMShsm)
An earlier version of IBM's Data Facility Hierarchical Storage Manager. Originally introduced in 1975 with the IBM 3850 Mass Storage Subsystem.

HSSI (High-Speed Serial Interface)
Standard for a serial interface used to connect to T3 lines. HSSI operates over a shielded cable at speeds of up to 52 megabits per second (Mbps) and distances of up to 50 feet. Functionally, it serves the same purpose as lower-speed serial interfaces such as V.35 and RS232, in that it provides the interface to DCE for wide-area-network (WAN) communications.

HTML (Hypertext Markup Language)
A scripting language for developing hypertext documents on the Web. It runs on a number of client hardware platforms and operating systems. It is the language that most Web sites use to write their applications. Its core capability is to link any textual information to another internal location or external page or file. In marketing terms, HTML is analogous to hypertext. One

of the more powerful features of HTML is the ability to create hyperlinks.

HTTP (Hypertext Transport Protocol)

The Internet standard for accessing and exchanging documents on the World Wide Web.

Huffman Code

A code used for one-dimensional data compression in the International Telecommunications Union Telecommunications Standards Sector Group III digital facsimile standard.

hybrid modeling

A term, coined by Gartner Group, that is used to signify second-generation, dimension-driven, constraint-based solids modeling technology beyond first-generation parametric modeling. Hybrid modelers offer multiple design input mechanisms, flexible constraint management, and robust interoperability with legacy computer-aided design (CAD) data.

hyperlink

A predefined link from one location to another. The link can jump within a particular location, to another location with the same computer or network site or even to a location at a completely different physical site. Hyperlinks are commonly used on the World Wide Web to provide navigation, reference and depth where published text cannot. A hyperlink can be created from text (which typically appears as blue underlined text within an HTML page) or from a graphic.

Hypermedia Management Schema (See HMMS)

Hypermedia Management Protocol (See HMMP)

HTML

```
<HTML>

<HEAD>
<TITLE>Welcome to Gartner Group</TITLE>
<SCRIPT LANGUAGE="JavaScript">
<!--
function makearray( n )
{
  this.length = n;
  for( var i = 1; i <= n; i++ )
    this[ i ] = 0;
  return this;
}
function other( img, len )



---------  [snip, snip]  ----------



//-->
</SCRIPT>
</HEAD>
```

HTML, a derived subset of SGML, defines a series of tags or codes that tell a Web browser how to interpret the text or image enclosed in the tags (**see <TITLE> Welcome to Gartner Group</ TITLE>**). Based on the simple ASCII text-based tags, the browser can adjust font size, display tables, or tell HTTP and other Web-related protocols to take an action (e.g., link to a given URL, send E-mail, or download a file). The benefits are HTML's relative simplicity and independence from operating-system, server or client platform. Since the browser is simply interpreting strings of ASCII characters, pages and basic form-based applications are inherently cross-platform.

The introduction of **JavaScript** (**see <SCRIPT LANGUAGE= "JavaScript"> code </SCRIPT>**) enables dynamic functionality, form and table manipulation, and interactive multimedia effects, as well as applet-based functionality.

ASCII = American Standard Code for Information Interchange
HTML = Hypertext Markup Language
HTTP = Hypertext Transport Protocol
SGML = Standard Generalized Markup Language
URL = Uniform resource locator

Source: Gartner Group

Hypertext Markup Language

Hypermedia Object Manager (See HMOM)

hypertext
Software technology used to create and store simple and complex navigational paths across computerized data. When the text is "clicked on," it can enable a user to navigate within or between Web pages.

Hypertext Markup Language (See HTML)

Hz (Hertz)
A measure of electromagnetic frequency equivalent to cycles per second.

IBG (interblock gap)
Space left unused between consecutive data blocks.

IBI (Information Builders Inc.)

IBM (International Business Machines)

IBM 3270 Pass-Through
A facility that enables attached terminals or PCs to connect to an IBM mainframe system through the midrange system and appear to the IBM system as 3278-type terminals.

IBU (independent business unit)

IC (integrated circuit)
An assembly of electronic circuits contained on a single piece of semiconductor material.

ICA (Intelligent Console Architecture — Citrix Systems)

ICA (International Communications Association)

I-CASE (integrated computer-aided software engineering)
Refers to the integration of lower-CASE tools with upper-CASE tools. (Upper-CASE tools are used in the analysis and design phases of a system's life cycle. Lower-CASE tools take the information contained in the upper-CASE tools and rapidly generate whole applications, or parts of an application.) I-CASE creates a bidirectional link that transfers information back and forth.

ICC (IBM Credit Corp.)

ICDA (Integrated Cached Disk Array)
A family of storage products for the IBM AS/400 from EMC. The ICDA Symmetrix product line provides three key benefits: 1) a high-performance read/write cache, 2) a "Perma Cache" (solid-state disk) option for ultra-high-performance data sets, and 3) a mirroring option for critical data sets requiring high availability.

ICMF (Integrated Coupling Migration Facility)
IBM's internal Coupling Facility product for Parallel Sysplex support.

ICMP (Internet Control Message Protocol)
A route management protocol.

iCOMP (Intel Comparative Microprocessor Performance)

icon

A symbol or pictorial representation of an object or idea in graphic interfaces, used to represent the different functions or applications available to the user. A mouse is typically used to select the desired operation by pointing to one of the icons on the screen.

ICR (intelligent character recognition)

A technology that employs either software alone or software and hardware to automatically recognize and translate raster images into structured data.

IDAPI (Integrated Database Application Programming Interface)

An API for data integration first promoted by Borland, IBM, Novell and WordPerfect in November 1992 to counter Microsoft's Open Database Connectivity.

IDE (Integrated Drive Electronics)

A legacy connectivity option.

IDEF (Integrated Definition Methodology)

IDH (integrated data hub)

IDL (interface definition language)

A standard language for defining objects' abstract descriptions in terms of their external interfaces (i.e., methods and parameters). The IDL compiler will create relevant runtime static and dynamic interface binding information.

IDM (integrated document management)

A vital class of middleware services that integrates library services, document-manufacturing and document-interchange technologies with critical business-process applications. The term "integrated" describes the transformation of document management from an end-user application to a network-based service integrated with a full complement of end-user personal-productivity and custom-developed applications.

IDMS (Integrated Database Management System — Computer Associates, also known as CA-IDMS)

The database management system introduced by Cullinet in 1973, based on technology acquired from B.F. Goodrich. Computer Associates acquired Cullinet and has maintained the product line since 1989.

IDNX (Integrated Digital Network Exchange)

IDRC (Improved Data Recording Capability)

IDRC is a 3480 feature announced in 1989 that improves the effective capacity of the cartridge.

IE (information engineering)

A methodology for developing an integrated information system based on the sharing of common data, with emphasis on decision support needs as well as transaction-processing (TP) requirements. It assumes logical data representations are relatively stable, as opposed to the frequently changing processes that use the data. Therefore, the logical data model, which reflects an organization's rules and policies, should be the basis for systems development.

IEEE (Institute of Electrical and Electronics Engineers)

An organization of engineers, scientists and students involved in electrical, electronics and related fields. IEEE also functions as a publishing house and standards body.

IEEE 802

An Institute of Electrical and Electronics Engineers standard for interconnection of local-area networking equipment dealing with the physical and link layers of the International Standards Organization (ISO) model for Open Systems Interconnection (OSI).

IEEE 802.3

The physical and medium-access control standards for CSMA/CD (carrier sense multiple access with collision detection) local-area networks (LANs) such as Ethernet.

IEEE 802.4

The physical and medium-access control standard for token bus local-area networks (LANs).

IEEE 802.5

The physical and medium-access control standard for Token Ring local-area networks (LANs).

IEEE 802.6

The physical and medium-access control standard for metropolitan-area networking.

IEEE 1394 (See FireWire)

IEF (Information Engineering Facility — Texas Instruments)

A life-cycle management computer-aided software engineering (CASE) product offered by Texas Instruments (TI) that focuses on Customer Information Control System/Database-2 (CICS/DB2) applications.

IETF (Internet Engineering Task Force)

IEW (Information Engineering Workbench — KnowledgeWare)

KnowledgeWare's upper-CASE (computer-aided software engineering) product that includes planning, analysis and design functions.

IFPUG (International Function Point Users Group)

IGES (Initial Graphics Exchange Specification)

A standard for the exchange of computer-aided design (CAD) geometry. IGES is largely superseded by STEP (Standard for the Exchange of Product Model Data) and PDES (Product Design Exchange using STEP). A vendor-neutral method of representing parts, geometrics and product dimensions, used as an intermediate system for transfer between specific computer-aided design (CAD) products.

IIA (Information Industry Association)

IIN (IBM Information Network)

IIOP (Internet Inter-ORB Protocol)

IMA (Information Management Associates)

Image Object Content Architecture (See IOCA)

ImagePlus

A document image package, introduced by IBM in 1988, that represented the commercial versions of image systems developed jointly by IBM and two customer "partners," USAA and Citibank. ImagePlus provided generic application software for using document images in common user environments.

image support

Hardware (scanner, workstation, printer) and software support for image as a system-recognized information type. Typically, although not necessarily, support for optical storage devices is included.

IMAP (Internet Message Access Protocol; also called Internet Mail Access Protocol)

A standard mail server that holds incoming E-mail messages until users log on and download them. It is more sophisticated and has more functionality than Post Office Protocol (POP).

IMAP4 (Internet Message Access Protocol 4)

Message-fetching protocol for client/server access to messages stored in an IMAP4 message store on a Simple Mail Transport Protocol (SMTP) system. This is a superset of the services provided by Post Office Protocol (POP3).

IMLC (Indexed Monthly License Charge)

An S/390 software licensing arrangement offered by IBM. It yields charges based on the machine capacity in millions of service units (MSUs), if the machine was not previously available, and has capacity greater than the newly defined upper limit to the Graduated Monthly License Charge (GMLC) Group 80 — approximately 480 million instructions per second (MIPS).

implementation inheritance

A relationship among classes in which a subclass shares, overrides or supplements operations or data values from one or more super-classes. A subclass is a specialization of one or more superclasses.

implode

Compression of detailed data into a summary-level record or report.

Improved Data Recording Capability (See IDRC)

IMS (Information Management System)

IMS is the name for two IBM Multiple Virtual Storage (MVS) products, a database management system (IMS/DB) and a transaction-processing monitor (IMS/TM), which are capable of accessing either Database-2 (DB2) or IMS/DB or both. IMS applications run in what are called message-processing regions, each in its own address space. They communicate as needed with the IMS control region, which can be located in a separate MVS address space. IMS is IBM's strategic subsystem for very high-speed Database Manager/Database Communications applications. DB2 is the vehicle chosen for normal database management system (DBMS) requirements. IMS involves customer-written application programs in response to transactions entered at teleprocessing terminals, and provides the services needed by those applications to retrieve and update data in Data Language/1 (DL/1) databases and respond to the terminal that invoked the data. Applications communicate as needed with the IMS control region, which is located in a separate MVS address space. This splitting of the program product into many components, called granularity, is one way IMS exploits the 3090 architecture more fully than does Customer Information Control System (CICS).

IMS/DB (Information Management System/Database Manager)

A Multiple Virtual Storage (MVS) database management system (DBMS) that supports the hierarchical data model (with optional extensions for some network data model features). IMS/DB may be used with either Information Management System/Transaction Monitor (IMS/TM) or Customer Information Control System (CICS) to provide online access to the database, or it may be used without a monitor for batch processing.

IMS/DC (Information Management System/Data Communication)

IMS/DC is the part of Information Management System (IMS) that is needed for the implementation of online transaction processing (OLTP) applications. Roughly speaking, IMS/DC is functionally equivalent to Customer Information Control System/Virtual Storage (CICS/VS), but is rarely used except in conjunction with Information Management System/Database Manager (IMS/DB). IMS/DC has a multiaddress space architecture and is quite fast — which explains why IBM tends to run its DB2 benchmarks with IMS/DC rather than CICS.

IMS/ESA DM (Information Management System/Enterprise Systems Architecture Database Manager)

IMS/ESA may be used with either IMS/DC (Information Management System/Data Communication) or CICS/VS (Customer Information and Control System/Virtual Storage) to provide online access to the database.

IMS/ESA TM (Information Management System/Enterprise Systems Architecture Transaction Manager)

The part of Information Management System (IMS) needed to create online transaction processing (OLTP) applications. Until the announcement of Information Management System/Enterprise Systems Architecture (IMS/ESA), IMS/TM was a feature of IMS, not a product separate from Information Management System/Database Manager (IMS/DB). IMS/TM, once called Information Management System/Data Communication (IMS/DC), has a multiaddress-space architecture. It is quite fast, which is why IBM runs its Database-2 (DB2) benchmarks with IMS/DC rather than Customer Information Control System (CICS).

IMS/FP (Information Management System/FastPath)

A functional extension to IBM's Information Management System (IMS) that improves performance for specific transactions, and features high data availability and specialized facilities for very large databases. It was introduced as a separately priced feature of IMS v.1.1.4. With IMS v.1.1.3, FastPath became part of Information Management System/Data Communication (IMS/DC).

in-band signaling

The method for telephone switches to communicate with one another by sending in-band (i.e., over each line connection) dial pulses or tones denoting the calling and called number. Signaling is generally performed this way in networks between the telephone instrument of private branch exchange (PBX) and the serving central office, among central offices in the same geographical area and throughout the local loop.

independent software vendor (See ISV)

Indexed Monthly License Charge (See IMLC)

Indexed Sequential Access Method (See ISAM)

industrial computer
A personal or process control computer that is designed to withstand the rigors of the factory floor. Some industrial computers are configured so that maintenance and cold start-up are relatively simple. These devices are used for applications such as data collection, monitoring and programming.

Industry Standard Architecture (See ISA)

Information Builders Inc. (See IBI)

information engineering (See IE)

Information Engineering Facility — Texas Instruments (See IEF)

Information Engineering Workbench — KnowledgeWare (See IEW)

Information Management System (See IMS)

Information Management System/Data Communication (See IMS/DC)

Information Management System/Database Manager (See IMS/DB)

Information Management System/Enterprise Systems Architecture Database Manager (See IMS/ESA DM)

Information Management System/Enterprise Systems Architecture Transaction Manager (See IMS/ESA TM)

Information Management System/FastPath (See IMS/FP)

information repository
Holds all the information needed to create, modify and evolve a software system, including information on the problem to be solved, problem domain, emerging solution, software process being used, project resources and history, and organizational context.

Information Resource Dictionary System (See IRDS)

information systems (See IS)

information superhighway
A proposed high-speed computing and communications network to deliver ubiquitous voice, telephony data, video graphics, and more, which was popularized by the United States' President Clinton and Vice President Gore. It was expected to provide education to U.S. citizens in the 21st century. The Internet itself was originally only cited as a model for the information superhighway, though the popularity of the World Wide Web made it the default successor to the concept. The Web currently falls short in comparison to the initial vision of the information superhighway due to the speed of communications (for instance, the Web does not provide rapid transfer of information and multimedia), though advancements in software, hardware and communications technology are quickly enabling the Internet to catch up to the original vision.

information technology (See IT)

**Information Technology Association of
America (See ITAA)**

**Initial Graphics Exchange Specification
(See IGES)**

**INMS (integrated network management
system)**

input/output (See I/O)

Inquire/Text
Content-based retrieval and document management product for IBM Multiple Virtual Storage (MVS) and Virtual Machine (VM) environments from Infodata of Falls Church, Va.

**INSM (integrated network
and systems management)**

INSPECT
Gartner Group's iterative framework for planning and executing application change. INventory, Scope, Parse, Examine, Consider options, Tactical solutions.

**Institute of Electrical and
Electronics Engineers (See
IEEE)**

**Integrated Cached Disk
Array (See ICDA)**

integrated circuit (See IC)

**Integrated Computer-Aided Software
Engineering (See I-CASE)**

**Integrated Coupling Migration Facility
(See ICMF)**

Integrated Database Application Programming Interface (See IDAPI)

**Integrated Database Management System
— Computer Associates (See IDMS)**

**integrated document management (See
IDM)**

Integrated Drive Electronics (See IDE)

INSPECT

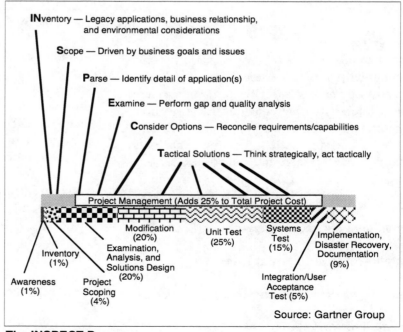

INventory — Legacy applications, business relationship, and environmental considerations

Scope — Driven by business goals and issues

Parse — Identify detail of application(s)

Examine — Perform gap and quality analysis

Consider Options — Reconcile requirements/capabilities

Tactical Solutions — Think strategically, act tactically

Project Management (Adds 25% to Total Project Cost)

Modification (20%)

Unit Test (25%)

Systems Test (15%)

Implementation, Disaster Recovery, Documentation (9%)

Inventory (1%)

Examination, Analysis, and Solutions Design (20%)

Awareness (1%)

Project Scoping (4%)

Integration/User Acceptance Test (5%)

Source: Gartner Group

The INSPECT Process

integrated E-mail

A facility that enables Macintosh users to create, send, receive, read, forward and file mail through the midrange system mail system directly from a Macintosh desk accessory or application, without terminal emulation log-on or other consideration for the midrange system. In the PC world, a facility that enables MS-DOS PC users to create, send, receive, read, forward and file mail through the midrange system mail system directly from a PC-resident menu system, without terminal emulation log-on or other consideration for the midrange system.

integrated office system (See IOS)

Integrated Services Digital Network (See ISDN)

Integrated Systems Solutions Corp. (See ISSC)

integrity

An operating system's ability to ensure that only authorized users can enter a privileged state (supervisor mode, protect key zero, superuser or root). Integrity is a prerequisite for security in an operating system. In Multiple Virtual Storage (MVS), it is the ability to ensure that only authorized users can enter a privileged state (e.g., protect key zero). The term is not synonymous with security, but security requires it.

intelligent character recognition (See ICR)

Intelligent Input/Output (See I₂O)

Intelligent Printer Data Stream (See IPDS)

intelligent workstation (See IWS)

interactive selling system (See ISS)

Interactive System Productivity Facility (See ISPF)

interactive television (See ITV)

interactive voice response (See IVR)

interblock gap (See IBG)

interexchange carrier (See IXC)

interface definition language (See IDL)

interface inheritance

An object request broker (ORB) technique for reusing the interface definition language (IDL) from another object implementation (program) in a new one. Unlike implementation inheritance, this does not make data and code visible and usable by another object.

International Standards Organization (See ISO)

Internet

A loose confederation of independent yet interconnected networks that use the Transmission Control Protocol/Internet Protocol (TCP/IP) protocols for communications. The Internet evolved from research done during the 1960s on a network called the ARPANet.

Internet Control Message Protocol (See ICMP)

Internet Message Access Protocol (See IMAP)

Internet Message Access Protocol 4 (See IMAP4)

Internet Protocol (See IP)

Internet Server API (See ISAPI)

Internet service provider (See ISP)

internetwork packet exchange (See IPX)

interprocess communications (See IPC)

intranet

A network internal to an enterprise that uses the same methodology and techniques as the Internet. It is not necessarily connected to the Internet and is commonly secured from it using firewalls. Intranets are often used an organization's local-area (LANs) or wide-area networks (WANs).

I/O (input/output)

The activity of sending information to or from peripheral devices, terminals, direct-access storage devices (DASDs), tape drives and printers. Physical I/O performance lags that of memory and logical technologies.

I$_2$O (Intelligent Input/Output)

The I$_2$O initiative seeks to change server I/O from a tightly

related driver-device structure to a more abstract, layered, message-oriented structure. Its key goals include:

- Faster I/O
- Reusable drivers
- Coexistence with legacy drivers
- Extensibility
- Peer-to-peer communications
- Ease of support of 64-bit architectures
- Faster adoption of new technologies such as Fibre Channel

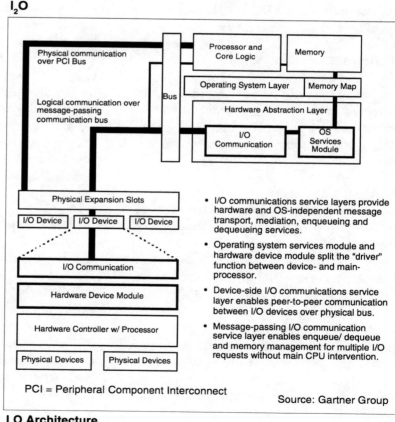

I$_2$O

- I/O communications service layers provide hardware and OS-independent message transport, mediation, enqueueing and dequeueing services.
- Operating system services module and hardware device module split the "driver" function between device- and main-processor.
- Device-side I/O communications service layer enables peer-to-peer communication between I/O devices over physical bus.
- Message-passing I/O communication service layer enables enqueue/ dequeue and memory management for multiple I/O requests without main CPU intervention.

PCI = Peripheral Component Interconnect

Source: Gartner Group

I$_2$O Architecture

Key early supporters include Intel, Microsoft, Novell, Hewlett-Packard, Compaq Computer, Symbios Logic, 3Com and NetFrame. It is being fostered by the I_2O Special Interest Group (I_2O SIG). The I_2O architecture is designed to facilitate the introduction of new I/O devices while offloading most I/O processing to intelligent I/O processors.

IOCA (Image Object Content Architecture)

A standard definition for the representation of images for interchange between environments. An element of Mixed Object: Document Content Architecture (MO:DCA), IOCA is used in ImagePlus and OS/2 Image Support.

IOS (integrated office system)

The label applied to second-generation office information systems (OISs) originating from the tight integration between the bundled applications, usually word processing, filing, E-mail, calendars, scheduling and basic decision support.

IP (Internet Protocol)

Transmission Control Protocol/Internet Protocol (TCP/IP) tracks the address of nodes, routes outgoing messages, and recognizes incoming messages. Current networks consist of several protocols, including IP, Internetwork Packet Exchange (IPX), DECnet, AppleTalk, Open Systems Interconnection (OSI) and LLC2. This wide diversity of protocols results from application suites that assume their own particular protocols. Collapse from this wide variety is inevitable, but users will only be able to reduce this diversity, not eliminate it. Most users will collapse networks into two main protocols: IP and IPX. Installed-base applications and the pain of change will prevent a total reduction to a single backbone protocol.

IPC (interprocess communications)

A system that lets threads and processes transfer data and messages among themselves; used to offer services to, and receive them from, other programs.

IPDS (Intelligent Printer Data Stream)

IBM format for sending files to a laser printer. It provides an interface to all-points-addressable printers that make possible the presentation of pages containing a mix of different types of data, such as high-quality text, raster image, vector graphics and bar codes. In addition, IPDS provides commands for the management of printing resources such as fonts and overlays; for the control of device functions such as paper sourcing and stacking; for the comprehensive handling of exception functions; and for a complete acknowledgment protocol at the data stream level. IBM has positioned IPDS as the ubiquitous enterprise data stream.

IPI (Intelligent Peripheral Interface)

IPV (in-place value)

IPX (Internetwork Packet Exchange)

Novell NetWare communications protocol used to route messages. From a user perspective, an IPX implementation allows concurrent dual access to both an application server and a native NetWare file server without imposing memory overhead on client workstations.

IR (information retrieval)

IRDA (Infrared Data Association)

IRDS (Information Resource Dictionary System)
A standard data dictionary specification from the American National Standards Institute (ANSI) X3H4 Committee.

IRI (Information Resources, Inc.)

IRLM (IMS Resource Lock Manager)

IS (information systems)
The use of and investment in computer technology by the principal or centralized organization formally charged with the responsibility for computer technology. Often the IS organization is led by a chief information officer (CIO), vice president of the IS organization or director of data processing.

IS is also often the formal name of the department within an enterprise that is responsible for information technology. Other common names for the IS department are:

• Management information systems (MIS)
• Data processing (DP)
• Information processing (IP)

ISA (Industry Standard Architecture)
Bus architecture originally developed and evolved by IBM for its PC, XT and AT lines. It comes in an eight-bit and 16-bit version; many machines with ISA compatibility have both eight- and 16-bit connectors on the motherboard.

ISA (Instrument Society of America)

ISAM (Indexed Sequential Access Method)
Disk access method that stores data sequentially, maintaining an index of key fields to all the records in the file.

ISAPI (Internet Server API)
A proprietary Web server application programming interface (API) from Microsoft. It is geared to provide direct function-level access to its Internet Information Server.

ISDN (Integrated Services Digital Network)
As a technical standard and design philosophy for digital networks, ISDN provides high-speed, high-bandwidth channels to every subscriber on the network, achieving end-to-end digital functions with standard equipment interface devices. ISDN networks enable a variety of mixed digital

IR

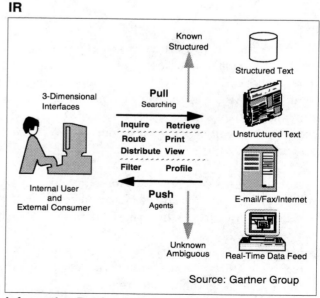

Information Retrieval

transmission services to be accommodated at a single interface (including voice, circuit-switched and packet-switched data). Access channels under definition include basic (144 kilobits per second or 2B+D) and primary (1.544 megabits per second or 23B+D in North America, and 30B+D or 2.048 megabits per second in Europe) interface rates. Signaling System 7 (SS7), an out-of-band signaling scheme, is key to current ISDN implementation.

ISO (International Standards Organization)

A voluntary, nontreaty organization established in 1949 to promote international standards.

isochronous

A transmission technique characterized by synchronization of the transmitter and receiver, so that packets are delivered to the destination at regular intervals, such as that required by voice or video.

ISP (Internet service provider)

A company that provides Internet access to its customers. The majority of ISPs are too small to purchase access directly from the network access point (NAP), and instead buy pieces of bandwidth that are available from larger ISPs. Access to the Internet can be provided in two principal ways:

- A modem uses common telephone lines to dial directly into the ISP, which then connects the user to the Internet. This is the slowest method of connection to the Internet, and the user often experiences delays in receiving information, particularly larger files such as graphics or programs with audio or video. Telephone service providers

also offer a digital communication service (called ISDN) that is capable of improving modem speed by anywhere from two to four times the normal speed of a modem. Unfortunately, setting up an ISDN service is often a complex and costly process.
- A direct connection to the Internet using a T1 line. This connection offers speeds far superior to a modem.

Internet service providers are different from online services such as America Online or Prodigy, though these services sometimes also provide access to the Internet. Online services provide access to exclusive content, databases and online discussion forums that are not available to people who do not use the service.

ISPBX (integrated services private branch exchange)

ISPF (Interactive System Productivity Facility)

ISPF is an IBM-licensed program that is used for writing application programs. It serves as a full-screen editor and dialogue manager and provides a means of generating standard screen panels and interactive dialogues between the application programmer and the terminal user.

ISPF/PDF (ISPF/Program Development Facility)

ISS (interactive selling system)

An ISS is the integration of a marketing encyclopedia system (MES), a sales configuration system, a proposal generation system and an order management system under a common user interface. It is used by organizations to streamline and enhance the selling process. The ISS effectively combines the application functionality that helps enterprises to configure solutions that meet customer needs, while avoiding data entry and business process errors. With an ISS, the salesperson can sit in front of the customer and pull up data to prove value, configure an order, create a proposal, and then turn the proposal into an order and book the order.

ISSC (IBM's Integrated Systems Solutions Corp.)
IBM's IT outsourcing business unit. Currently, it is the largest IT outsourcer in the world.

ISUP (ISDN User Part)

ISV (independent software vendor)
A software producer that is not owned or controlled by a hardware manufacturer; a company whose primary function is to distribute software. Hardware manufacturers that distribute software (such as IBM and Unisys) are not ISVs, nor are users (such as banks) that may also sell software products.

ISVs typically offer products that the primary vendor (i.e., IBM) does not offer, allowing clients of that vendor to round out their software needs. ISVs create price competition and also increase the pace of technology innovation in their markets.

IT (information technology)
This is the common title for the entire spectrum of technologies for information processing, including software, hardware, communications technologies and related services. In general, IT does not include embedded technologies that do not generate data for enterprise use.

IT asset management
A systematic approach to managing IT assets, including information systems (IS) department staff, end users performing IT support, technology procurement teams, suppliers, facilities, hardware and software.

IT infrastructure
The underlying technological components that constitute an organization's systems architecture. The seven components of IT infrastructure are hardware, operating system, network, database, development environment, user interface and application.

IT outsourcing
A contractual relationship with an outside vendor to assume responsibility of one or more IT functions. Outsourcing is usually, but not always, characterized by the transfer of assets — typically facilities, staff or hardware — and can include the data center, wide-area networks (WANs), applications development and maintenance, end-user computing, and IT-enabled business processes.

ITAA (Information Technology Association of America)

item master file
Typically, this computer file contains identifying and descriptive data, and control values (e.g., dead time and lot sizes). It may also contain data on inventory status, requirements and planned orders. There is normally one record in this file for each stock-keeping unit. Item master records are linked together by product structure records, thus defining the bill of material.

International Telecommunications Union
(See ITU)

ITU (International Telecommunications
Union)
Formerly the International Telegraph and Telephone Consultative Committee (Comite Consultatif International Telegraphique et Telephonique). In March 1993, the name was changed to the International Telecommunications Union Telecommunications Standards Sector (ITU-TSS) or just ITU. The ITU is a specialized Agency of the United Nations based in Geneva and coordinates and fosters cooperation in the use of international telecommunications systems.

ITV (interactive television)
Devices that allow for the passing of information back and forth through standard television delivery mediums like cable and satellites, using a TV-compatible interface.

IVR (interactive voice response)
A voice/call-processing option for improving call center functionality and integration. It enables callers to have more flexibility to access information or leave messages. Use of this option can "offload" call volume from agents to the IVR or improve load balancing by having agents handle recorded messages during slow periods. A slowly growing number of IVR developers are now using speech recognition in their applications.

IWS (intelligent workstation)
A term synonymous with programmable workstation (e.g., a personal computer).

IXC (interexchange carrier)
A long-distance telephone company in the United States that provides service between local access and transport areas (LATAs).

J

JAD (joint applications development)
An effective process for ensuring high levels of functional quality, since it requires participation of the prospective end user. It is especially effective in developing graphical user interface (GUI) requirements.

Java and JavaScript
A scripting language developed by Sun Microsystems that extends and complements the basic capabilities of Hypertext Markup Language (HTML). Originally developed as a language for consumer-oriented devices such as TV set-top boxes, Java became a viable alternative to other programming languages with the rapid growth of the Internet as it has the potential to work on an unlimited number of computing devices and operating systems. Java permits the creation of applications and application modules ("applets") that run in the Java virtual machine (JVM) on the browser, either as software on a PC or on the Sun picoJava chip, a piece of dedicated hardware. Browsers from both Netscape and Microsoft have a JVM. Java's platform-independence and security are designed-in, rather than added-on, so applications can run on a wide variety of desktop platforms as long as they can run a Java-enabled browser.

Java Beans
Similar to ActiveX, this lets external applications access each other's services.

Java virtual machine (See Java)

JBIG (Joint Bitonal Image Group)
Emerging standard for black-and-white, and gray-scale compression.

JCAHO (Joint Commission on Accreditation of Health Care Organizations)

JCALS (Joint Continuous Acquisition and Life-Cycle Support)

JCL (Job Control Language — part of MVS)
A language used to communicate with the operating system. JCL is used to tell the system who a user is, what program(s) are being invoked and what resources will be needed.

JDE (J.D. Edwards & Co.)

JES (Job Entry Subsystem — part of MVS)
The generic name for the operating system component that reads in jobs, interprets their Job

---

Control Language, schedules their execution, spools the print, and produces the output at the appropriate destination.

JIT (just in time)
A method of controlling and reducing direct and work-in-process inventory by having suppliers deliver material "just in time" to manufacturing.

JITT (just-in-time training)
A training methodology in which users are trained in a technology just when they begin using it.

JMAPI (Java Management API)

JMC (James Martin & Co.)

Job Control Language (See JCL)

Job Entry Subsystem (See JES)

joint applications development (See JAD)

Joint Bitonal Image Group (See JBIG)

Joint Photographic Experts Group (See JPEG)

JPEG (Joint Photographic Experts Group)
A widely accepted international standard for compression of color images.

jukebox
Automatic media handlers for optical disk drives, also called libraries.

Jupiter
The code name for IBM's system-managed storage project.

just in time (See JIT)

just-in-time training (See JITT)

JVM (Java virtual machine) (See Java)

K

Kbit (kilobit)
One thousand bits.

Kbyte (kilobyte)
One thousand bytes.

KBE (knowledge-based engineering)
A system that encapsulates design knowledge that can be recalled, reused and extended to create product designs.

KBMS (Knowledge Base Management System — Trinzic)

Kbps (kilobits per second)
A measure of data transmission rate — one thousand bits of information per second.

KBS (knowledge-based system) (See expert system)

Kbyte (Kilobyte)
One thousand bytes.

KHz (kilohertz)
A unit equal to 1,000 hertz (one thousand cycles per second).

KIF (Knowledge Interchange Format)

kilobit (See Kbit)

kilobyte (See Kbyte)

kilohertz (See KHz)

knowledge base
The knowledge, which may include assertion, rules, objects and constraints, used by the expert or knowledge-based system. Its organization is based on knowledge representations. The developer of the system or user may be unaware of the underlying knowledge representations, seeing only the domain knowledge representations.

Knowledge Capital

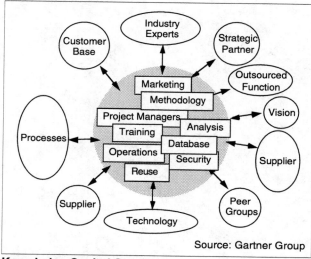

Source: Gartner Group

Knowledge Capital Structure

---

knowledge capital
The information available to an enterprise about best practices in all aspects of its operations.

knowledge representation
Structures used to store knowledge in a way that relates items of knowledge and permits an inference engine to manipulate the knowledge and the relationships.

Knowledge Sharing Effort (See KSE)

knowledge work management
A discipline that promotes an integrated approach to identifying, managing and sharing all of an enterprise's information assets. Knowledge work management focuses on extending knowledge management to business processes (i.e., policies and procedures as well as unwritten rules).

knowledge-based engineering (See KBE)

KQML (Knowledge-based Query Manipulation Language)

KSE (Knowledge Sharing Effort)
An initiative for building standard knowledge representation frameworks, led by a consortium of 18 university and industry research centers. It addresses the entire issues of standard knowledge representation schemes, standard interfaces between objects, the definition of a language that will map between various knowledge representation schemes, and work on standard application-specific ontologies.

L

LAN (local-area network)

A user-owned and user-operated data transmission facility connecting a number of communicating devices, such as, computers, terminals, printers and data storage units, within a single building or campus of buildings. LANs use gateways or communications servers to connect with other hosts. Some examples are Ethernet, AT&T's StarLAN and IBM's Token Ring Network (TRN).

LAN bridging

Multiple physical local-area networks (LANs) can be connected with local- or wide-area connections to support a single logical LAN environment.

LAN performance monitor

A tool or toolset (hardware/software) to allow local or remote monitoring of local-area network (LAN) traffic and problems.

LANE (local-area network emulation)

LAP-B (Link Access Procedure — Balanced)

A subset of High-level Data Link Control (HDLC) used in Open Systems Interconnection (OSI) to control Layer 2 functions.

LAP-D (Link Access Procedure — D Channel)

A data link layer procedure using D Channel communications, typical of Integrated Services Digital Network (ISDN).

laptop computer

A portable PC that can be easily transported and used in multiple environments. The portability of the laptop allows individuals to take all of their software, files and applications with them, whether they are in the office, at home or on an airplane. At minimum, laptops include the following components:

- Keyboard
- Display screen (typically smaller than a desktop monitor)
- Central processing unit (CPU)
- Battery and an AC adapter
- Hard disk

LAR (large-account reseller)

large-scale integration (See LSI)

laser

A device that emits a highly coherent beam of light. The name stands for light amplification by

---

stimulated emission or radiation. A typical laser has an active medium, which emits light, and a cavity structure, which selects certain wavelengths and directions for the emitted light.

LATA (local access and transport area)

A LATA is a local telephone network area controlled and operated by a local-exchange carrier (LEC), e.g., one of the Bell operating companies. A LATA is one of approximately 200 local telephone companies serving areas generally encompassing the largest standard metropolitan statistical areas. Circuits and calls within a LATA (intra-LATA) are generally the sole responsibility of the LEC, while interexchange carriers (IXCs), such as AT&T or MCI, handle circuits and calls that cross LATA boundaries (inter-LATA).

layer

In the Open Systems Interconnection (OSI) reference model, refers to a collection of related network-processing functions that constitute one level of a hierarchy of functions.

LCD (least common denominator)

LCD (liquid crystal display)

A low-powered flat-panel device that displays characters created from liquid crystal molecules that are controlled by an electrical field.

LD (long distance)

LDAP (Lightweight Directory Access Protocol)

A server-to-server interface for directory information exchange among directories, devised as a low-cost, simpler implementation of the X.500 protocol DAP. It facilitates the implementation of replication and chaining among dissimilar directories. Proposed by the University of Michigan, it was adopted by Netscape in 1996 for directory lookup, and has become the preferred access path for clients looking up directory information not only in X.500 directories, but in many other directory structures on the Internet.

lead time

A span of time required to perform an activity. In a production and inventory control context, the activity is normally the procurement of materials or products from either an outside supplier or a company's own manufacturing facility. The individual components of any given lead time can include some or all of the following: order preparation time, queue time, move or transportation time, and receiving and inspection time.

leased line

A line rented exclusively to one customer for voice or data communications; also called a private line, tie line or dedicated facility.

least total cost

A dynamic lot-sizing technique that calculates the order quantity by comparing the carrying cost and the setup (or ordering) costs for various lot sizes and selects the lot where comparisons are not nearly equal.

LEC (local exchange carrier)

The carrier or local telephone company that handles local access and transport area (LATA) traffic, e.g., one of the Bell operating companies (BOCs) or any of the independent telephone companies.

LED (light-emitting diode)
A semiconductor that produces light when activated.

LEN (Low-Entry Networking)
An IBM networking architecture introduced in 1986. It is an Advanced Program-to-Program Communications (APPC) application and a potential low-end alternative to Systems Network Architecture (SNA). SNA is complex and, for department environments, difficult to manage. LEN uses Synchronous Data Link Control (SDLC) as the backbone protocol and possesses a self-contained network management capability that is less comprehensive than IBM's traditional methods but is much easier to set up and operate.

lessee
An entity that contractually obtains use of equipment in return for payments over a specified time.

lessor
An entity that conveys a possession of specified property to a lessee for a period of time.

library
A data management system for documents frequently, though not necessarily, organized in a hierarchy of folders and drawers. Also called file cabinet.

light-emitting diode (See LED)

Lightweight Directory Access Protocol (See LDAP)

LIMS (laboratory information management system)

line of business (See LOB)

Link Access Procedure — Balanced (See LAP-B)

Link Access Procedure — D Channel (See LAP-D)

link layer
The logical entity in the Open Systems Interconnection (OSI) model concerned with transmission of data between adjacent network nodes. It is the second layer in the OSI model, between the physical and the network layers.

Links (See hot links)

Linpack
An early benchmark for scientific applications, now replaced by the SPECmark.

liquid crystal display (See LCD)

LMDS (local multipoint distribution service)

load
To copy a program into the memory of a computing device so that it can later be used for processing.

load balancing
The ability of processors to schedule themselves to ensure that all are kept busy while instruction streams are available.

LOB (line of business)
An organizational unit within IBM's new structure.

LOC (line of code)

local access and transport area (See LATA)

local exchange carrier (See LEC)

local-area network (See LAN)

local loop
That part of a communications circuit between the subscriber's equipment and the equipment in the local central office.

location broker
Middleware that automatically matches a client query with whichever server has the most suitable services, data and computing resources to accomplish the task.

lock
A means of preventing two users from trying to update the same data simultaneously.

Logical Unit (See LU)

Logical Unit 6.2 (See LU 6.2)

look and feel
The appearance and behavior of a graphical user interface (GUI) to the end user (who sees it as part of an application), determined by the tools and style guide provided by the vendor (and by whether the software developer obeys these guidelines).

loosely coupled multiprocessing
A configuration of several processors, each with its own memory, that execute user and operating system code independently.

Low-Entry Networking (See LEN)

lower-CASE tool
A tool for application generation rather than application modeling.

LPAR (logical partition)

LSI (large scale integration)
Between 3,000 and 100,000 transistors on a chip.

LU (Logical Unit — part of SNA)
IBM's term for a logical node that is the user's "port" into a Systems Network Architecture network. LU 1 is a high-performance print data stream and a 3270 data stream. LU 6 enables host-to-host data exchange, and provides a peer-to-peer data stream.

LU 6.2 (Logical Unit 6.2)
An IBM Systems Network Architecture (SNA) protocol. LU 6.2 is a strategic device-independent process-to-process protocol; it also supports asynchronous (store-and-forward) networking. It provides the facilities for peer-to-peer communications between two programs. Among other things, this means that programs and small/midrange computer systems can use LU 6.2 (along with PU 2.1) to establish and control sessions with each other, without host mainframe participation. When LU 6.2 is installed in devices such as PCs and cluster controllers, required functionality, such as multiple sessions among those devices and System/370 hosts, becomes available.

M

MAC (Media Access Control — IEEE)
The methods used to gain access to the physical layer of a local-area network (LAN).

MAC (message authentication code)
A way of confirming that a message has not been tampered with.

MAC (moves, adds and changes)

magnetic-ink character recognition (See MICR)

magneto-optic (See MO)

mail-aware application
A mail-enabled application that is complete without mail but can use messaging services.

mail-enabled application
An application that uses messaging services.

mail-reliant application
A mail-enabled product that is incomplete without mail.

mainframe
A computer system with large configuration capacity and processing power that is significantly superior to PCs or midrange computers.

Mainframes typically require skilled technicians to program and maintain, though client/server technology has made them easier to operate, from both the user's and programmer's perspectives. They are typically used by organizations to process very large tasks, such as payroll or accounts payable.

MAN (metropolitan-area network)
MAN is a technology that evolved from local-area network (LAN) designs, but is optimized for longer distances (more than 50 kilometers), greater speeds (more than 100 megabits per second) and diverse forms of information (e.g., voice, data, image and video).

managed network services (See MNS)

management consulting (Tier 1 segmentation)
Strategic consulting (enterprise): high-level corporate or business unit strategy, e.g., deciding what businesses to participate in or whether to make an acquisition.
Strategic consulting (operations improvement): targeted business issue analysis, e.g., an airline deciding how to improve customer service, or a bank deciding on the most effective type of retail delivery system.

Management Information Base — part of SNMP (See MIB)

management information systems (See MIS)

mandatory security controls
An operating system security rating of B1 or higher based on U.S. Department of Defense trusted-computer-system evaluation criteria.

Manufacturing Accounting and Production Information Control System (See MAPICS)

manufacturing execution systems (see MES)

manufacturing lead time
The total time required to manufacture an item. Included here are order preparation time, queue time, setup time, runtime, move time, inspection time and put-away time.

Manufacturing Message Service (See MMS)

manufacturing resource planning (See MRP II)

MAP (Manufacturing Automation Protocol)

MAP/TOP (Manufacturing Automation Protocol/Technical Office Protocol)

MAPI (Messaging Application Programming Interface)
Programming interface specification that enables an application to send and receive mail over a Microsoft Mail messaging system. It was designed to separate the mail engine from the mail client.

MAPI-WF (MAPI Workflow Framework)
A Microsoft framework originally intended to provide a standardized way for any Messaging Application Programming Interface- (MAPI-) capable application to be workflow-enabled and to support work item interchange between various workflow engines. It is now expected to be merged with standards based on Multipurpose Internet Mail Extensions- (MIME-) based standards.

MAPICS (Manufacturing Accounting and Production Information Control System)
IBM's material requirements planning software for the AS/400 and earlier System/36 and System/38 systems. The newest version, MAPICS/DDB, uses the relational-database capability of the AS/400.

MAPI-WF

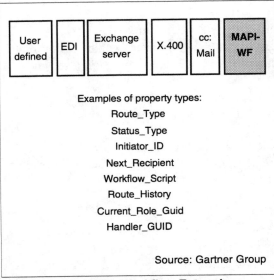

MAPI Message With Workflow Extensions

mapping
The transcription of functions into terms that make them equivalent on two different systems.

marketing encyclopedia system (See MES)

massively parallel processing (See MPP)

material requirements planning (See MRP)

materials management
A term to describe the grouping of management functions related to the complete cycle of material flow, from the purchase and internal control of production materials, to the planning and control of work in process, to the warehousing, shipping and distribution of the finished product. It differs from materials control in that the latter term, traditionally, is limited to the internal control of production materials.

MAU (multistation access unit)
A wiring concentrator in the IBM Token Ring Network (TRN) that can connect up to eight lobes to a ring.

MAW (Microsoft at Work)

Mbit (megabit)
One million bits of stored computer data. See also "bit."

Mbyte (megabyte)
One million bytes. This is the common way in which the size of files or computer random-access memory (RAM) is specified. Megabytes are also used to describe the size of storage space on storage devices such as floppy disks, hard disks or CD-ROMs. The relationship of the size of a file or accumulation of files to the size of the

RAM and storage space is critical because it determines the ability of a computing device to process a file.

Mbps (megabits per second)
A measure of data transmission rate, meaning one million bits per second.

MC (Memory Channel)
An additional level in the memory hierarchy of certain Encore computers, with an address space shared across clustered nodes. A write from local memory to the MC in one node simultaneously writes to reflective memories in all the other nodes. Each node can be attached to four separate MCs, allowing bandwidth scaling and substantial configuration flexibility. The MC also is used as a fast, low-latency transport for I/O transfer, remote procedure calls (RPCs) and general message passing.

MCA (Micro Channel Architecture)
The design specifications for subsystems to plug into IBM's 32-bit Micro Channel expansion bus. This architecture was introduced on the IBM PS/2, supporting peripheral operations on the bus.

MCI (MCI Communications)

MCO (managed care organization)

MCU (multipoint control unit)

MDA (Monochrome Display Adapter)

MDF (Multiple Domain Feature — Amdahl)

mean time between failures (See MTBF)

mean time to repair (See MTTR)

Measured Usage License Charge (See MULC)

Media Access Control — IEEE (See MAC)

media objects
Non-Hypertext Markup Language (HTML) files that can be displayed or executed as part of an HTML document or as a stand-alone file. Examples are Graphics Interchange Format (GIF) or Joint Photographic Experts Group (JPEG) graphic files; audio or video files; and Java applets.

medium-scale integration (See MSI)

megabit (See Mbit)

megabyte (See Mbyte)

mega-FLOPS (see MFLOPS)

MELP (Microsoft Enterprise License Pak)

memory in cassette (See MIC)

MES (manufacturing execution systems)
An integrated architecture that links applications residing within the seven agents of manufacturing. These agents are operations, job, material, equipment, labor, regulatory and

quality management. It encompasses any system not already classified in enterprise resource planning (ERP) or open control systems (OCS).

MES (marketing encyclopedia system)
Electronically distributes and consolidates up-to-date marketing information into a highly cross-referenced, single-source repository that is easy to use. An MES enables users to quickly locate and display information, thus shortening sales cycles and decreasing printing and distribution costs. An MES contains a database capable of storing all types of information that will be incorporated into the system (e.g., audio, video,

MES

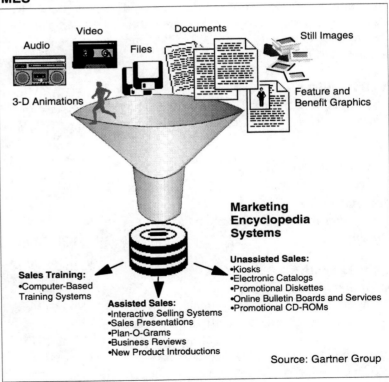

Marketing Encyclopedia Systems

sound, text and graphics). The system should have the capability to be used unconnected to a server and should include a remote communications mechanism for electronically downloading and uploading information.

message authentication code (See MAC)

message broker
A logical hub that copies and resends messages to one or more destinations. As a value-adding third party between information sources and information consumers, it can complement a service-oriented architecture.

A message broker encapsulates an entire application system in a virtual black box. All communication between the applications is through controlled, documented interface contracts. Data and program logic are hidden from external development groups so the edits, integrity checks and business rules within each application system are never bypassed.

A message broker, like a service-oriented architecture (SOA), is a design abstraction that may be implemented using component software for some or all of the connections. The interface from a message broker to the application may use an object request broker (ORB) or object transaction monitor (OTM); a request to the message broker may be implemented as a series of method calls to participating components.

**Message Handling Service — Novell
(See MHS)**

**message-passing operating system (See
MPOS)**

message transfer agent (See MTA)

messaging
In E-mail, messaging consists of moving messages from user to user, application to application, or place to place, providing a service analogous to that of the paper postal service and providing an infrastructure along which many other objects may be moved. The term is sometimes applied, with an entirely different meaning, to real-time interprocess communications in the transaction-processing (TP) environment.

Message Broker

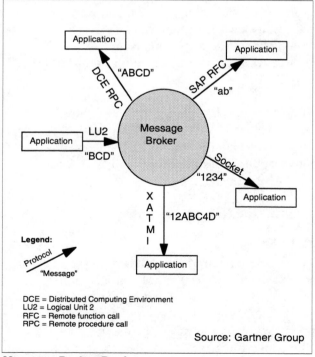

Message Broker Design

Messaging Application Programming Interface (See MAPI)

Messaging Application Programming Interface-Workflow Framework (See MAPI-WF)

metropolitan-area network (See MAN)

MFLOPS (mega-FLOPS)
Million floating-point operations per second, if used with a specific amount, e.g. 50 MFLOPS. A measurement for performance on compute-intensive, floating-point-intensive applications. The most commonly cited benchmark is Linpack.

MFJ (modified final judgment)
The U.S. District Court judgment under which AT&T began operating in 1984. Agreed to by the U.S. Justice Department and AT&T to settle the department's antitrust suit against AT&T, it divested AT&T of its Bell operating companies (BOCs).

MHS (Message Handling Service — Novell)
Utility in Novell NetWare platform providing a common format for exchanging information among applications. Used typically for electronic mail.

MHS (Message Handling System — X.400)

MHS SMF71
The current version of the standard messaging format used in the NetWare Message Handling Service (MHS) is a specification for a message data structure. There is no read/write utility. The application reads and writes the file to a known place on the file server.

MHz (Megahertz)
A unit equal to 1 million hertz (1 million cycles per second).

MIB (Management Information Base — part of SNMP)
A Simple Network Management Protocol (SNMP) flat-file, nonrelational database that describes devices being monitored.

MIC (Management Integration Consortium)

MIC (memory in cassette)
A media feature with which Sony has differentiated its Advanced Intelligent Tape (AIT) drive. It is a 16-Kbit E2PROM chip that indexes file locations, thus enabling faster access to data, and stores metadata about the media, allowing enterprises to track media life cycles in the physical cartridge.

MICR (magnetic-ink character recognition)
Machine recognition and digitization of magnetically charged characters printed on paper (typically bank drafts and deposit slips).

Micro Channel Architecture (See MCA)

microcode
The microinstructions, especially of a microprocessor, that govern the details of operation. For example, the hardware of the 3081 fetches and executes 108-bit microinstructions wholly different from the instruction set of System/370. Yet IBM supplies a microprogram that causes the 3081 to act like a System/370. The instructions in such a program are referred to as micro-

code. The execution of each System 370 instruction puts the hardware into a subroutine of microinstructions that execute the function defined for that instruction. Microcoded functions can improve performance but add a layer of complexity. For example, microcode errors appear to software as being hardware failures.

microfilm
A high-resolution film used to record images reduced in size from the original.

microprocessor
A central processing unit (CPU) on a single chip. Desktop and portable computers one microprocessor, while more powerful computers often make use of multiple microprocessors.

middleware
Originally, middleware was defined broadly as the runtime system software layered between an application program and the operating system. In that sense, database management systems (DBMSs) and transaction processing (TP) monitors represent middleware, but development tools or system management utilities do not, because they do not directly support the application at runtime. Now, middleware is more commonly and narrowly defined as the network-aware system software, layered between an application, the operating system and the network transport layers, whose purpose is to facilitate some aspect of cooperative processing. Examples of cooperative middleware include directory services, message-passing mechanisms, distributed TP monitors, object request brokers (ORBs), remote procedure call (RPC) services and database gateways.

midrange computer
A computer with an architecture similar to that of the minicomputer, which is used for multiple users.

Midrange System End-User Query
An end-user query facility on the midrange system that allows direct access to System/370 Virtual Storage Access Method (VSAM) or Database-2 (DB2) data using remote-access facilities.

MIF (management information file)

million instructions per second (See MIPS)

million of floating-point operations per second (See MFLOPS)

MIMD (multiple instruction, multiple data)
A design for parallel computers characterized by the simultaneous execution of many different instruction streams (programs) where the instructions in each stream handle different data.

MIME (Multipurpose Internet Mail Extensions)
Developed and adopted by the Internet Engineering Task Force, MIME enables mixed-media files to be transmitted across Transmission Control Protocol/Internet Protocol (TCP/IP) networks. This protocol, which is actually an extension of Simple Mail Transport Protocol (SMTP), covers binary, audio and video data, as well as electronic data interchange (EDI) and multiple body parts. SMTP only knows how to transfer a single file consisting of seven-bit American Standard Code for Information Interchange (ASCII) characters. MIME describes a way of

encoding the cover note and all attachments, or "body parts," so that they look to the system like a single file. A MIME object is carried with an SMTP message.

minicomputer

A computing device that is typically more powerful than a PC, but less powerful than a mainframe, and is therefore often referred to as "midrange." The minicomputer can support a single user or multiple users.

MIPS (million instructions per second)

An approximate figure to denote a computer's raw processing power. It is often misleading, since it does not necessarily provide a creditable throughput figure of merit.

MIPS RISC

A reduced instruction set computer (RISC) processor architecture designed and licensed by MIPS Computer Systems. Used by a number of midrange suppliers, it was the basis for the Advanced RISC Computing (ARC) definitions endorsed by the now-defunct Advanced Computing Environment (ACE) corsortium

MIS (management information systems)

This was once the predominantly-used name for the central data processing organization in a commercial enterprise. Today, information systems (IS) is the more commonly used term.

Mixed Object: Document Content Architecture (See MO:DCA)

MKS (Mortice Kern Systems)

MLA (Master License Agreement — Novell)

Novell's most popular licensing option under its "Customer Connections" program. It offers the highest discounts, and includes bundled Novell Premium Support and upgrade protection, but also requires the highest spending level for an organization to qualify.

MLC (monthly license charge)

A pricing structure for software licensing. Users can usually terminate their software licenses with a 30-day notice.

MMDS (multipoint multichannel distribution service)

A wireless technology used for broadcasting, personal communications and interactive-media services.

MMI (man-machine interface)

End-user interface.

MIME

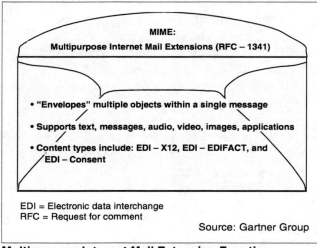

EDI = Electronic data interchange
RFC = Request for comment

Source: Gartner Group

Multipurpose Internet Mail Extension Functions

MMMC (minimum monthly maintenance charge)

MMS (Manufacturing Message Service)
Part of Layer 7 in the Open System Interconnection (OSI) seven-layer network protocol stack. MMS creates a common communications interface between application software and factory devices such as programmable logic controllers, numerical controllers and robots.

MNS (managed network services)
The vendor delivery of primarily operational support for a new environment in which the hardware assets, financial obligations and personnel still remain on the books of the customer.

MO (magneto-optic)
Information stored by local magnetization of a magnetic medium, using a focused light beam to produce local heating and consequent reduction of coercivity so that a moderately strong, poorly localized magnetic field can flip the state of a small region of high coercivity material. Reaching is done either magnetically, with inductive heads in close proximity to the medium, or optically, through rotation of the plan of polarization of probing light via the Faraday effect or Kerr effect.

MO:DCA (Mixed Object: Document Content Architecture)
The definition of the interchange data stream for documents containing a mixture of information types, such as text, image and graphics.

mobile satellite service (See MSS)

modem
A conversion device installed in pairs that allows a computing device to transmit information over analog communication lines (for example, traditional phone lines) through a modem at the opposite end by converting information that is digitally stored on the computer into transmission signals. The transmitting-end modem modulates digital signals received locally from a computer or terminal and sends analog signals over the line. The receiving-end modem demodulates the incoming signal, converting it back to its original (i.e., digital) format and passes it to the destination business machine. Modem speeds are measured in bits per second (bps). The higher the bit rate, the faster the modem can transmit information, and the shorter time a user needs to wait.

modified final judgment (See MFJ)

modulation
The application of information onto a carrier signal by varying one or more of the signal's basic characteristics (frequency, amplitude or phase); the conversion of a signal from its original (e.g., digital) format to analog format.

MOLP (Microsoft Open License Pak)

MOM (manufacturing operations management)

MOM (message-oriented middleware)

monitor
Computer hardware used for displaying digital output.

monthly license charge (See MLC)

Moore's Law
Moore's Law of semiconductor technology states that speed doubles and density quadruples every 18 months.

Mosaic
A user-friendly Internet front end developed at the University of Illinois.

MOSP (Multiple Operating System PR/ SM)

Motif
Graphical user interface (GUI) specified by the Open Software Foundation (OSF) and built on the Massachusetts Institute of Technology's (MIT's) X Windows.

Motion Pictures Experts Group (See MPEG)

MPC (Multimedia PC)
Specifications for a multimedia PC from the Multimedia PC Marketing Council, first published in 1990. Requires adherence to a minimum random-access memory (RAM), processor, CD-ROM transfer rate, sound-sampling, video and port standards.

MPE (Multiprogramming Executive)
A multitasking operating system that is used on the Hewlett-Packard 3000 series.

MPEG (Motion Picture Experts Group)
A digital video standard for compression of full-motion images driven by the same committee as the Joint Photographic Experts Group (JPEG) standard. The compression ratios achieved with MPEG encoding make it an ideal standard for delivery of digital video data.

MPN (multiprotocol network)

MPOA (multiprotocol over ATM)
A routing option that combines the second phase of local-area network (LAN) emulations with a route server, a route set cache of protocols where routing intelligence resides on the set server, and route cache devices or edge devices that maintain route tables updated by the server and that can forward traffic without going to the route server to obtain path information.

MPOS (message-passing operating system)
An operating system that enables a process anywhere in a network to communicate via messages with any other process in the network.

MPP (massively parallel processing)
An architecture that uses hundreds or thousands of parallel processors.

MPPC (multipurpose parallel computing)

MPS (master production scheduling)

MPTN (Multiprotocol Transport Networking)
Multiprotocol network support, including Transmission Control Protocol (TCP) over Systems Network Architecture (SNA), and SNA over Internet Protocol (IP), designed by IBM.

MQI (Message Queue Interface — IBM)

MQS (Message Queuing Series)

MRP (material requirements planning)
Original manufacturing business software that focused only on planning the manufacturing materials and inventories and did not integrate planning for other resources, like people and machine capacity.

MRP II (manufacturing resource planning)
A method for effective planning of all the resources of a manufacturing company. Ideally, it addresses operational planning in unitsand financial planning in dollars, and has a simulation capability to answer "what if" questions. It is made up of a variety of functions, each linked together: business planning, production planning, master production scheduling (MPS), material requirements planning (MRP), capacity requirements planning (CRP) and the execution systems for capacity and priority. Outputs from these systems will be integrated with financial reports, e.g., the business plan, purchase commitment report, shipping budget, and inventory projections in dollars. MRP II is a direct outgrowth and extension of MRP. MRP II is now migrating toward enterprise resource planning (ERP).

MS-DOS
MS-DOS stands for Microsoft Disk Operating System. It is an operating system written by Microsoft for personal computers and was the basis for IBM's PC-DOS. MS-DOS was used by all IBM PC-compatible machines. It was originally designed to organize how a computer reads, writes and interacts with its disks — floppy or hard — and how it talks to its various input/output (I/O) devices, such as keyboards, screens, printers and modems. Until the introduction of Windows-based operating systems, the most popular operating system for PCs was

MS-DOS. Unlike its successors, MS-DOS was character-based and did not use a graphical user interface (GUI).

MSI (medium-scale integration)
Between 100 and 3,000 transistors on a chip.

MSM (Microsoft Systems Management)

MSNF (Multisystem Networking Facility)
A facility of IBM's Network Control Program (NCP) that is used to control a multiple-domain network. It was an optional feature of telecommunications access method (TCAM) and Virtual Telecommunications Access Method (VTAM) version 1.

MSO (managed services organization)

MSS (mobile satellite service)
Mobile earth stations (e.g., on ships, survival stations and positioning radio beacons) that provide location identification using satellite service.

MSU (million service units)

MTA (message transfer agent)
The storing and forwarding part of an electronic-mail system.

MTBDU (mean time between data unavailability)

MTBF (mean time between failures)
The cumulative average time that a manufacturer estimates between failures or occurrences in a component, complete telephone system or printed circuit board.

MTO (master terminal operator)

MTTR (mean time to repair)
An estimated average time, by either the vendor or the manufacturer, required to do repairs on equipment.

MUD (multiuser domain)

MUI (multimedia user interface)

MULC (Measured Usage License Charge)
An S/390 software licensing arrangement offered by IBM. It yields charges based on the amount of processing capacity being used by selected software products. IBM provides a monitoring and measuring facility for establishing the charges for a system.

multimedia (See MM)
Applications and technologies that manipulate text, data, images, and voice and full-motion-video objects. Typically associated with PCs, but increasingly associated with network-based applications such as those residing on the Internet. Given the usage of multiple formats, multimedia is capable of delivering a stronger and more engaging message than standard text. Multimedia files are typically larger than text-based information, and therefore usually stored on CD-ROMs. Games and educational software commonly use multimedia.

Multimedia PC (See MPC)

multiple instruction, multiple data (See MIMD)

Multiple Virtual Storage (See MVS)

Multiple Virtual Storage/Enterprise Systems Architecture (See MVS/ESA)

multiplexer (See MUX)

multipoint multichannel distribution service (See MMDS)

multiprocessor
A computer that incorporates multiple processors with access to common storage.

Multiprogramming Executive (See MPE)

multiprotocol over ATM (See MPOA)

Multiprotocol Transport Networking (See MPTN)

Multipurpose Internet Mail Extensions (See MIME)

Multisystem Networking Facility (See MSNF)

multivendor network management
Support for integration of network management on a common workstation. The network management facility should enable user organizations or third-party vendors to integrate additional network management tools.

MUX (multiplexer)
A device that combines inputs from two or more terminals, computer ports or other multiplexers, and transmits the combined data stream over a single high-speed channel. At the receiving end, the high-speed channel is "demultiplexed," either by another multiplexer or by software.

MVLP (Microsoft Variable License Pak)

MVS (Multiple Virtual Storage)
IBM's flagship operating system. Essentially all the device support, software functions, time-sharing aids and reliability improvements that IBM produces are positioned most firmly within MVS. Many Virtual Machine (VM) microcode "assists" were designed so that MVS guests can run more effectively in that environment. Of all of IBM's software products, MVS has by far received the greatest investment for development, documentation and support. Unless qualified, MVS refers either to all versions of MVS currently in the field (and these are legion) or to the latest version (the context may be a guide).

MVS/370
A version of MVS limited to 24-bit addressing and lacking the dynamic channel subsystem. Dropped from support in the early 1990s.

MVS/ESA (Multiple Virtual Storage/ Enterprise Systems Architecture)
A version of MVS introduced by IBM in 1988. Capable of addressing up to 16 terabytes (Tbytes) of data. Runs on the 3090 E and S models, as well as on the 4381 E. Consists of MVS/SP1.3 plus the latest Data Facility Product (DFP) data management system.

N

N+1 disk shadowing/mirroring
A system or storage subsystem-level facility to provide significantly improved apparent disk reliability without the cost of two-times disk shadowing (e.g., N+1 redundant array of independent disks).

NACHA (National Automated Clearing House Association)

Named Pipes
One of several OS/2 facilities for interprocess communications.

naming service
A program that provides a mapping between a logical name and a physical address. It can be extended by a directory service (DS).

NAP (network access point)
The points from which Internet service providers (ISPs) drop down their lines and establish peering arrangements to provide Internet connectivity to their customers.

NAPLPS (North American Presentation Level Protocol Syntax)
A standard approach using vector graphics for the display and communications of text and graphics in a videotext system.

Narrowband ISDN (See N-ISDN)

narrowband PCS (See N-PCS)

NAS (Network Applications Support — Digital Equipment)
A collection of Digital Equipment architectures and development programs intended to provide a high degree of affinity between Virtual Address Extension (VAX) systems (both VMS- and Ultrix-based) and a variety of workstations, including Apple's Macintosh and IBM's PCs running MS-DOS and Operating System/2 (OS/2).

NAS (NetWare Access Server)

NAS (Networked Application Services — IBM division)

NAS (Numerical Aerodynamic Simulation — NASA program)
Located at NASA's Ames Research Center.

NASD (network-attached storage device)

NAT (Network Address Translation)
A functionality provided through the gateway Network Control Program (NCP) to protect the

internal Internet Protocol (IP) addressing structure from the Internet IP addresses.

**National Association of Securities Dealers
(See NASD)**

**National Institute of Standards and Tech-
nology (See NIST)**

national language support (See NLS)

NC (network computer)
Often called a "thin client," a network computer
is a limited-function desktop computer that is
designed to easily connect to networks. NCs
include a keyboard, mouse, monitor, memory
and a network connection but only limited, if
any, local disk storage. When end users want to
access software or databases using an NC, they
would use a graphical user interface (GUI) much
as they do now with a PC. However, the software
would be downloaded from a central server
instead of being resident on the desktop PC;
large databases would also be maintained on the
central server. All software backups, upgrades
and maintenance would therefore be performed
centrally on the network server.

NCD (networked computing device)

**N-channel metal-oxide semiconductor (See
NMOS)**

**NCP (Network Control Program — a k a
ACF/NCP)**
The IBM-licensed program that controls the
operation of an IBM 37xx front-end processor
(FEP). Communication with the host is through
Advanced Communication Function/Virtual
Telecommunications Access Method (ACF/

VTAM) via a channel interface, and communications with terminals or another FEP is via
telecommunication lines. NCP offloads certain
line protocol and routing functions from the host
central processing unit (CPU). Version 5 includes PU 2.1 support.

**NCQA (National Committee on Quality
Assurance)**

NCR (National Cash Register)

**NCS (Network Computing System — from
Hewlett-Packard)**

NCS (National Communications System)

NCSC (National Computer Security Center)

NDF (Network Distributed Function)

NDF (network dynamic functionality)
A software development and execution technology that allows applications to be written to a
model designed from the outset to achieve platform independence. It affords dynamic movement and invocation of code resources over a
network at runtime.

NDL (Network Data Language)
The skeletal standard developed by CODASYL
(Conference on Data Systems Languages) for an
application programming interface (API) to net-
work-model database management systems
(DBMSs). It has since been abandoned.

NDS (NetWare Directory Service)
The NetWare Directory Service is globally oriented and maintains information about network
resources, (including users, groups, servers, vol-

umes, printers and multiple servers) and provides a naming service. NDS replaces the binary file used in previous versions of NetWare.

NetBIOS (Network Basic Input/Output System)
An extension of IBM's PC BIOS. It was developed as the interface for the PC Network program, but is supported on the Token Ring Network (TRN) and a number of non-IBM systems. It will likely be a long-term tactical solution for local networking; the long-term strategic solution will be Advanced Program-to-Program Communications/Logical Unit 6.2 (APPC/LU 6.2).

NetView (See NV)

NetView Peer Interface
Network management as a peer Systems Network Architecture (SNA) node to the focal point of IBM's NetView.

NetView/PC Connect
A network management interface to IBM's NetView network management system through the IBM NetView/PC service point.

NetWare
A network operating system (NOS) by Novell. The dominant local-area networking system for peripheral sharing and application communications.

NetWare Directory Service (See NDS)

NetWare Loadable Module (See NLM)

network
Any number of computers (e.g., PCs and servers) and devices (e.g., printers and modems) joined together by a physical communications link. In the corporate context, networks allow information to be passed between computers, irrespective of where those computers are located. Networks provide the roads for information traffic (e.g., sending files and E-mail) within a corporate environment, and allow users to access databases and share applications residing on servers. If a network does not go outside of a company building, or campus, then it is known as a local-area network (LAN). If it has a bridge to other outside networks, usually via lines owned by public telecommunications carriers like AT&T, then it is known as a wide-area network (WAN).

network access point (See NAP)

Network Address Translation (See NAT)

Network Applications Support — Digital Equipment (See NAS)

Network Basic Input/Output System (See NetBIOS)

network computer (See NC)

Network Control Program — a k a ACF/ NCP (See NCP)

Network Data Language (See NDL)

network database
A database organized according to ownership of records, allowing records to have multiple owners and thus providing multiple access paths to the data. Database management systems (DBMSs) providing such capabilities are also known as CODASYL (Conference on Data Systems Languages) DBMSs.

network dynamic functionality (See NDF)

Network File System (See NFS)

network interface card (See NIC)

network layer
In the Open Systems Interconnection (OSI) model, the logical network entity that services the transport layer. It is responsible for ensuring that data passed to it from the transport layer is routed and delivered through the network.

network management
Administrative services performed in managing a network — e.g., network topology and software configuration, downloading of software, monitoring network performance, maintaining network operations, and diagnosing and troubleshooting problems.

network management vector tables (See NMVT)

Network News Transport Protocol (See NNTP)

network operating system (See NOS)

network performance tuning/configuring facilities
The ability to configure combinations of local-area networks (LANs) and wide-area networks (WANs) centrally and dynamically based on anticipation and prioritization of data traffic volumes. Physical data paths could be configured based on data traffic content (i.e., transaction type). This is particularly important for online transaction processing (OLTP) applications.

network service access point (See NSAP)

network-attached storage device (See NASD)

network-based storage backup facilities — midrange
A system facility for defining and executing predetermined backup processes of data from other midrange systems of the same supplier in the network.

network-to-network interface (See NNI)

networked systems management (See NSM)

networking (See also network)
The linking of a number of devices, such as computers, workstations and printers, into a network (system) for the purpose of sharing resources.

neural nets
A technique used to analyze elements that are organized in a random pattern. Using processes and feedback that are established by operational departments, neural nets can enable organizations to develop conclusions and action items from a complex and seemingly unrelated set of information.

NeWS
Sun Microsystems' initial graphical user interface (GUI) product.

NewWave
An environment that was developed by Hewlett-Packard in cooperation with Microsoft and built on Windows 2.0.

NewWave Office
Hewlett-Packard's third-generation office information system (OIS), which was built around the NewWave user environment on the workstation and HP-UX-, MPE/XL- and OS/2-based servers.

NFS (Network File System)
A method of sharing files across a computer network. Pioneered by Sun Microsystems, it is now a de facto standard in the Unix environment. NFS is built on Transmission Control Protocol/Internet Protocol (TCP/IP) and Ethernet.

NIC (network interface card)
An attachment that connects a device to a network, similar to an adapter.

NIH (not invented here)

N-ISDN (narrowband ISDN)
Integrated Services Digital Network (ISDN) speeds up to 1.544 megabits per second (Mbps). As speeds get faster, the definition of narrowband ISDN applies to faster speeds.

NIST (National Institute of Standards and Technology)
An agency of the U.S. Department of Commerce. Previously called the National Bureau of Standards.

NLM (NetWare Loadable Module)
Software that provides additional functions to a NetWare server — for example, an application (such as a DBMS) running directly under NetWare.

NLS (national language support)
Mechanisms provided for the straightforward internationalization of both system and application user-visible interfaces.

NLU (natural-language understanding)

NMF (Network Management Forum)

NMOS (N-channel metal-oxide semiconductor)
A microelectronic circuit used for logic and memory chips and in complementary metal-oxide semiconductor (CMOS) design. NMOS transistors are faster than the P-channel metal-oxide semiconductor (PMOS) counterpart, and more of them can be put on a single chip.

NMVT (network management vector tables)
A Systems Network Architecture (SNA) management protocol which provides alert problem determination statistics and network management data.

NNI (network-to-network interface)

NNTP (Network News Transport Protocol)
The discussion database standard that governs Usenet newsgroup distribution on the Internet.

node
A termination point for two or more communications links. The node can serve as the control location for forwarding data among the elements of a network or multiple networks, as well as performing other networking and, in some cases, local-processing functions. In Systems Network Architecture (SNA), it is an end point

of a link or a junction common to two or more links in a network. Nodes can be host processors, communications controllers, cluster controllers, workgroup computers or terminals.

NOLE (Network OLE)

nonreturn to zero inverted (See NRZI)

NonStop SQL (NonStop Structured Query Language)
Leading-edge relational database management system (RDBMS) software from Tandem Computers. Working in concert with Tandem's message-passing Guardian operating system, NonStop SQL supports near-linear expandability and high up-times for applications by tolerating single points of failure. NonStop SQL was the first DBMS to support engine-based (as opposed to front-end-tool-based), truly distributed databases.

NonStop Structured Query Language (See NonStop SQL)

nonvolatile (See NV)

North American Presentation Level Protocol Syntax (See NAPLPS)

NOS (network operating system)
A set of software utilities that, working in conjunction with an operating system (OS), provides the local-area network (LAN) user interface and controls network operation. A network operating system communicates with the LAN hardware and enables users to communicate with one another and to share files and peripherals. Typically, a NOS provides file-to-print services, directory services and security.

Novell NetWare Implementation
A facility that provides server functions and program-to-program application programming interfaces (APIs) on the midrange system.

NOW Index
An index devleoped by Real Decisions, a Gartner Group company. This metric is derived using normalized cost and work produced.

N-PCS (narrowband personal communications services)
N-PCS is similar to paging since it is used for short-message applications with a small "palm-of-the-hand" form factor. The addition of a response channel enables two-way paging capability and allows N-PCS to serve users that have more robust data and reliability requirements. N-PCS has been allocated a total of three megahertz (MHz) of spectrum in the 900-MHz block by the Federal Communications Commission (FCC).

NPSI (NCP Packet Switching Interface)

NPV (net present value)

NRZI (nonreturn to zero inverted)
Encoding by inverting a signal on a high-voltage (on) pulse, leaving the signal unchanged for the low (off).

NSAP (network service access point)
In the semantics of the Open Systems Interconnection (OSI) addressing scheme, the point at which the OSI network service is made available to the transport entity.

NSAPI (Netscape Server API)

NSM (networked systems management)
The intersection of networking, network management and systems management. The vision of NSM is to enable the management of a distributed set of systems in a fashion similar to that in which many centralized data centers are managed. This vision remains far from fulfillment.

NSO (Network Server Option)

NT (See Windows NT)

NTL (narrow track longitudinal)

NTSC (National TV System Committee)

NTT (Nippon Telephone and Telegraph)

Numerical Aerodynamic Simulation — NASA program (See NAS)

NV (NetView)
An IBM Systems Network Architecture (SNA) network management product that includes some of the functions of NCCF, NLDM, NPDA, NMPF and Virtual Telecommunications Access Method (VTAM) node control application. It was a key enabler to IBM's overall systems management strategy.

NV (nonvolatile)
A data store which retains data when power is off.

NW/IP (NetWare Internet Protocol)

OAG (Open Applications Group)

object
In its simplest terms, it means nothing more than "thing" or "entity." In the world of object-oriented programming and databases, it signifies an instance of a class, such as "IBM" being an instance of the class "hardware vendor." An object is the unit of information interchange in third-generation (3GL) office systems. An object contains both content and semantics describing how the content is to be interpreted or operated on. A network object is any entity in a network (e.g., a node, printer or file server). Software objects may be files or pieces of data.

object-based technologies
Technologies in which objects have encapsulation.

object class
A grouping of objects that can be described in terms of the attributes its members have in common. Generic electronic mail (E-mail) is a class. All E-mail systems have certain things in common. WordPerfect documents are a class.

Object Content Architecture (See OCA)

object data model
A data model based on object-oriented programming, associating methods (procedures) with objects that can benefit from class hierarchies. Thus, "objects" are levels of abstraction that include attributes and behavior. An object-oriented data model is one that extends the individual program space into the world of persistent object management and shareability.

Object

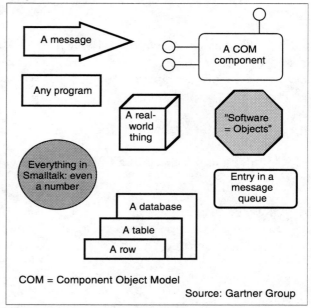

COM = Component Object Model

Source: Gartner Group

The Many Meanings of "Object"

Object Database Management Group (See ODMG)

object encapsulation
Hiding complexity. Data and procedures may be encapsulated to produce a single object.

Object File System (See OFS)

object inheritance
Inheritance defines a relationship among classes in which a subclass shares, overrides or supplements operations or data values from one or more superclasses. A subclass is a specialization of one or more superclasses.

object instance
A specific occurrence of an object. For example, a specific mail message from Betty to Sue is an instance; a specific WordPerfect document is an instance.

object late binding
Runtime interpretation of messages. Using late binding, objects are integrated at runtime, as opposed to compiling an integrated object. This greatly enhances flexibility.

Object Linking and Embedding (See OLE)

Object Linking and Embedding Database (See OLE DB)

object management
Middleware that manages the naming, location and invocation of objects in a system.

Object Management Group (See OMG)

object message passing
In object-oriented systems, one object never operates on another. Instead, one object may pass a message to another object requesting invocation of a method — e.g., "print yourself," "display yourself" or "file yourself."

object method
Methods define what can be done with an object. Methods for an electronic-mail document may be display, send, file or print.

object orientation (See OO)

object-oriented (See OO)

object-oriented database management system (See OODBMS)

object-oriented programming (See OOP)

object-oriented system
In an object-oriented system, all data is represented as discrete objects with which the user and other objects may interact. Each object contains data as well as information about the executable file needed to interpret that data. An object-oriented system allows the user to focus completely on tasks rather than tools. Examples of object-oriented programming language include C++ and Smalltalk.

OCA (Object Content Architecture)
The definition of the components, or objects, containing the data that comprises the document information carried by a Mixed Object: Document Content Architecture (MO:DCA) data stream.

object request broker (See ORB)

**Object Structured Query Language —
Hewlett-Packard (See OSQL)**

object transaction monitor (See OTM)

**OCE (Open Collaboration Environment)
(See AOCE)**

OCI (Oracle Call-Level Interface)

OC-N (Optical Carrier at Rate N)
The range of incremental rates defined for
SONET-based fiber-optic transmission. A
SONET/SDH term identifying the place in the
hierarchy or speed of such a channel (e.g., OC-
3 is 155 Mbps).

OCR (optical character recognition)
The ability of a computer to recognize written
characters through some optical-sensing device
and pattern recognition soft-
ware.

OCS (open control systems)
Systems that incorporate technologies generally perceived
as capable of integration
among themselves and with
other applications, without the
use of proprietary technology.
It refers to process control for
discrete, batch and continu-
ous-process industries as
implemented on platforms
that range from programmable
logic controllers and distributed control systems, to soft
control implemented on general-purpose computing platforms. It also includes computer numerical control and other
motion control.

OCX (OLE Custom Controls)
Visual Basic add-on components based on the
Object Linking and Embedding (OLE) set of
interfaces.

ODA (Open Document Architecture)
An international standard that enables users to
exchange texts and graphics generated on different types of office products.

ODBC (Open Database Connectivity)
A vendor-neutral interface based on the Structured Query Language (SQL) Access Group
specifications. Announced by Microsoft in De-
cember 1991, ODBC accesses data in a heterogeneous environment of relational and
nonrelational databases.

OCS

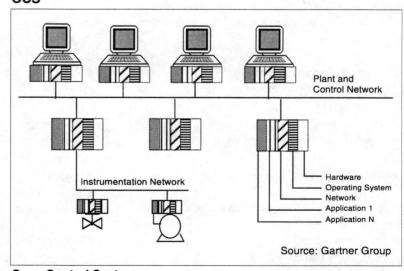

Open Control Systems

ODBMS (object-oriented database management system)
See OODBMS. Alternative acronym.

ODI (Object Design Inc.)

ODIF (Open Document Interchange Format)
Defines the Open Document Architecture (ODA) format in terms of interchanged data elements.

ODM (Open Document Management)

ODMA (Open Document Management API)
Provides standard interface between document management systems and end-user applications. ODMA is becoming a desktop application integration de facto standard.

ODMG (Object Database Management Group)
A group of object-oriented database management system (OODBMS) vendors assisting the Object Management Group (OMG) in defining object standards.

ODS (operational data store)
A new articulation of the perennial concept of shared production data. Different from a data warehouse, the ODS is an alternative to having operational decision support system (DSS) applications access data directly from the database that supports transaction processing (TP).

While both require a significant amount of planning, the ODS tends to focus on the operational requirements of a particular business process (for example, customer service), and on the need to allow updates and propagate those updates back to the source operational system from which the data elements were obtained. The data warehouse, on the other hand, provides an architecture for decision makers to access data to perform strategic analysis, which often involves historical and cross-functional data and the need to support many applications.

ODSI (Open Directory Services Interface)
A standard in the Microsoft Windows operating system that provides a generic application interface to any of a number of database systems that have a service provider interface (SPI) available in the architecture. Additional SPIs may be provided by the database vendor or a third party.

OEC (Open Environment Corp.)

OEM (original equipment manufacturer)
Refers to the manufacturer of a device that another vendor resells as part of a system.

office information system (See OIS)

OfficeVision
The name for IBM's Systems Application Architecture (SAA) office program, introduced in May 1989. It provides a common user interface across the various IBM office systems and removed from IBM's office systems the old stigma of poor usability. The front-end system is the PS/2 with Operating System/2 (OS/2) EE; the back-end system is based on Multiple Virtual Storage/Enterprise Systems Architecture (MVS/ESA), Virtual Machine (VM), OS/400 or a PS/2-based server.

offshore programming
The contracting by a company for software services to be carried out in a country other than

its own — e.g., a user located in North America may choose to have applications maintenance work carried out in India.

OFS (Object File System)
A file system conceived by Microsoft as a base for its Windows NT 5.0 directory, in which the name spaces of its file system and its Exchange electronic mail (E-mail) system would be unified.

OIS (office information system)
The architectural reference frame for the construction of an office solution that meets the needs that originate at all levels (individual, departmental and corporate), integrating them in a functional sense.

OLAP (online analytical processing)
A definition of multidimensional business intelligence (BI) servers that originated with a Code and Date white paper that defined 12 "OLAP product-evaluation rules" as the basis for selecting multidimensional products. OLAP is, in truth, only a new name for a class of BI products, some of which have existed for decades. The 12 evaluation rules for providing OLAP to user-analysts are:

1. Multidimensional conceptual view
2. Transparency
3. Accessibility
4. Consistent reporting performance
5. Client/server architecture
6. Generic dimensionality
7. Dynamic sparse matrix handling
8. Multiuser support
9. Unrestricted cross-dimensional operations
10. Intuitive data manipulation
11. Flexible reporting
12. Unlimited dimensions and aggregation levels

OLCP (online complex processing)
An extension of online transaction processing (OLTP) to include concurrent ad hoc query and batch processing.

OLE (Object Linking and Embedding)
A Microsoft protocol that enables creation of compound documents with embedded links to applications, so that a user does not have to switch from one application to another to make revisions. With OLE:

- It is easy for users to create compound documents using multiple applications.
- Compound documents may contain text and spreadsheet objects, graphic and chart objects, sound objects, and video and animated objects.
- Objects that support OLE automation may be scripted by OLE controllers, such as Visual Basic, and used in end-user-developed applications.

OLE Custom Controls (See OCX)

OLE DB (Object Linking and Embedding Database)
Microsoft's strategy is for OLE DB to provide much of the functionality previously expected to be in Windows NT 5.0. OLE DB is promoted as much more than an OLE interface to relational data. It has assumed the role of universal information access. OLE DB is perhaps better described as "OLE Information Access" because it provides more than database access. It provides access not only to relational data but also to other types of databases and to unstruc-

tured data and documents. The mechanism used to implement this functionality is OLE interfaces that manipulate underlying technology to provide access to the underlying information.

OLE DS (OLE Directory Services)

OLS (online service)

OLTP (online transaction processing)
A mode of processing that is characterized by short transactions recording business events and that normally requires high availability and consistent, short response times. This category of applications requires that a request for service be answered within a predictable period that approaches "real time." Unlike traditional mainframe data processing, in which data is processed only at specific times, transaction processing puts terminals online, where they can update the database instantly to reflect changes as they occur. In other words, the data processing models the actual business in real time, and a transaction transforms this model from one business state to another. Tasks such as making reservations, scheduling and inventory control are especially complex; all the information must be current.

OLTP monitor
Midrange system software designed to enhance the efficiency of online transaction processing applications by providing screen mapping, transaction queuing, service prioritization, communications buffering and security.

OLTP screen-formatting front end
A cooperative processing facility that offloads screen formatting from a midrange system-resident online transaction processing (OLTP) sys-

tem to a PC. The application programmer should be able to define a single set of screen-formatting maps without regard to whether the formatting is performed at the midrange system or at the PC.

OMG (Object Management Group)
A group, primarily of vendors, set up in 1990 to foster common definitions, understanding and standards for object-oriented computing. It has more than 100 members.

OMS (opportunity management system)
A system tied closely to the sales process; it is the framework for any sales force automation SFA design. All other applications are subordinate to the OMS. Transactions flow from the OMS to other applications on the users' portable computers. Applications can be integrated among vendors.

ONA (Open Network Architecture — from the FCC)

ONC (Open Network Computing — Sun Microsystems)

online analytical processing (See OLAP)

online complex processing (See OLCP)

online documentation
A consistent, system-supplied mechanism for online documentation of system and application programs, including provision of such documentation of vendor-provided software.

online processor hardware replacement
Replacement of failed processor components without disrupting system operation.

online services

These provide access to exclusive data, information and communications resources. Customers of online services often must use proprietary software to access these resources. Online services often provide access to the Internet in addition to their exclusive resources. America Online, Microsoft Network, Prodigy and Lexis-Nexis are examples of online services.

online transaction processing (See OLTP)

online transaction processing monitor (See OLTP monitor)

OO (object-oriented or object orientation)

An umbrella concept used to describe a suite of technologies that enable software to be highly modular and reusable; applications, data, networks and computing systems are treated as objects that can be mixed and matched flexibly rather than as components of a system with built-in relationships. As a result, an application need not be tied to a specific system or data to a specific application. The four central object-oriented concepts are encapsulation, message passing, inheritance and late binding.

OOA (object-oriented analysis)

OOD (object-oriented design)

OODBMS (object-oriented database management system)

A database management system (DBMS) that applies concepts of object-oriented programming, and applies them to the management of persistent objects on behalf of multiple users, with capabilities for security, integrity, recovery and contention management. An OODBMS is based on the principles of "objects," namely abstract data types, classes, inheritance mechanisms, polymorphism, dynamic binding and message passing.

OOP (object-oriented programming)

A style of programming characterized by the identification of classes of objects closely linked with the methods (functions) with which they are associated. It also includes ideas of inheritance of attributes and methods. It is a technique based on a mathematical discipline, called "ab-

OMS

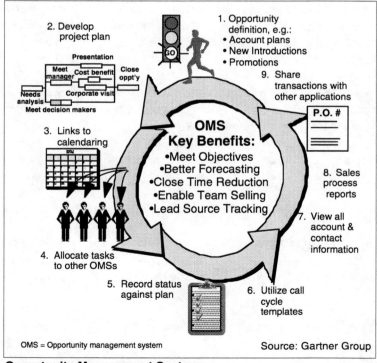

Opportunity Management Systems

---

stract data types," for storing data with the procedures needed to process that data. OOP offers the potential to evolve programming to a higher level of abstraction.

OOT (object-oriented technology)

open architecture
A technology infrastructure with specifications that are public as opposed to proprietary. This includes officially approved standards as well as privately designed architectures, the specifications of which are made public by their designers. The IBM PC, for example, was based on an open architecture, and spawned an entire industry of IBM clones.

OpenCIM
Hewlett-Packard's open-system manufacturing initiative, which serves as an umbrella for products like OpenMFG, Hewlett-Packard's Unix-based MRP II software.

Open Client/Open Server
A product (and set of interfaces) marketed by Sybase that allows for gateways to foreign information environments. It is flexible, and licensable, but still proprietary, and thus not truly "open."

open control systems (See OCS)

Open Database Connectivity (See ODBC)

Open Database Services Interface (See ODSI)

Open Document Architecture (See ODA)

Open Document Interchange Format (See ODIF)

Open Document Management API (See ODMA)

OpenLook
An X Windows-based graphical user interface (GUI) developed primarily by Sun Microsystems.

Open Server Offering (See OSO)

Open Software Foundation (See OSF)

open system
A system whose interfaces — for example, application programming interfaces (APIs) or protocols — conform to formal, multilateral, generally available industry standards. "Formal" implies that the standard is selected and maintained using a structured, public process (i.e., de facto standards, such as those developed by the Open Software Foundation). "Multilateral" implies that, while nothing is ever completely vendor-neutral, the standard is not controlled by a single vendor. "Generally available" implies that the specifications are fully published (preferably with source code of a reference implementation), and that anyone can readily obtain license rights for free or at low cost.

Open Systems Interconnection (See OSI)

OpenView
A network management system from Hewlett-Packard.

operating lease
A lease agreement that does not meet any of the criteria of a capital lease as defined by FASB 13 (Financial Accounting Standards Board Statement 13).

operating system (See OS)

Operating System/2 (See OS/2)

Operating System/400 (See OS/400)

operational data store (See ODS)

Optical Carrier at Rate N (See OC-N)

optical character recognition (See OCR)

optical disc
A disk read or written by light, generally laser light; such a disk may store video, audio or digital data.

ORB (object request broker)
A "standard" defined by the Object Management Group (OMG) that allows centralized communication among networked objects.

ORDBMS (object-oriented relational data base management system)

original equipment manufacturer (See OEM)

OS (operating system)
The operating system is the main control program that runs a computer and sets the standard for running application programs. It is the first program loaded when the computer is turned on, and it resides in memory at all times. An operating system is responsible for functions such as memory allocation, managing programs and errors, and directing input and output. It may be developed by the computer vendor or by a third-party independent software vendor.

OS/2 (Operating System/2)
An IBM operating system for personal computers featuring capabilities for large memory, multitasking and virtual machines.

OS/2 EE (OS/2 Extended Edition)
Extends the features of OS/2 to include integrated communications and database facilities.

OS/2 SE (OS/2 Standard Edition)
Operating System/2 Standard Edition. The IBM operating system (developed by Microsoft) for the PS/2. OS/2 represents a revolutionary (not evolutionary) advance over PC-DOS, and is the enabler for the transition of the desktop to a real computing environment, i.e., capabilities for large memory, multitasking and virtual machines. It also bundles database and communications facilities.

OS/400 (Operating System/400)
The operating system for IBM's AS/400.

OSF (Open Software Foundation)
A consortium formed to develop formal, multivendor standards. Its founding members included IBM, Digital, Hewlett-Packard, Apollo Computer (since acquired by HP), Siemens Nixdorf and Groupe Bull. OSF was founded in reaction to the pact between AT&T and Sun Microsystems to develop a Unix standard that favored Sun's hardware. Its role has since evolved to address issues of common technology beyond Unix environments.

OSF/1
The first Open Software Foundation operating system, based on Carnegie-Mellon's Mach kernel and announced October 1990 and shipped in

1992. Though it is a step in the right direction to unify the many flavors of Unix, convergence is far off. It is also unclear that vendors will abandon their own Unix for OSF/1.

OSF/Motif

The user interface developed by the Open Software Foundation (OSF). It is based on Digital Equipment's graphical user interface (GUI) toolkit, with a look and feel ported by Hewlett-Packard and Microsoft from Presentation Manager. It conforms to the X Windows standard, and is an implementation of the Motif GUI as defined by the Open Software Foundation Application Environment Specification User Environment Volume and Motif Style Guide.

OSI (Open Systems Interconnection)

A model developed by the International Standards Organization (ISO) for communications. It is similar in structure to Systems Network Architecture (SNA), but more open. A standard, modular approach to network design that divides the required set of complex functions into manageable, self-contained, functional layers. These layers, starting from the innermost, are:

1. Physical layer — concerned with the mechanical and electrical means by which devices are physically connected and data is transmitted.
2. Link layer — concerned with how to move data reliably across the physical data link.
3. Network layer — provides the means to establish, maintain and terminate connections between systems. Concerned with switching and routing information.
4. Transport layer — concerned with end-to-end data integrity and quality of service.
5. Session layer — standardizes the task of setting up a session and terminating it. Coordinates the interaction between end application processes.
6. Presentation layer — relates to the character set and data code that is used, and to the way data is displayed on a screen or printer.
7. Application layer — concerned with the higher-level functions that support application or system activities.

OSI X.400

Support for Open Systems Interconnection X.400 Message Handling System protocols verified under the Corporation for Open Systems Mark program.

OSI FTAM

Support for Open Systems Interconnection File Transfer, Access and Management protocols verified under the Corporation for Open Systems Mark program.

OSIS (operating-system-independent server)

OSI TP (OSI Transaction Processing)

OSM (operating-system service module)

OSO (Open Server Offering)

A process and marketing program from IBM, similar to its long-established Entry Server Offering (ESO), but with a focus on the network-computing and operating-systems environment.

OSPF (open shortest path first)

**OSQL (Object Structured Query Language
— Hewlett-Packard)**

An extension to Structured Query Language
(SQL) pioneered by Microelectronics & Computer Technology and delivered by Hewlett-
Packard. It provides object management capabilities to the SQL relational language.

OTM (object transaction monitor)

An application program — similar to the mainframe Customer Information Control System
(CICS) in function, but not in spirit — that
represents a consistent model of an application
for a modular and potentially highly distributed
environment.

outsourcing

A contractual relationship with an outside vendor that is usually characterized by the transfer
of assets, e.g., facilities, staff or hardware. It can
include facilities management (data center and/
or network), applications development/mainte-
nance functions, and end-user computing services.

End-user-computing outsourcing includes all
services to support end users from the workstation up to the front-end router. The scope ranges
from the end user's workstation to the shared
LAN and local network infrastructure of an
enterprise's distributed computing architecture.
It includes desktop services (implementation,
operations and management of desktop hardware, software and peripherals), network systems management (implementation and management of LANs, network-enabling hardware
and software) and help desks.

P

P7
X.400 protocol.

PA (Precision Architecture — Hewlett-Packard)

packet
An information block identified by a label at Layer 3 of the International Standards Organization (ISO) reference model for Open Systems Interconnection (OSI). It is a collection of bits that contains both control information and data, and is the basic unit of transmission in a packet-switched network. Control information is carried in the packet, along with the data, to provide for such functions as addressing sequence, flow control and error control at each of several protocol levels. A packet can be of fixed or variable length, but generally has a specified maximum length.

packet assembler/disassembler (See PAD)

packet format
The exact order and size of a packet's various control and information fields, including header, address and data fields.

packet overhead
A measure of the ratio of the total packet bits occupied by control information to the number of bits of data, usually expressed as a percentage.

packet switching
A technique in which a message is broken into smaller units called packets, which may be individually addressed and routed through the network, possibly using several different routes. The receiving-end node ascertains that all packets are received and in the proper sequence before forwarding the complete message to the addressee.

PAD (packet assembler/disassembler)
An interface device that buffers data sent to and from character mode devices, and assembles and disassembles the packets needed for X.25 operation.

page (See Web page)

PAM (pulse amplitude modulation)
Encoding of information in a signal based on the fluctuation of carrier waves.

PAMS (parallel application management system)

parallel processing
The solution of a single problem across more than one processor. Little parallel processing is

done today outside of research laboratories, because it is difficult to decompose tasks into independent parts, and the compiler technology does not yet exist that will extensively parallelize applications code.Parallel Query Server (See PQS)

Parallel Query Server (See PQS)

Parallel Reduced Instruction Set Multiprocessor (See PRISM)

Parallel Sysplex
The cornerstone of IBM's large-systems operating-system strategy. It is designed to allow multiple central electronics complexes (CECs) to share a common database so a transaction can execute on one of several processors that share a single view of the data. This implementation substantially improves parallelism, and therefore overall system throughput, at a multitasking level.

Parallel Sysplex License Charge (See PSLC)

parallel systems
Hardware configurations having nine or fewer central processing units (CPUs). Compare with highly parallel systems (HPS) and massively parallel systems.

Parallel Transaction Server (See PTS)

PARC (Palo Alto Research Center — Xerox)

PA-RISC (Precision Architecture Reduced Instruction Set Computer)
Hewlett-Packard's RISC-based processor architecture, the basis for its desktop-to-mainframe processor products. It serves as a single design point to consolidate Hewlett-Packard's three computer families: Hewlett-Packard 9000/800 Unix multiuser system and servers; Hewlett-Packard 9000/700 Unix servers and workstations; and Hewlett-Packard 3000 commercial MPE/XL multiuser system and servers.

partitioned data set (See PDS)

PBA (production business application)

PBX (private branch exchange)
A telephone switch located on a customer's premises that primarily establishes voice-grade circuits (over tie lines to a telephone company central office) between individual users and the

Parallel Sysplex

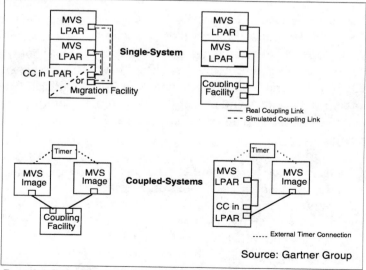

Parallel Sysplex Alternatives

public switched telephone network. The PBX also provides switching within the customer premises local area, and usually offers numerous enhanced features, including least-cost routing and call detail recording.

PC (personal computer)
A microcomputer designed primarily for individual use. Sharing resources with another computer is optional. The first PCs were introduced in the early 1980s.

PC ALL-IN-1
A Digital Equipment product that lets the user interface and other I/O-intensive portions of ALL-IN-1 reside on the PC.

PC-DOS
The original operating system that IBM supplied with its personal computers.

PCA (planning, control and administration)

PCB (printed circuit board)
A flat board made of fiberglass or plastic, on which chips and electronic components are interconnected via copper pathways. The primary PCB in a system is called a system board or motherboard, while smaller ones that plug into the slots in the main board are called riser boards or cards.

PCI (Peripheral Component Interconnect)
The industry standard system bus architecture that is prevalent in many vendors' desktop and server models. PCI provides faster communications between the processor and components (such as memory, disk and video) than Industry Standard Architecture (ISA).

PCL (Printer Control Language)
The set of commands used by Hewlett-Packard and compatible printers that governs how a document will be printed.

PCM (plug-compatible manufacturer)
A hardware vendor whose products are direct replacements for the products of a computer system manufacturer. Initially PCMs provided peripherals that were "plug-for-plug" compatible with IBM peripherals, but the PCM industry has since grown to include IBM-compatible mainframes and peripherals for other vendors' systems.

PCM (pulse code modulation)
A form of modulation in which the modulating signal is sampled and coded. It is the standard technique in telecommunications transmission.

PCMCIA (Personal Computer Memory Card International Association)
A nonprofit trade association founded in 1989 to standardize the PC card. The PCMCIA standard has since been renamed the PC Card standard. The standard cards are removable modules that can hold memory, fax/modems, radio transceivers, network adapters, solid-state disks or hard disks. They are 85.6 millimeters long by 54 millimeters wide (3.37 inches x 2.126 inches) and use a 68-pin connector. The original Type I card is 3.3 millimeters thick and is now used for memory in personal digital assistants (PDAs) and other lightweight applications.

PCN (personal communications network)
PCN is a highly functional technology that operates like digital cellular service, except that it uses cells with a much smaller radius, 600 feet.

PCS (personal communications services)
A new, lower-powered, higher-frequency competitive technology to cellular service. Whereas cellular technology typically operates in the 800 to 900 megahertz (MHz) range, PCS operates in the 1.5 to 1.8 MHz range.

PCS (Personal Conferencing Specification)

PCTE (Portable Common Tool Environment)

PDA (personal digital assistant)
A handheld, wireless computer that serves as an organizer, electronic book or note taker. It typically uses a stylus or pen-shaped device for data entry and navigation. Apple's Newton was an early example of a PDA.

PDES (Product Data Exchange Specification)
A standard format for the exchange of data between advanced computer-aided design (CAD) and computer-aided manufacturing (CAM) programs. It describes a complete product, including the geometric aspects of the images, manufacturing features, tolerance specifications, material properties and finish specifications.

PDF (Portable Document Format)
The title format used by Adobe Systems' Acrobat document exchange system.

PDI (personal data interchange)

PDL (page description language)
The programming language used to specify the way a document will be printed or displayed.

PDM (product data management)
A set of technologies and capabilities for comprehensively managing design intent and product development processes across the enterprise.

PDN (public data network)
A shared-use X.25 packet-switched network operated by a carrier. PDNs may offer value-added services at a reduced cost because of communications resource sharing and usually provide increased reliability due to built-in redundancy.

PDQ (Parallel Data Query)

PDS (partitioned data set)
A data set that is divided into physically distinct units, or members, which contain data or partial or complete programs.

Peer Process — APPC
LU 6.2 support. Midrange system peer communications support using IBM's Advanced Program-to-Program Communications (APPC) protocols.

Peer Process — CPI-C API
Support is provided for applications that use IBM's Common Programming Interface for Communications (CPI-C) for peer-to-peer communications.

peer-to-peer
Access to application-to-application facilities between network-attached midrange systems of the same supplier.

PEM (privacy-enhanced mail)
A method of interenterprise E-mail messaging that works with existing E-mail systems to en-

sure the authenticity, integrity and optional confidentiality, through encryption, of messages.

performance monitoring and tuning tools
Facilities that enable users to monitor midrange-system performance, identify system and application performance bottlenecks, and set optimal performance-tuning parameters.

Performance Optimized With Enhanced RISC — IBM (See POWER)

Peripheral Component Interconnect (See PCI)

peripheral device
A piece of hardware that is connected to a computer. Examples are:

- Monitor
- Keyboard
- CD-ROM drive
- Modem
- Floppy disk drive

permanent virtual circuit (See PVC)

personal communications network (See PCN)

personal communications services (See PCS)

personal computer (See PC)

Personal Computer Memory Card International Association (See PCMCIA)

personal digital assistant (See PDA)

personal information manager (See PIM)

PERT (Program Evaluation and Review Technique)
A management tool for graphically displaying projected tasks, milestones, schedules and discrepancies.

PES (Parallel Enterprise Server)
A label used by IBM for its CMOS-based mainframes.

PGP (Pretty Good Privacy)

PGS (proposal generation system)

PHIGS (Programmers' Hierarchical Interactive Graphics Standard)
A graphics system and language used to create 2-D and 3-D images that interface between the application program and the device-independent graphics subsystem. Graphics objects are managed in a hierarchical manner so that a complete assembly can be specified with all of its subassemblies. High-performance workstations and host processing are required to handle the standard.

physical layer
Within the Open Systems Interconnection (OSI) model, the lowest level of network processing concerned with the electrical, mechanical and handshaking procedures over the interface that connects a device to a transmission medium (e.g., RS-232-C).

Physical Unit (See PU)

picture element (See pixel)

PIM (personal information manager)
Software that organizes and manages random information for fast retrieval on a daily basis. It provides a combination of features, including telephone list with automatic dialing, calendar and scheduler.

PIN (personal identification number)

PIN (Processor Independent NetWare)

PIR (protocol-independent routing)
A method in which routing decisions are made with no reference to the protocol in use. Protocol-independent routers have the functionality of protocol-specific routers, but can also route nonroutable protocols.

PIX (private Internet exchange)

pixel (picture element)
The smallest resolvable dot in an image display.

Pixtext
Image-oriented document management product from Excalibur Technologies of Albuquerque, N.M.

platform
An individual hardware or software architecture or an operating system.

platform-independent
Software that can run on a variety of hardware platforms or software architectures. Platform-independent software can be used in many different environments, requiring less planning and translation across an enterprise. For example, the Java programming language was designed to run on multiple types of hardware and multiple operating systems. If Java platform-independence becomes a reality, organizations with multiple types of computers will be able to write a specialized application once and have it be used by virtually everyone, rather than having to write, distribute and maintain multiple versions of the same program.

PLC (programmable logic controller)
A specialized industrial computer used to programmatically control production and process operations by interfacing software control strategies to input/output (I/O) devices.

PL/SQL (Programming Language/Structured Query Language)
One of the two deliverables of Oracle Systems' Transaction Processing Option (TPO). It is a 3GL-level extension of Structured Query Language (SQL) that groups SQL statements for transmission across the tools/database management system (DBMS) interface or across a network. PL/SQL must be used to take advantage of the Oracle version 6 performance enhancements.

plug-compatible manufacturer (See PCM)

PM (Presentation Manager)
The OS/2 graphical user interface, which includes windowing, graphics, standards for the keyboard interface, and editors for icons and fonts. It was the first manifestation of IBM's User Interface Architecture, consistent with the Common User Access (CUA) component of Systems Application Architecture (SAA).

PM/X (Presentation Manager/X)
A graphical user interface (GUI) product developed by Hewlett-Packard and Microsoft that

provides an OS/2 Presentation Manager-compatible application programming interface (API) on Unix workstations.

PNNI (Private Network-to-Network Interface)

A standard that maps out the network from an asynchronous transfer mode (ATM) standpoint and, through multiple phases of the specification, will become the router-to-router protocol implementation in ATM switches.

PO (purchase order)

point of sale (See POS)

POMS (Process Operations Management System)

An IBM- and customer-supported initiative to link manufacturing resource planning (MRP) applications running on AS/400 minicomputers and shop floor data collection systems running on PS/2 computers. It is not an IBM product, although IBM funded its development and has exclusive marketing rights.

POLS (private online service)

polymorphism

The capability of an operation to accept arguments of different or unknown types. Parametric polymorphism executes the same operation on different types. Overloading polymorphism selects appropriate operations according to the type.

POP (Post Office Protocol)

An application protocol that provides a mailbox-retrieval service for Internet PC users. It is being replaced by Internet Message Access Prtotocol (IMAP).

POP3 (Post Office Protocol 3)

An access path for browser-enabled users to communicate with "mail to" requests from Hypertext Markup Language (HTML).

port

The entrance or physical access point to a computer, multiplexer, device or network, where signals may be supplied, extracted or observed.

Portable Document Format (See PDF)

ported proprietary

Refers to a system that is a compliant implementation of an evolving set of proprietary or vendor-neutral specifications (or both) for interfaces, services, protocols and formats. These specifications let a user configure and operate a system, its applications and its components only with other equally compliant implementations available from the same vendor or with licensed implementations from different vendors.

POS (point of sale)

POS systems use personal computers or specialized terminals in combination with cash registers, optical scanners or magnetic-stripe readers to capture and record data at the time of transaction. POS systems are usually online to a central computer for credit checking and inventory updating. Alternatively, they may be independent systems that store daily transactions until they can be transmitted to the central system for processing.

Posix

A Unix-based standard developed by the Institute of Electrical and Electronics Engineers (IEEE) Posix committee. Posix has been adopted as a Federal Information Processing Standard (FIPS), and is included in the Open Software Foundation's (OSF's) and X/Open's basic specifications.

Posix 1003.1 compliance

Operating-system compliance with the Institute of Electrical and Electronics Engineers (IEEE) Posix 1003.1 system services standard.

Post Office Protocol (See POP)

Post Office Protocol 3 (See POP3)

PostScript printer support

Support for the printing of compound document information, including "rich text," on PostScript printers.

POTS (plain old telephone service)

POWER (Performance Optimized With Enhanced RISC — IBM)

IBM's proprietary reduced instruction set computer (RISC) processor technology used in the RS/6000 and selectively licensed to other suppliers, including Motorola.

powerfail restart

Automatic restart initiation upon restoration of power after a power failure.

PPA (personal productivity application)

PQS (Parallel Query Server)

A product announced by IBM in April 1994 that uses complementary metal-oxide semiconductor (CMOS) technology to provide parallelism to Information Management System/Database Manager (IMS/DM) applications.

PRA (Primary Rate Access — known as PRI in United States) (See PRI)

Precision Architecture Reduced Instruction Set Computer (See PA-RISC)

predicate

A clause within a Structured Query Language statement (query) that specifies a constraint that the selected data (rows) must satisfy.

predicate transitive closure

The practice of adding semantically redundant predicates to a Structured Query Language (SQL) statement (query) to help the optimizer perform better. This can be done by application programmers or by the optimizer itself.

presentation layer

In the Open Systems Interconnection (OSI) model, the layer of processing that provides services to the application layer, enabling it to interpret the data exchanged, as well as to structure data messages to be transmitted in a specific display and control format.

Presentation Manager (See PM)

Presentation Manager/X (See PM/X)

Presentation Text Object Content Architecture (See PTOCA)

PRI (Primary Rate Interface — PRA in Canada and Europe)

An Integrated Services Digital Network (ISDN) interface that connects private branch exchanges (PBXs) to the network at the North American 1.544 megabits per second (Mbps) T1 rate. It is electrically identical to the ISDN Basic Rate Interface (BRI). North American standards for this interface specify 23 64-Kbps B, or bearer, channels, plus one 64-Kbps D, or delta, channel. Thus, it is also referred to as 23B+D. European standards call for 30B+D.

Primary Rate Access (See PRA)

Primary Rate Interface (See PRI)

printed circuit board (See PCB)

Printer Control Language (See PCL)

PRISM (Parallel Reduced Instruction Set Multiprocessor)

A reduced instruction set computer (RISC) architecture developed by Apollo for its high-end workstation products.

privacy-enhanced mail (See PEM)

private branch exchange (See PBX)

Private Network-to-Network Interface (See PNNI)

problem management

The core function of a customer service and support (CSS) application used by call centers.

Problem Management

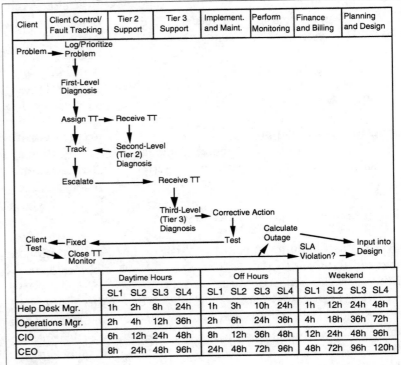

	Daytime Hours				Off Hours				Weekend			
	SL1	SL2	SL3	SL4	SL1	SL2	SL3	SL4	SL1	SL2	SL3	SL4
Help Desk Mgr.	1h	2h	8h	24h	1h	3h	10h	24h	1h	12h	24h	48h
Operations Mgr.	2h	4h	12h	36h	2h	6h	24h	36h	4h	18h	36h	72h
CIO	6h	12h	24h	48h	8h	12h	36h	48h	12h	24h	48h	96h
CEO	8h	24h	48h	96h	24h	48h	72h	96h	48h	72h	96h	120h

Severity Level (SL)

SL 1: Severe problem has disrupted user service. Business risk is high.
SL 2: Problem affecting production. Customer or IT service has been impacted. User can continue to process but at an inconvenience. Business risk is moderate to low.
SL 3: Low to moderate impact. Service has not been impacted. Low business risk.
SL 4: Low to negligible impact. Problem deferred to when time allows.

SLA = Service-level agreement
TT = Trouble ticket

Source: Gartner Group

The Problem Management Process

It coordinates a multitier, multiowner service and support environment, enables pattern analysis, provides management reports, and facilitates requesting additional service and support resources by providing hard numbers on the service workload and its changing nature. Because PM tools can also track service-level agreements (SLAs), they are valuable for monitoring compliance.

process
An interconnected network of activities that begins at the specification of a requirement for a product or service and terminates with the acceptance of consideration for providing the product or service.

process control
The regulation of variables that influence or control the conduct of a process so that a specified quality and quantity of product are obtained.

process coordination
The class of applications that exploits workflow technology.

Process Operations Management System (See POMS)

Processor Resources/Systems Manager (See PR/SM)

product data management (See PDM)

Professional Office System (See PROFS)

PROFS (Professional Office System)
Office system facilities for the Virtual Machine (VM) environment. The E-mail function is particularly strong, but the user interface is not oriented toward novice users.

PROFS Document Exchange
A facility to exchange documents to or from the midrange system with IBM's Professional Office System (PROFS). PROFS document content can be compatible with DISOSS (Document Content Architecture), although distribution and exchange of documents or notes requires a different approach.

program
An organized list of instructions that, when executed, causes a computer to behave in a predetermined way. Without programs, computers are useless. A program is like a recipe that contains a combination of two things:

1. A list of ingredients (called variables). Variables represent numeric data, text or graphical images.
2. A list of directions (called statements). Statements provide the instructions for what to do with the variables. There are many programming languages that are used to create this combination of variables and statements.

Program Evaluation and Review Technique (See PERT)

programming language
A defined group of commands and syntax that a program developer uses to write software. Languages range from primitive (similar to machine code) to high-level (closer to standard written language and somewhat automated) and have been classified into generations, the fifth being the most recent. C, C++, Pascal, BASIC, FOR-

TRAN, COBOL, LISP and Java are examples of programming languages.

Programming Language/Structured Query Language (See PL/SQL)

programmable logic controller (See PLC)

Programmers Hierarchical Interactive Graphics Standard (See PHIGS)

project management
A distributed-computing help desk strategy for achieving appropriate service levels. Processes include: management control, problem impact reduction, and effective problem resolution.

proprietary software
Software that is owned by an organization or an individual, as opposed to "public-domain software," which is freely distributed. The explosion in the use of the Internet has expanded the reach of public-domain software since it is now much easier to transmit these programs. While many commercial software developers have developed software that has become the de facto standard (e.g., Microsoft's Windows programs), proprietary software that is based on proprietary protocols, or standards, can create obstacles for applications development and usage.

protected mode
A mode of the Intel 80286, 80386 and 80486 microprocessors with hardware memory protection, which has been important for multitasking and for escaping the 640K memory barrier.

protocol
A set of procedures for establishing and controlling data transmission. Examples include IBM's Binary Synchronous Communications (BSC) and Synchronous Data Link Control (SDLC) protocols.

protocol-independent routing (See PIR)

PR/SM (Processor Resources/Systems Manager)
IBM's logical-partitioning facility that allows the computer architecture to be separated from its physical implementation to provide a logical organization of resources that allows multiple operating systems (or copies of the same system) to run on one physical central processing unit (CPU) or complex.

PSI (Performance Systems International)

PSLC (Parallel Sysplex License Charge)
A software licensing arrangement available to vendors if the pieces making up their Parallel Sysplex (PS) complex have been qualified by IBM. Charges are based on the total machine capacity.

PSTN (public switched telephone network)
A worldwide voice telephone network.

PTO (public telecommunications operator)

PTOCA (Presentation Text Object Content Architecture)
Describes character data, position, controls and attributes that represent a formatted text presentation.

PTS (Parallel Transaction Server)
A product announced by IBM in April 1994 that introduces CMOS-based parallelism to Information Management System/Database Manager (IMS/DB) applications.

PTT (postal, telegraph and telephone)
A term used to refer to the agency responsible for postal, telegraph and telephone services at a governmental level.

PU (Physical Unit)
A physical device used in IBM Systems Network Architecture (SNA) communications; includes the software in an SNA node controlling the node's communications hardware. PU is synonymous with "node type" within SNA. PU 2 devices are intelligent cluster controllers/terminals. A PU 2.1 node enables local user ports to communicate without going through a host node's services.

public data network (See PDN)

public switched telephone network (See PSTN)

pulse amplitude modulation (See PAM)

pulse code modulation (See PCM)

PVC (permanent virtual circuit)
A virtual circuit established through manual or protocol interaction rather than via a call establishment sequence.

Q.2931
The broadband out-of-band signaling standard for call management. Also known as Q.93 broadband.

QA (quality assurance)

QA/QC (quality assurance/quality control)

QCIF (Quarter Common Intermediate Format)
Part of the International Telecommunications Union Telecommunications Standards Sector's H.261 video format standard, centered on Common Intermediate Format (CIF), which is a compromise between National Television Standards Committee (NTSC) and phase alteration line (PAL). In the H.261 standard, only QCIF is specified (176x144 pixel resolution).

QIC (quarter-inch cartridge)

QMF (Query Management Facility)
IBM's strategic query and report-writing product for relational database management systems (RDBMSs). Its main objective is to widen the RDBMS user base, i.e., to allow anyone to use relational data. QMF has basic analysis and graphics features.

QOS (quality of service)
A negotiated contract between user and network that renders some degree of reliable capacity in the shared network.

QPSX (Queued Packet Synchronous Exchange)
A metropolitan-area network (MAN) based on the Institute of Electrical and Electronics Engineers (IEEE) 802.6 Distributed Queue Dual Bus (DQDB) standard for speeds up to 150 megabits per second (Mbps).

QR (quick response)

QR (queuing requirements)

QSAM (Queued Sequential Access Method)
An extended version of the Basic Sequential Access Method (BSAM), which queues up input data blocks pending processing and output data blocks pending transfer.

quality of service (See QOS)

Quarter Common Intermediate Format (See QCIF)

Quel (Query Language)

A relational data manipulation language that was a rival to Structured Query Language (SQL) but has now fallen into general disuse. It was used for the University of California at Berkeley Ingres prototype and adopted for the early version of Relational Technology and Birtton-Lee products. IBM's endorsement of SQL killed Quel, despite its popularity among many relational partisans.

Query Language (See Quel)

Query Management Facility (See QMF)

query/report tools

Basic interactive and batch facilities that allow users to query files and databases and create terminal and printed-report output.

Queued Packet Synchronous Exchange (See QPSX)

Queued Sequential Access Method (See QSAM)

RAAD (rapid architected applications development)

RAAD is an approach to large-scale AD that includes the following phases, which are executed by up to 10 teams of 10 people each during a period of no more than 18 months:

Phase 1: Business and technical architecture reconciliation

Phase 2: Functional requirements gathering and specification

Phase 3: Initial architecture design, building and implementation

Phase 4: First building and testing of application, including user interface, data access and business logic

Phase 5: Initial installation of application

Phase 6: Concurrent engineering for subsequent builds

Phase 7: Rapid release plan

RACE (R&D for Advanced Communications in Europe)

RACF (Resource Access Control Facility)

The IBM product offering back-end security in the System/370 Multiple Virtual Storage (MVS) and Virtual Machine (VM) envi-

ronments. RACF had been difficult to use, but release 1.7 achieved a level of flexibility and usability close to what is offered by leading-edge, third-party software. Computer Associates' Top Secret and Access Control Facility-2 (ACF2) are the leading independent software vendor (ISV) offerings.

RAD (rapid applications development)

RAD is an AD approach that includes small teams (typically two to six persons, but never more than 10) using joint applications develop-

RAD

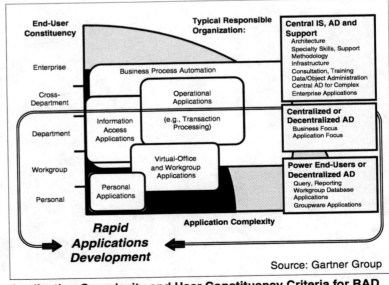

Application Complexity and User Constituency Criteria for RAD

ment (JAD) and iterative-prototyping techniques to construct interactive systems of low to medium complexity within a time frame of 60 to 120 days.

radio frequency (See RF)

RAID (redundant array of independent disks)

A method of mirroring or striping data on clusters of low-end disk drives; data is copied onto multiple drives for faster throughput, error correction, fault tolerance and improved mean time between failures.

With the exception of RAID 0, all RAID levels provide automated recovery of data in the event of a disk failure. The RAID levels and their key features are:

- RAID-0 — provides disk striping without parity information; data is written by segment across multiple disks sequentially until the end of the array is reached, and then writing starts at the beginning again. Provides greater logical disk capacity with faster access time on reads (multiple segments read simultaneously). However, RAID-0 provides no data redundancy — if one drive fails, the entire disk array subsystem is unavailable.
- RAID-1 — provides fault tolerance by using disk mirroring (also called shadowing). Each byte of data on a disk is duplicated on another physical drive, thus providing 100-percent data redundancy. RAID-1 provides immediate access to data when either the primary or secondary drive fails, but it has the highest cost of all RAID types, since duplicate hardware is required.

- RAID-2 — eliminates the 100-percent redundancy overhead of RAID-1 by using a powerful error detection and correction code (Hamming), with bits of the data pattern written across multiple disks.
- RAID-3 — similar to RAID-2, but uses a single check disk per group that contains the bit parity of the data disks; data is interleaved across all disks. Because disk reads are performed across the entire array and all data is transferred to the controller in parallel, RAID-3 is well suited for applications that require high data read/write transfer rates for large sequential files.
- RAID-4 — instead of interleaving blocks of data across all drives, writes the first block on drive 1, the second block on drive 2, and so on. This technique dramatically improves read time, since many reads are single block (single drive), freeing other drives for additional read requests.
- RAID-5 — eliminates the dedicated parity drive by writing parity with the data across all drives in the array. Consequently, the single-write restriction and some performance degradation of RAID-1 through RAID-4 are eliminated. If a drive fails, the controller can rebuild the data from the parity and data on the remaining drives.
- RAID-6 — provides two-disk parity and one spare, so that two simultaneous disk failures per array of disks can be tolerated. With the occurrence of a failure, a spare is brought online and transparent reconstruction begins automatically in the background with negligible impact on performance.
- RAID-10 — a combination of RAID-0 and RAID-1 that provides the benefits of striping and fault tolerance (disk mirroring).

RAM (random-access memory)
The primary memory in a computer. Memory that can be overwritten with new information. The "random access" part of the name comes from the fact that the next bit of information in RAM can be located — no matter where it is — in an equal amount of time.

RAMP-C
An IBM proprietary benchmark constructed to measure performance on online transaction processing (OLTP) workloads. IBM has used RAMP-C both to measure the relative performance of its processors and architectures and to compare its processors to the competition. It has not released the code, so independent judgments on the relevance of the benchmark are impossible.

random-access memory (See RAM)

rapid applications development (See RAD)

rapid architected applications development (See RAAD)

RARP (Reverse Address Resolution Protocol)
A Transmission Control Protocol/Internet Protocol (TCP/IP) protocol for translating a Data Link Control address to an IP (Internet Protocol) address. RARP can be used to obtain a logical IP address. Responding to a RARP broadcast from a workstation, a RARP server can send back the IP address.

RAS (reliability, availability and serviceability)
A reference to a product's quality, availability of optional features, and ease of diagnosis and repair.

raster
Originally a German word naming the screen used in photoengraving; now, the array of scan lines used to cover a planar area to read or depict image information on that area. The electron beam of a TV picture tube writes a raster on the phosphor screen.

raster image processor (See RIP)

RCS (Revision Control System)
A Unix utility that provides version control. The majority of Unix developers rely on basic utilities such as RCS for version control.

R&D (research and development)

RDA (Remote Data Access)
A standard (ISO/JCTI/SC21 WG3) to address the interconnection of applications and databases. The standard originally attempted to cover any kind of data access and concerned itself only with effective dialog management, but inherent complexity has encouraged it to focus more on Structured Query Language (SQL).

Rdb
Digital Equipment's strategic database management system (DBMS). Rdb is integrated with the other Virtual Address Extension (VAX) Information Architecture products, and is designed to provide true multiplatform, distributed-database capabilities.

RDBMS (relational database management system)

A DBMS that incorporates the relational-data model, normally including a Structured Query Language application programming interface. It is a DBMS in which the database is organized and accessed according to the relationships between data items. In a relational database, relationships between data items are expressed by means of tables. Interdependencies among these tables are expressed by data values rather than by pointers. This allows a high degree of data independence.

RDLAP (Radio Data Link Access Protocol)

RDM (remote data management)
A form of cooperative-processing in which the database management system (DBMS) or file management system executes on a different node than the rest of the application logic.

RDM (Relational Document Manager — Interleaf)

RDS (report distribution system)

read-modify-write (See RMW)

read-only memory (See ROM)

real time
The description for an operating system that responds to an external event within a short and predictable time frame. Unlike a batch or time-sharing operating system, a real-time operating system provides services or control to independent ongoing physical processes. It typically has interrupt capabilities (so that a less important task can be put aside in deference to a more pressing job) and a priority-scheduling management scheme.

Record Management System – part of VMS (See RMS)

reduced instruction set computer (See RISC)

redundant array of independent disks (See RAID)

referential integrity
The underlying rules defining the semantic interdependencies among items in a database. The goal is to have those items defined declaratively (i.e., as business-oriented assertions) rather than through procedural logic. A relational database management system (RDBMS) should enforce referential integrity as defined by Addendum 1 (X3.135.1-1989) to the American National Standards Institute (ANSI) Structured Query Language (SQL) standard.

relational database management system (See RDBMS)

reliability, availability and serviceability (See RAS)

remote access
The ability to log on to a network from a distant location. Generally, this requires a computer, a modem and remote-access software to allow the computer to dial into the network over a telephone line and connect.

remote console operation
A remote-operator console facility that enables the remote operator to perform normal operational tasks, including storage backup, on a running system.

Remote Data Access (See RDA)

remote data management (See RDM)

Remote DB2 Read-Only Access
Program-level calls allowing midrange-system applications remote but direct access to IBM Database-2 (DB2) databases on a System/370 mainframe. At least read-only access is supported.

Remote DB2 Update Access
Program-level calls allowing midrange-system applications remote but direct access to IBM Database-2 (DB2) databases on a System/370 mainframe. Both read-only and update are supported.

remote environmental monitoring
Hardware and software facilities to permit monitoring of computer room environment from a remote site, and to notify remote operators and sound alarms on conditions outside of selectable parameters.

remote file access
Cross-network file access from a process on the midrange system without special coding in the application. Directories or control statements external to the application would be used by the system to locate the file within the network.

Remote IMS Read-Only Access
Program-level calls allowing midrange-system applications remote but direct access to IBM Information Management System (IMS) databases on a System/370 mainframe. At least read-only access is supported.

Remote IMS Update Access
Program-level calls allowing midrange-system applications remote but direct access to IBM Information Management System (IMS) databases on a System/370 mainframe. Both read-only and update are supported.

remote initial program load
A remote-operator console facility that enables the remote operator to initiate as well as continue systems operation after power-on or abnormal system failure.

remote job entry (See RJE)

Remote Job Entry — Binary Synchronous Communication (See RJE — BSC)

remote log-on
A facility to allow an interactive user on one midrange system to log on to any other midrange system of the same supplier in the network.

Remote Monitoring (See RMON)

remote peripheral access
The ability to attach peripherals logically on other midrange systems in the network to a user's local process or program.

remote power-off
A system command facility that when executed results in a full power-off of the midrange system. The command could be invoked by local or remote terminal access to the system or could be time-released as an unattended processing task.

remote presentation
A form of cooperative processing in which the presentation executes on a different node than

the rest of the application logic and data management.

remote procedure call (See RPC)

remote software maintenance — applications

A form of cooperative processing that allows user support groups to control updates and distribution of application system libraries. A facility for predefining the selection and distribution criteria that should be included.

remote software maintenance system

A facility available to a user support group providing for distribution to selected remote midrange-system nodes of both new versions and "fixes" to midrange system software (e.g., operating system, database and communications).

remote SQL database calls

The availability of Structured Query Language (SQL) database calls on a PC that provide cross-network access to a relational database on a midrange system. The calls most likely would be syntactically and semantically equivalent to similar calls available on the midrange system.

remote system monitoring

Software facilities to enable monitoring of systems operation from a remote site, and to notify remote operators on conditions outside of selectable parameters.

Remote VSAM Read-Only Access

Program-level calls allowing midrange-system applications remote but direct access to IBM Virtual Storage Access Method (VSAM) files on a System/370 mainframe. At least read-only access is supported.

Remote VSAM Update Access

Program-level calls allowing midrange system applications remote but direct access to IBM Virtual Storage Access Method (VSAM) files on a System/370 mainframe. Both read-only and update access are supported.

replicated-site applications

Identical versions of applications that are distributed to remote sites (e.g., sales offices, bank branches, field service offices, insurance agencies, supermarkets and pharmacies) to perform identical roles.

repository

A facility for storing descriptions and behaviors of objects in an enterprise, including requirements, policies, processes, data, software libraries, projects, platforms and personnel, with the potential of supporting both software development and operations management. As single point of definition for all system resources, it should stimulate both program and installation management productivity. A system repository would include configuration definitions, tuning parameters and performance goals, while an application repository would include data definitions.

request for comment (See RFC)

request for information (See RFI)

request for proposal (See RFP)

request for quotation (See RFQ)

requester/server

A type of relationship between two independent programs in which:

- Two programs interoperate to carry out the processing for a single unit of application work.
- One invokes and directs the other; i.e., the requester program specifies a function to be performed and the server program fulfills that service.

Resource Access Control Facility (See RACF)

resource accounting and chargeback

Mechanisms for recording the utilization of resources such as processor time, physical memory, transactions, logical or physical input/output (I/O) operations, disk storage and licensed software, and then reporting such utilization as charged against users, projects, applications or cost centers.

resource requirements planning

The process of converting the production plan or the master production schedule into the impact on key resources, e.g., man hours, machine hours, storage, standard cost dollars, shipping dollars and inventory levels.

response time

The time period between a terminal operator's completion of an inquiry and the receipt of a response. Response time includes the time taken to transmit the inquiry, process it by the computer, and transmit the response back to the terminal. Response time is frequently used as a measure of the performance of an interactive system.

Restructured Extended Executor (See REXX)

return on investment (See ROI)

reuse

An applications development methodology that catalogs and makes available application components so that they may be incorporated into other applications.

Reverse Address Resolution Protocol (See RARP)

Revisable Form Text: Document Content Architecture (See RFT:DCA)

Revision Control System (See RCS)

REXX (Restructured Extended Executor)

A "command language" (job control language). A structured, interpretive language used to create operator-level command streams to manage and link applications. Introduced in the Virtual Machine (VM) environment.

RF (radio frequency)

1. In general terms, RF refers to the electromagnetic frequencies used for radio communications.
2. RF is also now used to refer to a class of peripheral devices communicating with a warehouse management system (WMS) on a local-area network (LAN) or a shipping system on a wide-area network (WAN) via RF communications means. It allows real-time interaction between the peripheral devices and the server without physical connection via wire.

RFC (request for comment)

A document submitted for comment and put through a review process under the auspices of the Internet Engineering Task Force (IETF). When accepted, it has the weight of a standard in the Internet community. Each RFC is given a tracking number by which it is known. For example, RFC 822 describes the address format and data definitions for addressing electronic messages over the Internet.

RFI (request for information)

Notification of an intended acquisition sent to potential suppliers to determine interest and gather general descriptive product materials, though not prices.

RFP (request for proposal)

An invitation for vendors to bid on supplying goods and services.

RFQ (request for quotation)

Solicitation for pricing for a specific component software product, service or system.

RFT (request for technology)

RFT:DCA (Revisable Form Text: Document Content Architecture)

The data stream for passing text documents in revisable form under IBM's second-generation Document Content Architecture.

RHC (regional holding company)

RHCs are the companies that were created from the AT&T divestiture (originally, there were seven; now there are five), each of which acts as a holding company within a region of the United States for one or more of the divested Bell operating companies, as well as for their unregulated subsidiaries. The RHCs are: Ameritech, Bell Atlantic, BellSouth, SBC Communications and US West.

RIP (raster image processor)

A device that converts computer graphics into a raster image — grids of small dots — from which the printing device will re-create them on paper.

RIP (Routing Information Protocol)

An internal router protocol used for informing network computers of changes in configuration.

RFP

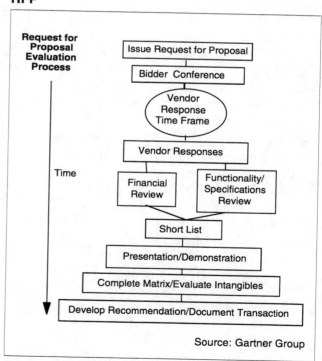

The Request for Proposal Process

RISC (reduced instruction set computer)

A processor architecture that shifts the analytical process of a computational task from the execution or runtime to the preparation or compile time. By using less hardware or logic, the system can operate at higher speeds. RISC cuts down on the number and complexity of instructions, on the theory that each one can be accessed and executed faster, and that less semiconductor real estate is required to process them. The result is that for any given semiconductor technology, a more powerful microprocessor can be produced with RISC than with complex instruction set computer (CISC) architectures.

This simplification of computer instruction sets gains processing efficiencies. That theme works because all computers and programs execute mostly simple instructions. RISC has five design principles:

- Single-cycle execution — In most traditional central processing unit (CPU) designs, the peak possible execution rate is one instruction per basic machine cycle, and for a given technology, the cycle time has some fixed lower limit. Even on complex CPUs, most compiler-generated instructions are simple. RISC designs emphasize single-cycle execution, even at the expense of synthesizing multi-instruction sequences for some less-frequent operations.
- Hard-wired control, little or no microcode — Microcode adds a layer of interpretive overhead, raising the number of cycles per instruction, so even the simplest instructions can require several cycles.
- Simple instructions, few addressing modes — Complex instructions and addressing modes, which entail microcode or multicycle instructions, are avoided.
- Load and store, register-register design — Only loads and stores access memory; all others perform register-register operations. This tends to follow from the previous three principles.
- Efficient, deep pipelining — To make convenient use of hardware parallelism without the complexities of horizontal microcode, fast CPUs use pipelining. An n-stage pipeline keeps up to "n" instructions active at once, ideally finishing one (and starting another) every cycle. The instruction set must be carefully tuned to support pipelining.

RISC System 6000 (See RS/6000)

RJE (remote job entry)

Refers to a set of communications protocols for input and output of information to a mainframe in a batch mode (as opposed to interactive).

RJE – BSC (Remote Job Entry — Binary Synchronous Communication)

Emulation in the midrange system of IBM bisynchronous 2780 or 3780 protocols allowing terminal operators to exchange job control and job output with the mainframe processing queues.

RMF (Resource Measurement Facility)

RMON (Remote Monitoring)

A network management protocol that remotely manages networks providing multivendor interoperability between monitoring devices and management stations.

RMS (Record Management System — part of VMS)

The basic data management system under Digital Equipment's Virtual Memory System (VMS).

ROA (return on assets)

ROE (return on equity)

A measure of a company's financial performance (net income divided by the value of the stockholders' equity, and expressed in percent).

ROI (return on investment)

Financial gain expressed as a percentage of funds that were invested to generate that gain.

rollback recovery

"Before" and "after" images of a transaction are maintained in a log file such that, if the system fails, the unsuccessful updates can be backed out, or rolled back.

ROM (read-only memory)

Data stored in computer memory that can be accessed and read by the user but not modified.

router

A device that connects two networks, performing a function similar to a local or remote bridge. Routers receive packets of information from computers or other routers on the network; they then send these packets to their destinations based on "addresses" at the beginning of the packets and a road map of the other computers and peripherals on the network.

Routing Information Protocol (See RIP)

RPC (remote procedure call)

A mechanism that extends the notion of a local (i.e., contained in a single address space) procedure call to a distributed computing environment, enabling an application to be distributed among multiple systems in a way that is highly transparent to the application-level code. Examples of RPCs are Sun Microsystems' Open Network Computing, Sybase's Open Client/Open Server and the Open Software Foundation's (OSF's) Distributed Computing Environment (DCE) RPC.

RS-232-C

A technical specification published by the Electronic Industries Association (EIA) that establishes mechanical and electrical interface requirements between computers, terminals and communications lines.

RS-422

A technical specification published by the EIA that establishes mechanical and electrical interface requirements between digital devices. It is incompatible with, and has a higher speed capability than, RS-232-C.

RS-449

A technical standard published by the EIA that provides more-extended mechanical and electrical interface functions than those provided by RS-232-C.

RS/6000 (RISC System/6000)

IBM's 32-bit technical workstation introduced in mid-1990. It is based on reduced instruction set computer (RISC) architecture and runs the Unix-based Advanced Interactive Executive (AIX) operating system.

RSA (Rivest-Shamir-Adelman)

RSP (remote store procedure)

RTCP (Real-Time Control Protocol)

RTP (Real-Time Transport Protocol)

**RTR (Reliable Transaction Router —
Digital Equipment)**

runtime component
A dynamically bindable package of one or more programs managed as a unit and accessed through documented interfaces that can be discovered at runtime.

RUOW (remote unit of work)

RV (residual value)

S

S3 (stand-alone shared storage)

S3 (S3 Inc., San Jose, Calif.)

S/370 (See System/370)

S/390 (See System/390)

SAA (Systems Application Architecture)
IBM's name for the architecture once intended to unify its disparate computer architectures.

SAD (slow applications development)

SAG (Software AG)

sales force automation (See SFA)

SAM (software asset management)
A process for making software acquisition and disposal decisions. It includes strategies that identify and eliminate unused or infrequently used software, consolidating software licenses or moving toward new licensing models.

SAP (SAP AG)

SASD (server-attached storage device)

SATAN (Security Administrator Tool for Analyzing Networks)

SBA (strategic business application)

SBM (skills-based management)
A program that objectively defines what skills an enterprise possesses, what skills it will need going forward, when it will need those skills, what strategic value it will place on those skills and how the information technology (IT) employees' competency levels match the value of the strategically significant skills. It is, in effect, a road map for developing competency improvement programs and other methods to fill any skill gaps.

SCADA (supervisory control and data acquisition)
System to enable real-time monitoring of events occurring in remote locations, and to transmit this data to a database where they can provide alert and process management control information. SCADA data can be used to build a computerized model of the process, establish alarm criteria and prepare management reports on the performance of the system. Applications for SCADA include pipeline management, environmental management and industrial process management. Components of SCADA systems include a remote terminal unit, a central-site computer system (ranging in size from a PC to a mainframe, depending on processing require-

---

ments) and associated SCADA management software. Communications alternatives for SCADA systems run the gamut from none, (i.e., the service personnel collect data manually) to satellite communications. Microwave, very small aperture terminals (VSATs), telephone lines and mobile radio are also used.

scalability
The measure of a system's ability to increase or decrease in performance and cost in response to changes in application and system processing demands.

Scalable Processor Architecture (See SPARC)

scanner
A device that resolves a two-dimensional object, such as a business document, into a stream of bits by raster scanning and quantization.

SCCS (Source Code Control System)
A Unix software configuration management utility used for source code version control.

SCE (System Control Element)
The SCE's major function is to provide paths and controls for the communications between the major functional units and central storage within the 308, 3090 and ES/9000 processor families.

SCM (software change management)
A methodology that includes problem/change request initiation and tracking; change impact analysis; version control;

security administration of software assets; software promotion; quality reviews; and software distribution.

SCM (supply chain management)

SCO (Santa Cruz Operation)

SCP (service control point)
The database machine at the apex of the Signaling System 7 (SS7) network containing information on how to process, route and bill calls.

SCS (sales configuration system)

SCM

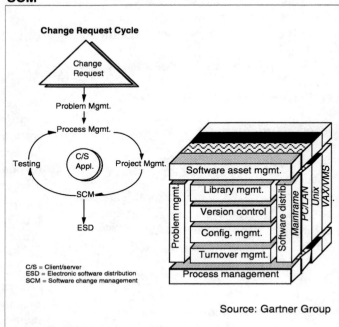

Software Change Management Structure

SCSA (Signal Computing System Architecture)

A hardware and software architecture, defined by Dialogic, that specifies interfaces between components of a call-handling system, including media control. Media management is a missing component of Computer Supported Telephony Architecture (CSTA), Telephony Application Programming Interface (TAPI) and Telephony Services Application Programming Interface (TSAPI). Applications must make assumptions about the type of call (i.e., voice, data, fax or image) or interface with another piece of hardware to determine the type of call. SCSA can mesh with CSTA, TAPI and TSAPI. SCSA can provide computer-telephony integration (CTI) applications with the interfaces needed to identify and manage different call types.

SCSI (Small Computer Systems Interface)

A peripheral interface for up to seven devices. SCSI provides a high-speed, parallel data transfer of up to four megabits per second (Mbps) and has the advantage of connecting multiple peripherals while taking up only one slot in the computer.

SDH (Synchronous Digital Hierarchy)

The European equivalent of the Synchronous Optical Network (SONET) standard, with transmission speeds and network management suited to the European standards.

SDK (software development kit)

A set of development utilities for writing software applications, usually associated with specific environments (e.g., the Windows SDK).

SDLC (Synchronous Data Link Control)

IBM's subset of HDLC (High-level Data Link Control). The protocol is used for serial (by bit) information transfer over a data communications channel. Concerned with the lower two layers of the Open Systems Interconnection (OSI) model (physical and link control), SDLC was half of the Systems Network Architecture (SNA) attack on the diverse link controls, access methods and terminal types that existed in the pre-SNA era. IBM's strategy with SNA was to establish a single S/370-based access method (Virtual Telecommunications Access Method, or VTAM) and a single device-independent line discipline (SDLC). IBM has included SDLC in Systems Application Architecture (SAA), but has also designated the X.25 and Token Ring protocols, which operate at the same level. Those two are special-purpose, while SDLC is general-purpose.

SDRAM (synchronous dynamic random-access memory)

SDV (switched digital video)

search

Software used for randomly accessing textual information.

second generation

The class of multiuser time-sharing integrated office systems including Digital Equipment's ALL-IN-1, IBM's PROFS and Data General's CEO. These products, introduced around 1983, were largely superseded by client/server third-generation products in 1989.

Secure Electronic Transactions (See SET)

Secure Socket Layer (See SSL)

SEI (Software Engineering Institute)

selling, general and administrative (See SG&A)

semantic data model

A method of organizing data that reflects the basic meaning of data items and the relationships among them. This organization makes it easier to develop application programs and to maintain the consistency of data when it is updated.

Sequenced Packet Exchange (See SPX)

Serial Storage Architecture (See SSA)

server

1. A system or a program that receives requests from one or more client systems or programs to perform activities that allow the client to accomplish certain tasks. A processor that provides a specific service to systems on a network. Routing servers connect subnetworks of like architecture; gateway servers connect networks of different architectures by performing protocol conversions; and terminal, printer and file servers provide in-terfaces between peripheral devices and systems on the network.

2. Can refer to a physical computer ("the server is down..."), but more commonly to any machine that serves applications or information on the World Wide Web.

service control point (See SCP)

service desk

A help desk that is equipped with the resources for resolving service requests and problem calls. It gives the customer service representative or end user the ability to efficiently diagnose,

SFA

Generation	1st	2nd	3rd	4th	5th	6th
Key Application Components (Additive by Generation)	•Word Processor •Spreadsheet •E-Mail	•Contact Manager •Expense Reports	•Account/ Territory Manager •Order Entry •Call Reporting •Sales Analysis	•Configurator •Telesales •Telemarketing •Opportunity Management System •Marketing Encyclopedia	•Enterprise Team Selling •Integrated Telemarketing/Field Sales •System Administration	•Inter-enterprise Team Selling •Virtual Sales Organizations
Focus	Administrative →			Selling →		
	Point Solutions →				Data Model →	
	Package →		Database →		Workflow →	
	Stand-Alone →		Networked →			
Adoption (60 percent of Sites)	Now	Now	Now	1998	2001	2005

Maximum Effectiveness Zone

Return on Investment   LOW → HIGH

Source: Gartner Group

The Evolution of Sales Force Automation Systems

troubleshoot and correct technical-support problems, rather than being a "pass through."

service-level agreement (See SLA)

Service Level Reporter (See SLR)

SET (Secure Electronic Transactions)
A multiparty protocol that secures online communication between all parties in a payment card transaction. It encrypts access to sensitive credit card information throughout the card processing network, thus reducing potential points of exposure to online theft from the buyer or merchant.

SFA (sales force automation)
The process of providing information technology (IT) to an outside sales force.

SFDR (software failure detection and recovery)
Should support the concept of a transaction, including atomicity (either all changes take place or none take effect) to enable operating-system or application data recovery mechanisms to be implemented.

SFS (Structured File Server — Transarc)

SG&A (selling, general and administrative)
An expense category on a company's income statement.

SGI (Silicon Graphics Inc.)

SGML (Standard Generalized Markup Language)
An international standard of identifying the basic structural elements of a text document. SGML addresses the structure of a document, not its format or presentation.

shadow/mirror databases
A system-level facility to enable shadowing or mirroring of selected databases to a separate disk or disk set. The purpose is to minimize the space required for backup data while providing for the continuation of critical processing in the event of the loss of a disk containing related databases.

shell
A cross-application operating environment accessed through a single user interface. A network connectivity shell is the environment used to access network resources — e.g., a suite with a single user interface for host, Transmission Control Protocol/Internet Protocol (TCP/IP) and Web access.

shielded pair
A pair of conductors in a cable that are wrapped with metallic foil designed to insulate the pair from interference.

shielded twisted pair (See STP)

SHTTP (Secure Hypertext Transport Protocol)

Signal Computing System Architecture (See SCSA)

signal-to-noise ratio (See SNR)

Signaling System 7 (See SS7)

SIMD (single instruction, multiple data)
A design for parallel computers characterized by instructions that can directly trigger a large number (in parallel) of data operations on different data. Vector processors fall into this category.

SIMM (single in-line memory module)
A small printed circuit board that plugs into a socket on a personal computer and increases the available random-access memory (RAM).

Simple Internet Protocol Plus (See SIPP)

Simple Mail Transfer Protocol (See SMTP)

Simple Network Management Protocol (See SNMP)

simulation
The use of a mathematical or computer representation of a physical system for the purpose of studying constraint effects.

single large expensive disk (See SLED)

single in-line memory module (See SIMM)

single-image mode
A mode of operation in which multiple physical central processing units (CPUs) within a complex logically appear as one system running under control of a single copy of the operating system.

single instruction, multiple data (See SIMD)

SIPP (Simple Internet Protocol Plus)
A proposed revision to the Internet Protocol (IP). IP must be modified to support an address threshold capable of supporting the exponential growth of the Internet. SIPP would increase the address space to eight bytes.

SITA (Societe Internationale de Telecommunications Aeronautiques)

skills-based management (See SBM)

SLA (service-level agreement)
An agreement that sets the expectations between the service provider and the customer and describes the products or services to be delivered, the single point of contact for end-user problems and the metrics by which the effectiveness of the process is monitored and approved.

SLC (subscriber loop carrier)

SLED (single large expensive disk)
Traditional disk drive. That is, a conventional large-system disk system that has, on average, almost twice the diameter of a lower-cost redundant array of independent disks (RAID) system and, as its name implies, is significantly more expensive to manufacture.

SLIP (Serial Line Internet Protocol)

SLM (software license management)
A mechanism for systematically ensuring compliance with system vendor and independent software vendor (ISV) software licenses — for example, maximum users, maximum nodes and maximum MIPS. Examples include Digital Equipment's License Management Facility and Hewlett-Packards's Network License Server.

SLO (service-level objective)

SLR (Service Level Reporter)
An IBM product that provides direct-access storage device (DASD) administrators with predefined storage report formats. (Storage reports are used for identification of exception conditions, capacity planning, trend analysis, cost accounting and standards enforcement.)

Small Computer Systems Interface (See SCSI)

smart card
A card embedded with either a microprocessor and a memory chip or just a memory chip. The microprocessor card has the ability to add, delete and otherwise manipulate information on the card, while a memory chip card — such as the popular "phone card" — can only add information on the card. Smart cards do not require access to remote databases.

SMB (Server Message Block)

SMDR (station message detail reporting)
A means of capturing telephone system information on calls made, including who made the call, where it went and what time of day it was made, for processing into meaningful management reports. With such information, it is easier to spot exceptions to regular calling patterns such as out-of-hours calling, international calls, significant variances from previous reporting periods and call destinations that do not reflect normal calling patterns for the enterprise.

SMDS (Switched Multimegabit Data Service)
A Bell Communications Research-originated standard providing DS-1 and DS-3 access to a high-speed metropolitan-area network (MAN).

It is based on the Institute of Electrical and Electronics Engineers (IEEE) 802.6 standard and on early MAN work by QPSX Communications of Australia. SMDS is based on the data connectivity portion of the 802.6 MAN standard (but does not provide isochronous circuits). SMDS is a high-volume, high-speed, switched digital service. Supported speeds range from 1.544 megabits per second (Mbps) to 45 Mbps (with 155 Mbps possible in the future). Several local exchange carriers (LECs) and interexchange carriers (IXCs) are now offering or testing SMDS services. Additionally, the service description for public networking includes an addressing capability, enabling users to interoperate with other SMDS users. Asynchronous transfer mode (ATM) is the underlying protocol of Broadband Integrated Services Digital Network (B-ISDN). It is dependent on the B-ISDN addressing scheme and needs to rationalize addressing schemes for non-B-ISDN implementations.

SMF (Standard Message Format)
A file format protocol for NetWare Message Handling Service (MHS).

SMF Min.
A message using the minimal submission format, or minimum set of header fields required by Standard Message Format (SMF).

SMG (Storage Management Group)

SMI (server management interface)

SMP (symmetric multiprocessing)
A multiprocessor architecture in which all processors are identical, share memory and execute both user code and operating-system code.

SMR (specialized mobile radio)

A wireless communications technology in competition with analog cellular services. In an SMR system, the base station equipment supplier is the licensee of the transmitters. Users have access to the multiple channels of the network rather than the limited number of channels of a private mobile radio network. Many users share all of the available channels. Sharing is accomplished on a first-come, first-served basis. When users want to initiate a call, they activate the push-to-talk button on the handset. Assuming the portable unit (and dispatcher or other portable unit) is tuned to an available channel, a communication path is established. If channels that the sender and receiver can use are not available, the call cannot be completed, and the operator must wait for another opportunity to try again.

SMS (Systems Management Server— Microsoft)

SMS is systems management software that runs under Microsoft's Windows NT Server 3.5. It is used for the distribution of software, monitoring and analyzing network usage, and performing a variety of other network administration functions. Using SMS requires a Microsoft SQL Server database.

SMS (system-managed storage)

The term used for the conceptualization of an architecture for attachment, management and reconfiguration of secondary storage. Among the SMS basic design goals is the separation of logical-device management from physical-device management.

SMS (Storage Management Subsystem — IBM)

A component of IBM's Multiple Virtual Storage/Data Facility Product (MVS/DFP) that is used to automate and centralize the management of storage by providing the storage administrator with control over data class, storage class, management class, storage group and ACS routine definitions.

SMTP (Simple Mail Transfer Protocol)

A messaging protocol governing electronic-mail transmission in Transmission Control Protocol/Internet Protocol (TCP/IP) networks. It is used to transfer E-mail between computers. It is a server-to-server protocol. SMTP supports only text and cannot handle attachments. It supports negative delivery notifications, not the positive notifications required by electronic data interchange (EDI).

SNA (Systems Network Architecture)

An IBM-developed layered network architecture. The layers isolate applications from system network services, enabling users to write applications independent of the lower networking software layer.

SNA APPN — Intermediate Node

Support for connecting and exchanging information with IBM systems using IBM's Advanced Peer-to-Peer Networking (APPN) protocols. Support should be extended to include an intermediate-node (data forwarding) role.

SNA Distribution Services (See SNADS)

SNA LEN PU 2.1 End Node

Support for connecting and exchanging information with IBM systems using IBM's Low

Entry Networking (LEN) PU 2.1 protocols. Support should be for at least an end-node LEN role.

SNADS (SNA Distribution Services)

An architecture for interchanging data through a Systems Network Architecture (SNA) network in a store-and-forward fashion. SNADS is an SNA extension that provides an asynchronous interface. It is mostly appropriate for applications without strong time requirements, such as document distribution, file transfer and E-mail. SNADS requires that LU 6.2, and the software that implements SNADS, reside in the same processor as the LU 6.2 support.

SNI (Siemens Nixdorf Informationssysteme AG)

SNMP (Simple Network Management Protocol)

A TCP/IP derived protocol governing network management and the monitoring of network devices.

SNR (signal-to-noise ratio)

The power of a signal relative to channel noise.

software

Programs that control computer hardware. The two primary categories are system software (which governs the workings of the computer itself, such as the operating system and utilities) and applications software (which performs specific tasks for the user, such as word processing, spreadsheets and accounts payable).

software asset management (See SAM)

software change management (See SCM)

software development

Project management, specifications, design, programming, testing, installation and training associated with a specific applications development project of any size.

software development kit (See SDK)

software failure detection and recovery (See SFDR)

Software License Management (See SLM)

software maintenance

Updating software, adding new functions, fixing bugs and solving problems. Technology vendors often sell a maintenance contract with their software. This contract is usually calculated as an annual fee based on some percentage of the total software cost. It generally provides for overall support and maintenance of a software product, including applications. Support may include telephone assistance time as well.

SOGA (SNA Open Gateway Architecture)

SOHO (small office/home office)

solid-state disk (See SSD)

SOM (System Object Model)

IBM's object model designed to provide users with scalability, portability and interoperability of distributed applications across Hewlett-Packard and IBM platforms.

SONET (Synchronous Optical Network)

A International Telecommunications Union Telecommunications standard for synchronous transmission up to multigigabit speeds. The standard includes multivendor interoperability, improved troubleshooting and network survivability. As a Layer 1 standard, it is a foundation for Broadband Integrated Services Digital Network (B-ISDN) services.

Source Code Control System (See SCCS)

SPARC (Scalable Processor Architecture)
A reduced instruction set computer (RISC) architecture developed by Sun Microsystems and used in the Sun workstation family. SPARC chips are available from several semiconductor manufacturers, as Sun positions SPARC as a de facto standard.

SPC (statistical process control)
The identification and control of process variations so that a change in some process parameter (and faulty outcome) can be avoided. In practice, significant inputs to a process are measured or sampled. Out-of-control conditions are recorded, either because the value of the measurement falls outside a control limit, or a pattern in the time series indicates an unusual and undesirable event, such as a trend or a process shift. When an out-of-control condition is identified, the production line can be stopped and an effort made to fix the process. SPC within manufacturing practices can: 1) reduce scrap/rework; 2) reduce or eliminate inspection; and 3) increase production.

SPEC (System Performance Evaluation Cooperative)
A vendor consortium that selects and standardizes benchmark programs submitted by members or others.

SPECfp (SPEC floating point)
The CFP92 test of floating-point computations, established by the System Performance Evaluation Cooperative (SPEC). Because the decimal point is not fixed, but can move left or right, calculations involving very large or small numbers can be made more precisely.

specialized mobile radio (See SMR)

specialty center
A specialty center, or center of excellence, is a group of people dedicated to identifying best practices in an area of expertise and to building an internal service organization around that expertise. A center of excellence is a central clearinghouse for knowledge capital that is used across all business transformation projects. Specialty centers are an excellent means to leverage specialized skill sets, and are typically staffed to address a known demand.

specification, tracking, evaluation, production (See STEP)

SPECint (SPEC integer)
SPEC benchmark to measure the integer performance of a processor.

SPI (service provider interface)

SPMD (single program, multiple data)

SPX (Sequenced Packet Exchange)
A Novell NetWare session-based communications protocol used to govern the transport of messages across a network. It is designed to provide reliable end-to-end data transport, including error detection between two end-user devices.

SQC (statistical quality control)

SQL (Structured Query Language)
A relational data language that provides a consistent, English keyword-oriented set of facilities for query, data definition, data manipulation and data control. It is a programmed interface to relational database management systems (RDBMSs). IBM introduced SQL as the main external interface to its experimental RDBMS, System R, which it developed in the 1970s. SQL statements include:

- Data manipulation language statements: SELECT, INSERT, UPDATE and DELETE
- Data definition language statements, including the CREATE and DROP statements for tables and indexes
- Statements that control data consistency, and grant and revoke authority

SQL statements are called "dynamic" when they are not completely specified until the program is executed. They are called "static" when they are completely specified when the program is compiled. SQL is precise, because it is based on predicate logic, but is difficult for average users to deal with, and its most fruitful position is as a protocol for software-to-software connectivity, rather than for human-to-software access.

SQL/400
The IBM relational database management system (RDBMS) for the AS/400.

SQL Access Group
A consortium of vendors set up in November 1989 to accelerate the development of Remote Data Access (RDA) standards, deliver protocols for interconnectivity among multiple SQL-based products, and define the application programming interfaces (APIs) necessary for the interoperability of heterogeneous SQL implementations in a network environment and the portability of applications developed for those same implementations.

SQL DB Access (SQL Database Access)
Availability of a relational interface to a midrange system database that is compliant with Level 1 of the American National Standards Institute (ANSI) X3.135-1986 or International Standards Organization (ISO) 9075 SQL standard. Both a command (interpretive) and programming (compiled) implementation of the interface should be available.

SQL/DS (SQL/Data System)

SQL Services
Digital Equipment's implementation of a Structured Query Language application programming interface (API) that was distributed from Virtual Memory System (VMS) servers to Disk Operating System (DOS), Macintosh, OS/2, VMS or Ultrix desktops.

SRM (System Resource Manager)

SRPI (server/requester programming interface)

SRT (Source Routing Transparent)

SS7 (Signaling System 7)
An out-of-band signaling scheme, typically with a 64-kilobits per second (Kbps) transmission rate, used in the United States. It is designed for digital networks, and is key to current Integrated Services Digital Network (ISDN) implementa-

tions. Also called Common Channel Signaling No. 7 (CCS7).

SSA (Serial Storage Architecture)
IBM's disk storage technology and product line of disk subsystems. For most purposes, it is a single-sourced proprietary interface, especially useful for users who have standardized on RS/ 6000 systems with applications that require very high data rates that are not particularly cache-friendly.

SSD (solid-state disk)
An electronic semiconductor memory-based storage device that appears, to the computer system, to be a fast conventional direct-access storage device (DASD).

SSI (single-system image)

SSL (Secure Socket Layer)
An Internet security standard from Netscape Communications, used for its browser and server software.

ST (synchronous transport)

STAIRS (Storage and Information Retrieval System)
IBM's mainframe contextual search and library package (STAIRS/VS for MVS and STAIRS/ CMS for VM).

Standard for the Exchange of Product Model Data (See STEP)

Standard Generalized Markup Language (See SGML)

Standard Message Format (See SMF)

standards
Specifications or styles that are widely accepted by users and adopted by several vendors. Standards are critical to the compatibility of hardware, software and everything in between. Industry standards enable the essential elements of a computer and related infrastructure to work together. Standards provide specifications to hardware manufacturers and software developers that allow them to create products that will work together.

station message detail reporting (See SMDR)

statistical process control (See SPC)

statistical quality control/statistical process control
A set of techniques based on statistical principles and methods used to regulate the quality of products and processes.

STEP (specification, tracking, evaluation, production)
The four stages on which essential activities in the successful deployment of advanced technology are based. They are:

- Specification — which aligns corporate strategy and technology focus
- Tracking — which assesses individual technologies for maturity and business impact
- Evaluation — which involves prototyping and other in-depth evaluation activities to further gauge the readiness and relevance of the technology
- Production — which sees the technology being piloted and, if successful, rolled out into full deployment.

STEP (Standard for the Exchange of Product Model Data)

An international standards effort for defining the exchange of complete, unambiguous product model data. The goal of STEP is not only neutral file exchange, but also to serve as the basis for implementing, sharing and archiving entire product databases.

STK (StorageTek — for Storage Technology Corp.)

Storage and Information Retrieval System (See STAIRS)

Storage Management Subsystem — IBM (See SMS)

stored procedures

A limited form of remote procedure call (RPC) that enables procedural code (e.g., referential integrity constraints) to be stored and, thus, shared in the kernel of the database management system (DBMS). The DBMS provides a facility for storing procedural code associated with the database, and enforces its use during any database operation.

STP (signal transfer point)

STP (shielded twisted pair)

A pair of twisted transmission wires with a metallic shield to minimize interference.

StP (Software through Pictures — Interactive Development Environments)

Structured Query Language (See SQL)

Summit

Also referred to as FS/Summit. Summit is the name used to denote the IBM high-end processor series that follows the 3090. The FS/Summit processors are the ES/9000 Models 820 and 900.

Sun Microsystems Operating System (See SunOS)

Super Video Graphics Array (See SVGA)

supervisory control and data acquisition (See SCADA)

SunOS (Sun Microsystems Operating System)

Based on Berkeley 4.2; merged with AT&T's SVR4 Unix operating system.

STEP

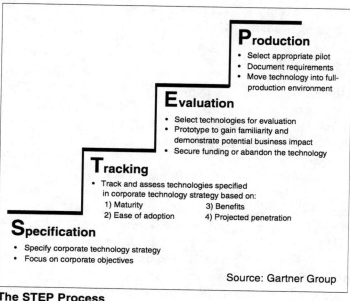

The STEP Process

Supra
Cincom Systems' overall environment that includes productivity tools and database managers.

SVC (switched virtual circuit)
A virtual connection with a call establishment and tear-down procedure to allow its temporary use.

SVGA (Super Video Graphics Array)
A Video Electronics Standards Association (VESA) display standard that provides much higher resolution than the Video Graphics Array (VGA) standard. It can support as many as 16 million colors, depending on the computer system and amount of available memory.

SVID (System V Interface Definition)
The specifications for Unix System V, set by AT&T. The fear that SVID might become a de facto standard, though not vendor-independent, was one reason for the creation of the Open Software Foundation (OSF).

SVR4 (System V Release 4)

switched virtual circuit (See SVC)

symmetric multiprocessing (See SMP)

synchronous
Having a constant time interval between successive bits, characters or events. Synchronous transmission uses no redundant information to identify the beginning and end of characters, and thus is faster and more efficient than asynchronous transmission, which uses start and stop bits. The timing is achieved by transmitting sync characters prior to data; usually synchronization can be achieved in two- or three-character times.

Synchronous Data Link Control (See SDLC)

Synchronous Digital Hierarchy (See SDH)

Synchronous Optical Network (See SONET)

Sysplex
A system complex of closely coupled Multiple Virtual Storage (MVS) processors sharing status information over a channel-to-channel link using the MVS Cross-System Coupling Facility (XCF) component. Sysplex became available with the first release of MVS/ESA SP 4.

System Control Element (See SCE)

system-managed storage (See SMS)

System Object Model (See SOM)

System Performance Evaluation Cooperative (See SPEC)

System R
Prototype version of the relational model developed by IBM, of which the important result was the precursor of Structured Query Language (SQL).

System V
AT&T's Unix operating system, introduced in 1983.

System V Interface Definition (See SVID)

System/370
A generic term for IBM's older mainframe architecture. Families with 370 architecture include 370/xxx, 9370, 43xx, 303x and 3090. The

term System/370, if not qualified, generally refers to all large IBM computers except for the S/390 family.

System/390
The generic term for IBM's processor family announced in September 1990, which replaced the S/370 family. S/390 consists of the ES/9000 mainframes.

Systems Application Architecture (See SAA)

systems integration
A large (more than $3 million), complex information systems (IS) project that includes designing or building a customized architecture or application, as well as integrating it with new or existing hardware, packaged and custom software, and communications. There is heavy reliance on an external contractor for program management of most or all phases of system development. This external vendor generally also assumes a high degree of the project's risks.Systems Management Server—Microsoft (See SMS)

Systems Network Architecture (See SNA)

System View
IBM's initiative for systems management.

T

T1

A digital carrier facility used to transmit digital signals at 1.544 megabits per second (Mbps) using 24-channel pulse code modulation (PCM). T1 lines are the most prevalent form of dedicated network connection. They are leased from a network provider like AT&T, MCI or Sprint.

T3

A digital carrier facility used to transmit digital signals at 44.74 megabits per second (Mbps). The king of Internet connections, a T3 line is realistically about 30 times faster than a T1 line.

TA (telecommunications administration)

Also called a PTT (postal, telephone and telegraph), a TA is an agency in a European or Asian country that is usually a government-run monopoly. It is responsible for all postal, telegraph and telephone services. It also has certain regulatory functions for telecommunications, such as providing specifications for modems and certifying that equipment may connect to the telephone network. In some countries, the TA also provides its own line of equipment, e.g., modems. TAs are undergoing varying amounts of structural change.

TA (terminal adapter)

An interfacing device for an Integrated Services Digital Network (ISDN) environment. It enables non-ISDN terminals to connect at the physical layer.

Tag Image File Format (See TIFF)

T&C (terms and conditions)

T&M (time and materials)

TAPI (Telephony Application Programming Interface)

An interface standard from Microsoft and Intel that brings a well-defined computer/telephone application programming interface (API) to the desktop. TAPI's initial release offered drivers that could be added to Microsoft's Windows 3.1. The desktop linkage for TAPI can be accomplished via serial RS-232 interfaces. Additionally, it also allows for a board associated with the telephone to plug into the desktop computer's bus. The telephone station does not disappear from the desktop for several reasons (e.g., computer and application up-time, and handset requirement). The stable APIs that exist between Windows and the Nx64 Kbps circuit-switching systems are not limited to voice; they can accommodate data, images and video.

tariff

The formal process whereby services and rates are established by and for communications com-

---

mon carriers. Carriers submit tariffs to the appropriate regulatory agencies, which then review, amend and then approve or disallow them.

Tariff No. 12

AT&T's tariff offering to large users whose requirements were ostensibly unique enough to require a custom network design and price. The custom designs included voice and data requirements; each is subject to the Federal Communications Commission's approval.

TAXI (transparent asynchronous transmitter/receiver interface)

A 100-megabits per second (Mbps) multimode fiber interface.

Tbyte (terabyte)

One trillion bytes.

TCB (transaction control block)

TCI (Tele-Communications Inc.)

TCM (Thermal Conduction Module or Thermo-Conductive Module)

The basic building block technology of the IBM 308X, 3090 and ES/9000. The TCM is a sealed container enclosing a multiple-chip carrying substrate amid a chip interconnection structure.

TCMP (tightly coupled multiprocessing)

A configuration in which all processors share a single pool of memory.

TCO (total cost of ownership)

The useful life-cycle cost of a system. In practice, in addition to hardware and software configuration prices, maintenance costs are added as computer system TCO factors.

TCP (Transmission Control Protocol)

A communications protocol based on the U.S. Department of Defense's standards for reliable internetwork delivery of data.

TCP/IP (Transmission Control Protocol/ Internet Protocol)

A set of protocols covering (approximately) the network and transport layers of the seven-layer Open Systems Interconnection (OSI) network model. TCP/IP was developed during a 15-year period under the auspices of the Department of Defense. It has achieved de facto standard status, particularly as higher-level layers over Ethernet. TCP/IP implementations are available on products from more than 80 vendors, including IBM, Digital Equipment, AT&T, Data General and Sun Microsystems. The biggest issue for TCP/IP is potential migration to the International Standards Organization (ISO) protocols for layers 3 and 4.

TDD (telephone device for the deaf)

TDI (technical data interchange)

TDL (Teknekron Data Language)

TDM (team data management)

Systems for managing computer-aided design (CAD) files and the activities of small work groups.

TDM (time division multiplexing)

A data, voice and video communications technique that interleaves several low-speed signals into one high-speed transmission.

TDMA (time division multiple access)

TDS (telecommunications data systems)
A frequency allocation technique based on allotting discrete time slots to users, permitting many simultaneous transmissions.

team data management (See TDM)

TEC (Tivoli Enterprise Console)

technical license management (See TLM)

Technology Upgrade Option (See TUO)

telco
A contraction of the term "telephone company." It generally refers to the local-exchange carrier (LEC).

telecommunications administration (See TA)

telecommuting
Any significant portion of working hours spent at a remote site (for example, home) using communications lines to send and receive information, interact with customers and peers, and deliver work projects.

Telephony Application Programming Interface (See TAPI)

Telephony Services Application Programming Interface (See TSAPI)

telpak
A discount schedule for volume voice-grade channel users.

terabyte (See Tbyte)

tera-FLOPS (See TFLOPS)

terminal
A device, combining keyboard and display screen, that communicates with a computer. Terminals are divided into different classes depending on whether they are able to process data on their own.

- Dumb terminals—display monitor or simple input/output (I/O) devices that send and accept data from a network server or mainframe. They have no built-in processing capabilities. Workers enter data and commands, which are sent to a computer located elsewhere.
- Smart terminals — monitors that process limited amounts of information.
- Intelligent terminals—devices that contain main memory and a central processing unit (CPU) to perform special display functions. Examples include an information kiosk and AT&T Display Phones.
- 3270 terminals—IBM display stations used to communicate with mainframes made by IBM and other manufacturers. They are in widespread use, and are widely copied

text information management system (See TIMS)

text retrieval
Software used for finding units of textual information such as documents by matching a user's search terms to those in a full-text index derived from the collection of textual units.

TFLOPS (tera-FLOPS)
Trillion floating-point operations per second.

Thermal Conduction Module or Thermo-Conductive Module (See TCM)

THF (time horizon to failure)

third generation
The class of client/server office systems introduced beginning in 1989, including IBM's OfficeVision, Digital Equipment's ALL-IN-1 Phase II and Hewlett-Packard's NewWave Office. Third-generation office systems are targeted at the knowledge worker delivering improvements in usability and new classes of applications with mission-critical implications.

three-schema architecture
A framework for managing access to data that involves three layers or schemas: the external or programming view, the conceptual or data administration view, and the internal or database administration view. Such ideas were developed by an American National Standards Institute/Scalable Processor Architecture subcommittee in 1971 but received little practical implementation by database management system (DBMS) vendors. The principle is that the conceptual schema consists of business rules derived from a semantic data model, which provides independence between programs and data structures. The emphasis has since shifted to computer-aided software engineering (CASE) tools and "repository" standards.

throughput
A computer term for the volume of work or information flowing through a system. Particularly meaningful in information storage and retrieval systems, in which throughput is measured in units such as accesses per hour.

TI (Texas Instruments)

TIFF (Tag Image File Format)
A de facto standard format for image files.

tightly coupled multiprocessing (See TCMP)

time division multiplexing (See TDM)

time division multiple access (See TDMA)

time sharing
An operating environment that supports many users by allocating small time slices so that each user appears to have the dedicated resources of the machine.

Time-Sharing Option (See TSO)

TIMS (text information management systems)
The genre of products that combines content-based retrieval and document database functions.

TLM (technical license management)
The management and control of software via a platform-independent automated facility that:

1. Ensures that access and use are in alignment with associated licensing agreements
2. Provides the basis for determining enterprise use requirements
3. Integrates with systems and network management tools

TLMS (tape library management system)

TMC (Thinking Machines Corp.)

TME (Tivoli Management Environment)

Token Ring Network (See TRN)

TOP (Technical Office Protocol)

total cost of ownership (See TCO)

total quality control (See TQC)

Total Solutions Lease (See TSL)

TP (transaction processing)
A mode of processing characterized by short transactions recording business events that normally requires high availability and consistent, short response times. A category of application that requires a request for service to be answered within a predictable period that approaches real time, and a transaction transforms this model from one business state to another. Tasks such as making reservations, scheduling and inventory control are especially complex; all the information must be current.

TPC (Transaction Processing Performance Council)
An organization that has developed several standardized transaction processing (TP) benchmarks, among which are TPC-A, TPC-B, and TPC-C. TPC prohibits testing systems that are specially optimized for benchmarking or lack real-world applicability.

TPC-A (Transaction Processing Performance Council Benchmark A)
A revised and superior version of the debit/credit online transaction processing (OLTP) benchmark. Ratified in late 1989, it came into widespread use in 1990. The major improvements in TPC-A were the requirements for full disclosure and the inclusion of the front-end network and terminals. TPC-A is intended to replace debit/credit as the only industrywide measure for OLTP performance and price/performance. It is a good test since it measures end-to-end performance, but it still is only one test reflecting a single type of transaction.

TPF (Transaction Processing Facility)
A high-availability, high-performance IBM system designed to support real-time, transaction-driven applications with maximum efficiency.

TPF2 (Transaction Processing Facility 2)
TPF2 is a low-function, high-cost set of control blocks and macro instructions that is positioned as IBM's highest-performance transaction-processing environment. Its users include many banks and airlines.

TPM (third-party maintenance)

TPM (transaction-processing monitor)
A process whereby the computer handles each instruction or query individually as it is entered.

tpm (transactions per minute)

tps (transactions per second)

TQC (total quality control)
A theory of quality whereby the maker of the part has responsibility for the quality of that part.

TQM (total quality management)

traditional processing
The availability of traditional and basic data processing facilities at the midrange system.

Examples include sequential and keyed files, compilers such as COBOL, FORTRAN, PL/I, BASIC and C, interactive access, batch processing, multiprocessing, and multitasking.

transaction
A logical update that takes a database from one consistent state to another.

transaction feed
The capability of passing, to the mainframe, midrange system transactions predetermined for Multiple Virtual Storage/Customer Information Control System (MVS/CICS) or Virtual Machine/Customer Information Control System (VM/CICS) processing with replies returned to the midrange system user. The IBM "intersystem communication" facility of CICS could be the technique used for implementation.

transaction logging
A concept in which a detailed record is kept of all operations in a transaction; in case of a failure, the transaction could be backed out and the former state reconstructed.

transaction monitor
A subsystem that ensures that all transactions against a database leave it in a consistent state or, in case of a transaction failure, returns the database to its pre-transaction state.

transaction processing (See TP)

Transaction Processing Performance Council (See TPC)

Transaction Processing Performance Council Benchmark A (See TPC-A)

Transaction Processing Facility (See TPF)

Transaction Processing Facility 2 (See TPF2)

transaction-processing monitor (See TPM)

Transmission Control Protocol (TCP)

Transmission Control Protocol/Internet Protocol (See TCP/IP)

transparent asynchronous transmitter/ receiver interface (See TAXI)

transport layer
In the Open Systems Interconnection (OSI) model, the network processing entity responsible — in conjunction with the underlying network, data link and physical layers — for the end-to-end control of transmitted data and the optimized use of network resources.

TRN (Token Ring Network)
A local-area network (LAN) topology and protocol in which all stations actively attached to the ring listen for a broadcast token or supervisory frame. Stations wishing to transmit must receive the token before doing so, and when done, must pass the token to the next station on the ring. IBM promotes TRN as its strategic LAN architecture.

TSAF (Transparent Services Access Facility)

TSAPI (Telephony Services Application Programming Interface)
A computer-telephony integration (CTI) application programming interface (API) developed

by Novell and AT&T that provides a client/server implementation and supports first- and third-party call control. The major benefit of third-party call control is that, via the command link to the switch, it is possible to control calls between third parties (much like an operator does today). This permits CTI applications to provide multiparty services, call routing based on automatic number identification and other advanced features. However, TSAPI requires a Novell NetWare networking environment. TSAPI does not require additional hardware in each PC, but does require a server CTI connection to the private branch exchange (PBX) equipment.

TSL (Total Solutions Lease)
An IBM ESO/ICC (Entry Service Offering/IBM Credit Corp.) marketing program that rolled the price of hardware, software, maintenance and certain services into a multiyear contract with a fixed monthly payment.

TSO (Time-Sharing Option)
The name originally given to IBM's compatible extension of Multiple Virtual Storage (MVS) background facilities into foreground execution. The name has stuck, although TSO is no longer an option in MVS.

TSO/E (Time-Sharing Option/Extended)

TSR (terminate and stay resident)

TT (trouble ticket)

TUO (Technology Upgrade Option)
An CMOS-based offering from IBM Credit Corp. that gives the user the option to upgrade to a larger processor, increasing the performance of the system for an increase in the monthly payment, which includes hardware, software services and maintenance costs.

two-phase commit
A method for coordinating a single transaction across two or more database management systems (DBMSs) or other resource managers. Two-phase commit guarantees the logical integrity of data by ensuring that transaction updates are finalized in all of the separate databases or are fully backed out of all participating databases, i.e., all or nothing based on transaction boundaries. Two-phase commit is a necessary component of distributed database and is implemented in "transaction management" software, which may be part of a DBMS, online transaction processing (OLTP) monitor, or front-end application tool.

Two-Phase Commit Protocol
Handshaking semantics across more than one participating node or database on a network involved in a transaction update such that, if a failure occurs at any point in the middle, all record updates are automatically rolled back.

U

UCC (Uniform Commercial Code)

UCD (universal call distribution)

UDF (user-defined functions)

UDP (User Datagram Protocol)
A Transmission Control Protocol/Internet Protocol (TCP/IP) technology that enables an application to send a message to one of several applications running in a destination machine. Some problems arise because Internet applications are not exclusively TCP-based. UDP is stateless — it differentiates sources and destinations within hosts and provides no other services. Often services do not use predefined port numbers, so filtering on the basis of "well known ports" will not work.

UHF (ultra-high frequency)

UI (Unix International)
A Unix development company formed principally by AT&T and Sun Microsystems as a counter to the initiatives of the Open Software Foundation. Now part of Novell.

UI (user interface)
The connection between the user and a computer's hardware or software that permits the user to work productively with a system or a program. User interface design requires significant skill and attention and has become a recognized specialty.

ultra large scale integration (See ULSI)

Ultrix
Digital Equipment's version of Unix, built on a University of California at Berkeley 4.2 Berkeley Software Distribution (BSD) base.

UMA (unified memory architecture)
A memory subsystem design for PCs. It eliminates the "graphics frame buffer," the additional memory for graphics used in typical PC designs, and consolidates graphics memory and main memory into a single physical memory array.

UNI (user-to-network interface)

unified memory architecture (See UMA)

uniform resource locator (See URL)

uninterruptible power supply (See UPS)

Universal Networked Object (See UNO)

Universal Serial Bus (See USB)

Universal Time-sharing System (See UTS)

Unix

A family of operating systems originally developed by AT&T in 1968 that is known for its relative hardware independence and portable applications interface. This time-sharing operating system is widely used in technical and scientific computing applications and has gone through a multitude of upgrades and enhancements. It has made great strides in entering mainstream commercial computing because of its scalability and support of complex processing.

Unix International (See UI)

UNMA (Unified Network Management Architecture)

AT&T's scheme for integrated network management.

UNO (Universal Networked Object)

Object Management Group's (OMG's) approval of the Universal Networked Object (UNO) proposal on Dec. 6, 1994, mandates that CORBA2-compliant object request brokers (ORBs) must be able to interoperate with other, heterogeneous ORBs using a particular lightweight, TCP/IP-based protocol ("GIOP").

unshielded twisted pair (See UTP)

upper-CASE tool

A tool for modeling applications requirements, systems analysis and data structure. Examples are Index Technologies' Excelerator and Knowledge-Ware's Information Engineering Workbench.

UPS (uninterruptible power supply)

A device that provides temporary power upon failure of the main power source.

URL (uniform resource locator)

The character string that identifies an Internet document's exact name and location.

USB (Universal Serial Bus)

A commercial desktop standard input/output (I/O) bus that provides a single peripheral connection and vastly increases bus speed. It simplifies peripheral connections via a "daisy chaining" scheme whereby the desktop system has only one I/O port to which all peripherals are connected in a series. Up to 120 peripherals can be connected to a single system.

USB

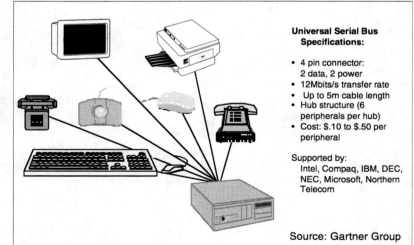

Universal Serial Bus Specifications:

- 4 pin connector: 2 data, 2 power
- 12Mbits/s transfer rate
- Up to 5m cable length
- Hub structure (6 peripherals per hub)
- Cost: $.10 to $.50 per peripheral

Supported by:
Intel, Compaq, IBM, DEC, NEC, Microsoft, Northern Telecom

Source: Gartner Group

Universal Serial Bus

user

An individual who interacts with a computing device through applications. Technical personnel are not considered to be users when they are programming or operating the computer.

User Datagram Protocol (See UDP)

user-friendly

Any system, software or device that is easy to learn and use. Graphical user interfaces (GUIs) are designed to be user-friendly.

user interface (See UI)

user workbench

A vision to guide the implementation of end-user computing, providing a multimedia integrated work environment, an omnipotent tool for gaining, using and communicating information, and a high level of job support to the office worker.

USL (Unix System Laboratories)

USLI (ultra-large-scale integration)

More than 1 million transistors in a chip.

UTP (unshielded twisted pair)

Two insulated wires twisted together, that is, wiring with one or more pairs of twisted insu-lated conductors housed in a single plastic sheath. The wires are twisted around each other to minimize interference from other twisted pairs in a cable bundle. UTP has no coaxial shielding.

UTS (Universal Time-sharing System)

In January 1986, Amdahl introduced a version of its UTS that can run stand-alone (not just as a guest under VM) on Amdahl 580 Series processors. UTS has been verified by AT&T as a Unix System V implementation. It initially ran in three modes:

1. As an operating system on an Amdahl 580 Series processor
2. In a domain under Amdahl's 580/Multiple Domain Feature (MDF)
3. As a guest under VM/SP or VM/SP HPO. Amdahl has now restricted UTS to its own machines. UTS's principal advantages over IBM's AIX/370 product are: efficiency, support for 327x terminals and ability to run natively as an operating system (i.e., without a hypervisor such as VM). UTS 2.1 is the first and only Unix offering to run native on large-scale S/370-type processors.

V

V.34
High-speed modem standard, also known as V. Fast, governing speeds up to 28,800 bits per second (bps) as set by the International Telecommunications Union (ITU).

V.42
International Telecommunications Union (ITU) standard for error correction

value-added network (See VAN)

value-added reseller (See VAR)

VAM (Vendors Against Microsoft)
A de facto coalition that has formed around Netscape Communications, Sun Microsystems and Oracle, with dozens of informal members, loosely united against Microsoft. VAM has: engaged the imagination of entrepreneurs, inventors and some early adopters; fostered tremendous creativity, reinvention and relearning; and provided a new source of leadership attempting to counterbalance Microsoft. Intel is equally a target, since Microsoft and Intel control critical industry software and hardware standards.

VAN (value-added network)
A private network through which value-added carriers provide special data transmission services.

VAR (value-added reseller)
An organization that buys equipment from a vendor at a discount, adds value (such as application software that is packaged and sold with underlying systems software, often including a database management system) and remarkets it.

VAX (Virtual Address Extension)
The Digital Equipment architecture that was the company's principal product line prior to the Alpha. VAX was enormously successful in Digital's traditional engineering and scientific customer base and, more significantly, enabled Digital to penetrate the commercial data-processing and office-automation markets.

VAX IBM Data Access (See VIDA)

VAX unit of performance (See VUP)

VB (Visual Basic)
A high-level programming language used in developing applications for Microsoft Windows 95.

VBA (Visual Basic for Applications)
A Visual Basic system included with Windows 95 applications and used for creating basic and customized programs.

VBR (virtual bit rate)

VBVA (visual builder of virtual applications)

VBX (Visual Basic Extension)
A Visual Basic add-on which Microsoft is converting to an OLE Custom Controls (OCX) infrastructure. The OCX/OLE standard interface is replacing the VBX interface.

VC (virtual circuit)
In packet switching, network facilities that appear to users to be an end-to-end circuit, but are in fact a dynamically variable network connection in which sequential user data packets may be routed differently during the course of a "virtual connection." Transmission facilities may be shared by many virtual circuits simultaneously.

VDT (video display terminal)

vector facility (See VF)

VEM (vendor evaluation model)

Vendor Independent Messaging (See VIM)

vendor-neutral
A state in which no one vendor can control the definition, revision or distribution of a specification. Vendor-neutral specifications encourage the development of competing yet compatible implementations, freeing the purchaser to choose from a multitude of vendors without suffering a loss of functionality. Vendor-neutral specifications must be comprehensive, consistent, and either publicly available or licensed at a nominal fee. Additionally, they must be defined by a multilateral association that is representative of a broad cross-section of the computer industry, open to new members, publishes the rules of membership and operates according to democratic principles. Preferably, a vendor-neutral specification is supplemented with at least one reference implementation. This reference would be available in a format that allows re-creation — that format would be source code for software implementations — and a set of conformance tests that sufficiently ensure the implementation's integrity under all reasonable conditions of projected use.

Vendors Against Microsoft (See VAM)

very large database (See VLDB)

very large-scale integration (See VLSI)

very small aperture terminal (See VSAT)

VESA (Video Electronic Standards Association)

VESA local bus (See VL bus)

VF (vector facility)
An attachment to a processor that enables the processor to run programs that issue vector instructions, which are particularly useful in scientific calculations, but are not particularly useful for database operations.

VF (voice frequency)

VGA (Video Graphics Array)
A hardware display and software resolution standard for personal computers.

VHDL (VLSI Hardware Description Language)
An industry standard format for describing integrated circuit logic and behavior.

VHDL Initiative for the Standardization of ASIC Libraries (See VITAL)

VHF (very high frequency)

VIDA (VAX IBM Data Access)
Digital Equipment's Rdb to DB2 interoperation software.

Video Graphics Array (See VGA)

video random-access memory (See VRAM)

view
An alternative representation of data from one or more tables. A view can include all or some of the columns in these tables.

VIM (Vendor Independent Messaging)
An application programming interface (API) that allows the exchange of electronic mail among programs from different vendors. Members of the Vendor Independent Messaging (VIM) Consortium are in the process of internally standardizing on VIM across all their networking products as they roll out their new product releases. VIM is designed to work across desktop platforms on Windows, Macintosh, DOS and OS/2.

Vines
Banyan Systems' network operating system (NOS).

Virtual Address Extension (See VAX)

virtual circuit (See VC)

Virtual Machine (See VM)

Virtual Memory System (See VMS)

virtual private network (See VPN)

virtual reality (See VR)

Virtual Reality Modeling Language (See VRML)

Virtual Storage Access Method (See VSAM)

Virtual Storage Extended (See VSE)

virtual tape subsystem (See VTS)

Virtual Telecommunications Access Method (See VTAM)

virus
Software used to infect a computer. After the virus code is written, it is buried within an existing program. Once that program is executed, the virus code is activated and attaches copies of itself to other programs in the system. Infected programs copy the virus to other programs.

Visual Basic (See VB)

Visual Basic Extension (See VBX)

Visual Basic for Applications (See VBA)

VITAL (VHDL Initiative for the Standardization of ASIC Libraries)
A standard for defining the format of integrated-circuit simulation libraries.

VL bus (VESA local bus)
A local bus architecture introduced by the Video Electronic Standards Association (VESA) to work with the Intel 486.

VLA (Volume License Agreement — Novell)
A software licensing option offered under the Novell "Customer Connections" program, with an entry point that opens discounts to smaller organizations.

VLDB (very large database)
A database greater than 100 gigabytes.

VLF (very low frequency)

VLSI (very large-scale integration)
A technology that makes it possible to place the equivalent of between 100,000 and 1 million transistors on a chip.

VLSI Hardware Description Language (See VHDL)

VM (Virtual Machine)
The IBM VM set of operating system products (VM/SP, VM/HPO, VM/XA, VM Migration and VM/ESA) manages a system so that all its resources — processors, storage and input/output (I/O) devices — are available to many users at the same time. Each user has at his disposal the functional equivalent of a real dedicated system. Because this functional equivalent is simulated by VM and does not really exist, it is called a "virtual" machine.

VMEbus
A high-speed parallel backplane system bus originally developed by Motorola, and now widely used on technical workstations and small multiuser systems.

VMS (Virtual Memory System)
Digital Equipment's traditional mainstay operating system. Virtual Address Extension (VAX) computers that play a role for Digital similar to the one that Multiple Virtual Storage (MVS) plays for IBM.

voice response unit (See VRU)

voice-grade channel
A channel with bandwidth equivalent to a telephone line obtained through the public telephone network. The maximum potential bandwidth of a voice-grade channel is approximately 20 kilohertz (KHz); however, most voice grade channels in a transmission facility are usually spaced 4,000 hertz (Hz) apart, and not all of that bandwidth is generally available to a user due to the presence of noise-limiting loading coils. The telephone network itself is usually defined in terms of channels, with frequencies from 300 to 3,400 Hz.

Volume License Agreement — Novell (See VLA)

volume purchase agreement (See VPA)

volume table of contents (See VTOC)

VPA (volume purchase agreement)
An agreement between a computer vendor and a customer under which the vendor grants discounted prices in return for the customer's commitment to purchase a minimum quantity of products.

VPN (virtual private network)
A system that delivers corporation-focused communications services on a shared public network infrastructure, and provides customized operating characteristics uniformly and universally across an enterprise.

VPO (Volume Purchase Option — Lotus)

VR (virtual reality)
A computerized process, usually including special equipment, that projects the user into a simulated three-dimensional space. It gives the user the sensation of being in the simulated environment and the ability to respond to the simulation.

VRAM (video random-access memory)
A type of dynamic random access memory (DRAM) used in high-speed processing of visual data.

VRML (Virtual Reality Modeling Language)
A means of rendering 3-D worlds from mathematical equations or descriptions. A VRML browser can create shapes and text within a navigable 3-D context. The v.2.0 specifications further enhance the immersive experience, allowing for such real-world events as interaction between "visitors" and collision-detection when a user bumps into an object or other users.

VRU (voice response unit)
An automated telephone answering system consisting of hardware and software that allows the caller to navigate through a series of prerecorded messages and use a menu of options through the buttons on a touch-tone telephone or through voice recognition.

VSAM (Virtual Storage Access Method)
IBM's chosen access method for direct-access files. It is optimized for a virtual storage environment. Multiple Virtual Storage (MVS), Data Facility Product (DFP), Information Management System (IMS), Customer Information Control System (CICS), and DB2 all use VSAM.

VSAT (very small aperture terminal)
Small earth station for data transmission to and from orbiting satellites.

VSE (Virtual Storage Extended)
VSE (formerly DOS/VSE) is a multitasking, 370-architected operating system akin to Multiple Virtual Storage (MVS). VSE work runs in partitions rather than address spaces, and uses Performance Optimized With Enhanced RISC (POWER) for input/output (I/O) rather than Job Entry Subsystem (JES), but is largely similar to MVS. Subsequent VSE/ESA releases gave VSE the XA-370 channel architecture, 31-bit virtual and real storage support, and data spaces. VSE is the IBM operating system on one-third of installed 4381s and a significant proportion of 9370s as well. It offers transaction and batch

processing capabilities well beyond Virtual Machine's (VM's) current capabilities, and has a close affinity with MVS.

VTAM (Virtual Telecommunications Access Method)

The main Systems Network Architecture (SNA) subsystem resident in an IBM mainframe that manages session establishment and data flow between terminals and application programs, or between application programs.

VTOC (volume table of contents)

The data structure on a direct-access volume that describes each data set on that volume.

VTS (virtual tape subsystem)

Tape library hardware and software extensions that utilize direct-access storage device (DASD) buffers to multiply the tape device count, throughput and storage density of tape library systems.

VUP (VAX unit of performance)

The average compute-bound performance of a Virtual Address Extension (VAX) processor relative to a VAX-11/780. One VUP is equivalent to between 0.7 and 1.0 IBM System/370 MIPS, depending on the compute-bound benchmarks chosen. Multiuser benchmark results vary much more widely, due to different input/output (I/O) architectures and software path lengths on Digital Equipment and IBM systems.

W-4GL (workgroup fourth-generation language)

WAN (wide-area network)
A communications network that connects computing devices over geographically dispersed locations. While a local-area network (LAN) typically services a single building or location, a WAN covers a much larger area such as a city, state or country. WANs can use either phone lines or dedicated communication lines.

WAN performance monitor
A tool or toolset (hardware and software) to allow monitoring of wide-area network (WAN) traffic and problems.

WAPI (Workflow API)
The Workflow Management Coalition's application program interface (API), designed to enable workflow application interoperability in a heterogeneous workflow environment in five key areas between: business process re-engineering (BPR)/modeling tools and workflow systems; workflow systems and workflow-client applications; workflow systems and desktop applications; workflow engines; and common workflow administration and monitoring services.

warehouse management system (See WMS)

WATS (wide-area telephone service)
A telephone company service providing reduced costs for certain telephone call arrangements. It may be IN-WATS or 800-number service, for which calls can be placed to a location from anywhere at no cost to the calling party, or OUT-WATS, for which calls are placed from a central location. The cost is based on hourly usage per WATS circuit and on distance-based zones, or bands, to which (or from which) calls are placed.

WBEM (Web-Based Enterprise Management)

WBEM

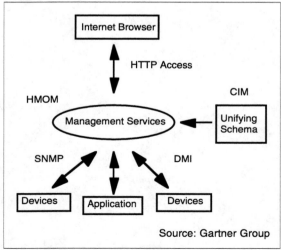

Components of the WBEM Initiative

WBEM is an initiative launched in July 1996 by a consortium of five vendors: BMC Software, Cisco Systems, Compaq Computer, Intel and Microsoft. Its intention was to create a new set of networked systems management (NSM) middleware services based on Internet technologies. As a part of the proposal, three components of an NSM architecture were introduced: Hypermedia Management Schema (HMMS), Hypermedia Management Protocol (HMMP) and Hypermedia Object Manager (HMOM).

WCL (Windows Communication Library)

wearable computer
Typically consists of a belt-mounted PC and a head-mounted, voice-activated screen over one eye. Originating in the military, wearable systems are commercially available in the $5,000 to $10,000 price range.

Web page
A World Wide Web document — usually based on Hypertext Markup Language (HTML) — that may contain text, graphics, online audio, video, Java or ActiveX objects. The most basic elements of Web marketing, these pages are linked to other pages using hypertext to form a Web site. Web pages can be designed for virtually any purpose, and many third-party organizations have evolved services that assist marketers in page content development and layout. WF (workflow framework)
A set of proposals that allow applications to deliver "workflow information" to a user or workflow engine.

WfMC (Workflow Management Coalition)
Headquartered in Brussels, Belgium, a non-profit, international consortium of more than 180 workflow vendors, users, service providers and analysts, founded in July 1993 to address the standardization of workflow technology. The WfMC's goal is to document an agreed-upon set of terminology, application programming interfaces (APIs), protocols and formats that allow workflow products to interoperate.

WfMC API (See WAPI)

WGS (workgroup systems)
A future-oriented, vendor-independent model for office information systems (OIS). Key WGS proposals include a complete, cohesive architecture, distributed-logic client/server technology and interenterprise-capable, enterprise-class platforms for communications, collaboration, word and knowledge reuse.

wide-area network (See WAN)

WIMPS (windows, icons, menus, pointers, scroll bars)
A style of graphical user interface (GUI) originally developed by Xerox and popularized by the Apple Macintosh.

windowing
A display technique that uses multiple screen segments to display different items of information. The display can take two forms: tiling (breaking up the screen into discrete segments) and overlapping (producing a three-dimensional effect by having a screen segment partially or fully obscure another segment).

Windows CE (See CE)

windows, icons, menus, pointers, scroll bars (See WIMPS)

Windows Open Services Architecture (See WOSA)

Windows

The family of operating systems written by Microsoft to manage the graphical user interface (GUI) and all related functionality for IBM-compatible personal computers. The various versions of the Windows product have become the dominant operating system for PCs.

Windows NT

Microsoft's 32-bit operating system for client/server computing. Offered in two versions: Windows NT Workstation for the client, and Windows NT Server for the server.

Windows 95

A 32-bit operating system introduced by Microsoft in 1995, it offered significant enhancements over prior releases of Windows, with features like memory protection, multithreading, integrated networking and pre-emptive multitasking.

WINS (Windows Internet Naming System)

Wintel

Refers to the personal computer (PC) environments composed of a Microsoft Windows operating system running on an Intel microprocessor. This environment dominates the personal-computing market, and therefore Microsoft and Intel together control many aspects of the PC industry. The widely accepted standards of this environment have encouraged significant software development for this de facto standard platform, allowing software, files and data to be more easily shared among users and enhancing productivity. However, some have claimed that the dominance of Microsoft and Intel in the PC marketplace has reduced innovation and allowed Microsoft and Intel to set guidelines that enhance their corporate profits rather than benefit users.

WIP (work in progress)

WIP (Windows Interface Protocol)

wireless LAN (See WLAN)

WK1

The specification for the structure of data stored on disk by Lotus 1-2-3 releases 1 and 2.

WK3

The specification for the structure of data stored on disk by Lotus 1-2-3 release 3.

WLAN (wireless LAN)

A wireless local-area network (LAN) communications technology, WLANs represent a full system extension to the enterprise network. Three physical media types of WLAN systems are available. The first two — direct-sequence spread spectrum (DSSS) and frequency-hopping spread spectrum (FHSS) — are based on radio technologies which are not interoperable. The third is based on infrared, a non-radio technology which is based on light waves. Infrared can coexist with DSSS and FHSS radio-based systems in one enterprise network; however, internetworking issues between access points (APs) prevent an enterprise from mixing and matching WLAN devices from multiple vendors; other criteria are needed for interoperability to occur.

WMS (warehouse management system)

A real-time execution management system designed to receive, store and ship products in the most efficient, yet compliant, way possible. It enables the enterprise to ensure, with its own resources, that the customer receives what it wants when it wants, and in the form and by the methods specified.

work in progress (See WIP)

work management
A set of software products and services that apply workflow structure to the movement of information as well as to the interaction of business processes and human-worker processes that generate the information. Work management streamlines and transforms crucial business processes and thus can improve results and performance.

workflow
The automation of work among users where the system is intelligent enough to act based on the definition of work types, users and tasks, and the recognition of dynamic processing conditions.

workflow framework (See WF)

Workflow Management Coalition (See WfMC)

workgroup systems (See WGS)

workstation
1. In general terms, a workstation is a human-to-machine interaction device, usually a PC, that is composed of coordinated input/output (I/O) devices (including video displays, keyboards and functional menus) and that may include offline storage capabilities. It may be used for graphics, text, data and retrieval functions.

2. More specifically, a workstation is the term often applied to a high-performance computer designed for use with personal applications that require significant processing power, such as graphics or computer-automated design. Many software programs originally designed for use on a workstation are designed to run using a Unix operating system.

World Wide Web
A hypertext-based global information system developed at the European Laboratory for Particle Physics (CERN) in Geneva, Switzerland. It uses the Internet to transport data and documents formatted in a language called Hypertext Markup Language (HTML) among users.

WORM (write once, read many)
A digital, optical storage medium on which information can be recorded once and read many times. Provides for extremely compact storage of data at relatively low prices compared to traditional magnetic storage.

WOSA (Windows Open Services Architecture)
An architecture and set of application programming interfaces (APIs) that position Windows as a universal client. It standardizes the interfaces that developers can use in accessing underlying network services.

WP (word processing)

wpm (words per minute)

write once, read many (See WORM)

WYSIWYG (what you see is what you get)

X.25

An International Telecommunications Union interface standard for connection of data terminal equipment to a public packet-switching network. X.25 defines the services that the user can expect from a public packet-switching network, including the establishment of virtual circuits through the network to exchange packets with other users.

X.25 WAN

Support of the X.25 wide-area network (WAN) protocol for system and network interconnection.

X.400

The International Telecommunications Union guidelines that define the basis for providing message handling services, such as store-and-forward electronic mail.

X.400 Application Programming Interface (See XAPI)

X.500

The International Telecommunications Union standard for directory services.

XA (Extended Architecture)

System/370 XA is the second major extension of IBM's System/360 architecture. It was de-livered in 1983 on the 308x processors, and is now available on the 3090 and 4381. The major new features in XA were 31-bit addressing and a more sophisticated input/output (I/O) subsystem. It is supported by the MVS/XA and VM/XA operating systems.

X.500

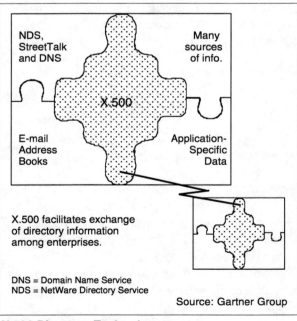

X.500 facilitates exchange of directory information among enterprises.

DNS = Domain Name Service
NDS = NetWare Directory Service

Source: Gartner Group

X.500 Directory Technology

XAPI (X.400 Application Programming Interface)

APIs developed by the X.400 API Association (XAPIA) to sit on top of the X.400 protocols, simplifying the task of submitting and fetching X.400-compliant messages. The message submitted is transported by an X.400-compliant message transfer agent.

XAPI file-based API

An unofficial file-based API used to submit and deliver messages with X.400 features to an X.400 message transfer agent.

XAPIA (X.400 API Association)

XDS

An interface that connects to X.500 directory services, designed by XAPIA.

XFN (X/Open Federated Naming)

Sun Microsystems' federated-naming service specification, similar to Messaging Application Programming Interface (MAPI) and Apple Open Collaborative Environment (AOCE), for the Unix environment. XFN first shipped with Sun's Solaris operating system in 1994. XFN was accepted as a prototype of an X/Open federated-naming service standard in 1995.

XICS (Xerox Integrated Composition System)

XIE (X-Windows Image Extensions)

Extensions that support client compression/decompression.

X/Open

An international consortium of computer vendors that aims to create and promote a vendor-independent interface standard called the Common Applications Environment (CAE). CAE addresses the operating-system interface, data management and languages, and includes networking and graphical user interfaces (GUIs). X/Open was founded in Europe by European vendors, but has expanded to include a number of U.S. companies (AT&T, Digital Equipment, Hewlett-Packard, NCR, Unisys and Sun Microsystems) and an office in the United States.

X/Open branding

Verified midrange-system software compliance, in accordance with the X/Open branding program, with the X/Open consortium's Common Applications Environment (CAE) X/Open Portability Guide release 3 (XPG3) base profile.

X/Open

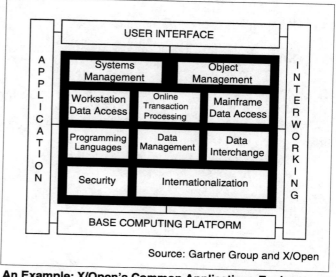

Source: Gartner Group and X/Open

An Example: X/Open's Common Applications Environment

X/Open Distributed Transaction Processing
An online transaction processing (OLTP) monitor compliant with the X/Open "XA" distributed transaction-processing advance specification.

X/OPEN Federated Naming (See XFN)

X/Open ISAM
Support, compliant with X/Open XPG volume 5, for Indexed Sequential Access Method (ISAM) files.

X/Open NLS
National language support (NLS) compliant with the X/Open XPG3 NLS specification.

X/Open Portability Guide (See XPG)

X/Open Transport Interface (See XTI)

XPAF (Xerox Printer Access Facility)

XPG (X/Open Portability Guide)

XPG3 (X/Open Portability Guide release 3)

XPG4 (X/Open Portability Guide release 4)

XRF (Extended Recovery Facility)
A reliability enhancement for an Information IMS/VS database/data communications environment. It provides the capability of creating a "mirror" IMS system and synchronizing it to the primary subsystem. The mirror IMS/VS system takes over the workload from the primary subsystem in the case of some, but not all, disruptive events, thereby improving availability. XRF will also facilitate testing and installation of new software releases. It has also been extended to Customer Information Control System (CICS).

XTI (X/Open Transport Interface)
Support provided for applications that use the X/Open XTI programming interface for peer-to-peer communications.

XUI
An X Windows-based graphical user interface (GUI) developed by Digital Equipment as part of its DECwindows program.

X Windows
The software system written for managing windows under Unix. A graphics architecture, application programming interface (API) and prototype implementation developed by the Massachusetts Institute of Technology, X Windows defines a client/server relation between the applications program and the workstation. It is not, however, a complete graphical user interface (GUI), but rather the basis upon which one can be built.

X-Windows Image Extensions (See XIE)

Y & Z

year 2000 compliance
Confirmation that applications are free from the year 2000 problem, i.e., that they do not abnormally end or produce erroneous results as the result of incorrectly interpreting the year 2000 as "00" due to the use of only two digits to represent the year.

year 2000 problem
The year 2000 problem is the result of an industry practice that for more than 35 years has represented dates in applications as only six digits (i.e., yy/mm/dd, assuming in application logic that the first two digits of the year are one and nine). A variety of errors are introduced once such applications must deal with dates beyond Dec. 31, 1999.

ZAK (Zero Administration Kit)
Microsoft product designed to reduce the management complexity associated with the Windows platform. Initially announced as an offering for Windows NT 4.0, ZAK is an early component of Microsoft's Zero Administration Windows (ZAW) initiative.

ZAW (Zero Administration Windows)
Microsoft initiative to lower the total cost of ownership associated with the Windows platform by reducing costs associated with administration. ZAW is expected to take the form of a set of features to be deployed across a variety of Windows platforms over a period of years.

Zero Administration Kit (see ZAK)

Zero Administration Windows (see ZAW)

About Gartner Group

⑤ GartnerGroup

Your Personal Information Technology Advisor

**Members of the Worldwide
Information Technology Community:**

As you are aware, information technology (IT) is fast becoming one of the key drivers in today's rapidly changing corporate environment. No longer the bastion of management information systems (MIS) managers and computer engineers alone, IT is now a major concern to business managers and to every corporate employee.

At the same time, the IT market sector is exploding with new products, new technologies and new capabilities. Some of these innovations will live up to their promises and some will not. And that's where Gartner Group comes in.

As the leading advisor on the IT industries, Gartner Group is uniquely positioned to guide you through this changing landscape with our commitment to provide you with personalized service.

Gartner Group has invested in the intellectual assets of our more than 430 analysts, innovative delivery mechanisms and a worldwide research network in order to personalize our service for you and the individual IT issues you face. And we provide the broadest and deepest range of services in the IT advisory services industry, covering all of IT from a global perspective.

Everything we do is designed to provide you with concise, actionable advice to help you optimize your time, money and resources, not to mention your own and your company's success. We at Gartner Group look forward to being of service to you.

**The Value of a Relationship
with Gartner Group**

Gartner Group provides a wide range of IT advisory services for executives who use, purchase or provide IT products and services. Through the research, analysis and recommendations of Gartner Group analysts, clients can measurably improve the effectiveness of their decisions. The benefits that Gartner Group provides to clients include:

Saving Money
Extending the value of your IT dollars through a complete understanding of areas to improve, alternatives and means of negotiating leverage.

Staff Extension
Having access to Gartner Group's more than 430 analysts can extend your staff resources to better utilize your time and budget.

Accountability Insurance
Ensuring your IT decisions are made with the best possible information and planning assump-

---

tions from the experience of the world's leading analysts.

Supporting Strategic and Tactical Plans

Keeping you in a position of power with minimal risks, Gartner Group outlines evolving markets and vendor strategies, giving you a constant flow of analysis of market forces and trends that has become a prerequisite for changing strategic and tactical plans.

Staff Training

Gartner Group training on technology provides your staff with state-of-the-art tools and techniques to help them keep pace with technology. The focus is technology-based training courses that provide you with enterprisewide solutions.

Core Areas of Expertise

Gartner Group provides vital advice to professionals making key decisions about IT. Its subscription-based products and services include qualitative research and analysis on trends and developments, quantitative market research, and benchmarking services. In addition, Gartner Group provides consulting services, technology-based training products, worldwide conferences and events, research reports and newsletters.

Gartner Group has more than 80 product service offerings, each concentrating on specific issues and how they affect individual clients. The company matches its services to clients' personal IT needs.

Management of Technology

Like all key business functions, information technology must be tightly managed if it is to return the greatest benefit. Services in this segment provide clients with integrated and comprehensive information analysis and advice to enhance their decision-making process. The focus of these services is on management skills and objective analysis.

Application of Technology

Business executives need to know how best to apply IT to their needs. This segment focuses on business applications of both existing and emerging technologies. Coverage includes the application of specific technologies within a business environment, and strategic considerations involved in aligning IT with business objectives.

Direction of Technology

To compete effectively, companies of all sizes must understand the evolution of IT. Having current and objective information about product features, vendor strategies and technological developments is critical when making important purchasing decisions. The services in this segment provide clients with key trends relating to the direction of technology, enabling them to make decisions that work today and in the future.

Market Research on Technology

Dataquest, a Gartner Group company, is a global market research and consulting company serving the IT vendor, manufacturer and financial communities.

Dataquest provides worldwide market coverage on computer systems and peripherals, document management, semiconductors, services and support, online, multimedia and software, and telecommunications sectors of the IT industry.

Dataquest products concentrate on quantitative market research, statistical analysis, growth projections and market share rankings of IT manufacturers and vendors. Other services include custom research, consulting and a wide array of supplemental research-based reports, vendor profiles and newsletters.

Training on Technology

IT professionals struggle to keep pace with new and evolving technologies. To meet this need in a cost-effective manner, the $10 billion education and training industry is evolving from instructor-led classes to technology-based training, multimedia, and interactive products. Gartner Group Learning offers self-paced, interactive training courses for IT professionals and end users.

Measurement & Evaluation of Technology

These services provide quantitative and qualitative analysis and recommendations for continuous IT improvement to IT and business professionals. Through a complex and well-established comparative benchmark methodology, Real Decisions services enable companies to comprehensively assess and measure performance, understand their position vis-à-vis other like organizations, leverage strategies for improving performance, and share best practices with peers.

Gartner Group Makes IT Advisory Services Personal

By matching the services offered from its core areas of expertise with clients' IT needs, and delivering advice through six major mechanisms, Gartner Group gives truly personalized service.

Product and Services Delivery Systems Advisory Services

Gartner Group's subscription-based information services combine bottom-line, business-oriented analysis with in-depth knowledge of technology trends and developments. These services are delivered through telephone consultations with its analysts, and through audioconferences, briefings and research reports. The research and analysis from these services provide clients with a continuous stream of information to help them gain a complete view of their present condition, create a strategic vision for the future, and implement sound technology strategies and migration plans.

Interactive Services

Gartner Group uses leading-edge technology, including Internet and intranet, to increase the value of its research and advisory services, making them easier to search, use, share and personalize. Access to Gartner Group and Dataquest research is available through these Gartner Group Interactive Services:

- Gartner CD-ROM™
- Gartner on Lotus Notes®
- GartnerFLASH™
- Dataquest on Demand
- MarketViews
- GartnerWeb
- Gartner Group Government Technology Strategies on @vantage™
- Gartner Group Premium on @vantage™
- Dataquest Interactive
- @xpo™

Consulting Services

Gartner Group consulting services provide customized consulting engagements: 1) for end users of technology on the management of the IT infrastructure within the enterprise; and 2) for information and communication technology providers and investors on the delivery, deployment and management of IT products and services.

Events

Recognized as the premier in industry forums, Gartner Group annually hosts more than two dozen conferences, annual symposia/ITxpo in the United States, Europe, the Pacific and Asia regions, as well as numerous seminars, briefings, audioconferences and video-conferences for IT professionals worldwide.

Newsletters and Reports

A complete range of research reports and newsletters is available to help keep you informed in the ever-evolving IT industry. With Gartner Group analysts based around the world, the company offers global reports and newsletters with the most accurate, in-depth and up-to-date information available in a vast marketplace. The Newsletters Program's new Webletter product is a customized electronic publication, accessible only through the World Wide Web.

At Gartner Group, we see the world through your eyes.

We understand the business issues driving your technology strategies, the importance of ROI, the impact that right and wrong IT decisions can have on the future of your business, and the critical need to continuously measure and benchmark the effectiveness of your systems. Perhaps most importantly, we understand the human issues, the angst that often accompanies a transition to new technologies and processes. Many of our analysts have direct experience in corporate IT decision making, and others have had personal involvement in hardware and software development companies. Their collective experience ensures you of a complete breadth and depth of IT knowledge.

Personal Advisory Services
The following list represents Gartner Group's extensive product service offerings*:

Integrated Business Solutions

EEMI	Executive Edge: IT Management Insights
EE2000	Executive Edge: Year 2000 Solution
MECS	Management Edge: Customer Service
ME2000	Management Edge: Year 2000

Application of Technology

AAS	Administrative Application Strategies
CS3	Customer Service and Support Strategies
CIM	Computer Integrated Manufacturing
ECS	Electronic Commerce Strategies
FSIR	Financial Services Industry-Retail
HETS	Higher Education Technology Strategies
ILS	Integrated Logistics Strategies
IRCM	Information Resource Center Management
MKT	Marketing Knowledge & Technology
SLS	Sales Leadership Strategies

Healthcare Advisory Services

DSAV	Delivery System Applications and Vendors
HEMS	Healthcare Executive and Management Strategies
HT	Healthcare Technologies
MCAV	Managed Care Applications and Vendors

Direction of Technology

ADM	Applications Development & Management Strategies
APV	Asia Pacific View
ATA	Advanced Technologies & Applications
C/S	Client/Server
DCP	Distributed Computing Platforms
DCS	Data Center Strategies
ENS	Enterprise Network Strategies
ENSC	Enterprise Network Strategies Canada
ENSE	Enterprise Network Strategies Europe
ENSP	Enterprise Network Strategies Pacific
IDOM	Integrated Document & Output Management
IM	Interactive Media
INET	Internet Strategies
ISS	Information Security Strategies
ITD	Industry Trends & Directions
LAN	Local Area Networking
MBS	Mobile Business Strategies
NSM	Networked Systems Management
OIS	Office Information Systems
PC	Personal Computing
RDS	Rapid Development Solutions
SDM	Strategic Data Management

SSA	Systems Software Architectures
STOR	Storage Technologies, Operations & Resources

Information Technology Management

ITM	Information Technology Management
ITM-D	ITM-Distributed
ITM-D4	ITM- Distributed for AS/400
ITM-G	ITM-Growth
ITME-E	ITM Europe-Executive
ITME-D	ITM Europe-Distributed
ITME-D4	ITM Europe-Distributed for AS/400
ITME-G	ITM Europe-Growth

Market Research on Technology

See Dataquest 1997 Research Programs List or DAS Book 970101

Training on Technology
Talking Technology Series

TTS	Talking Technology Series
TTF	Talking Technology Fundamentals
TTG	Talking Technology Government

Gartner Group Learning

See Curriculum/ Main Catalogue for List

Gartner Group Learning Suites

GGL-C/S	Client/Server Suite
GGL-LN4	Lotus Notes 4 Suite
GGL-M	Microsoft Migration Suite
GGL-MW	Microsoft Windows Programming Suite
GGL-O7D	Oracle7 Database Administration Suite

GGL-O	Oracle Programming Suite
GGL-OD2000	Oracle Developer/2000 Suite
GGL-OOT	Object-Oriented Technology Suite
GGL-PB	PowerBuilder Suite
GGL-UA	Unix System Administrators Suite
GGL-UF	Unix Foundations Suite
GGL-UP	Unix Programmers Suite

Measurement & Evaluation of Technology

Real Decisions

RDAD	Applications Development & Support Management
RDCC	Call Center
RDCSS	Centralized Systems and Servers
RDDC	Data Center
RDDT	Distributed Computing
RDEMAP	Executive Market Analysis Program
RDESAP	Enterprise Software: SAP
RDGWAD	Global View: Wide Area Data
RDITIV	Information Technology Integrated View
RDITOA	Information Technology Overview Analysis
RDLAD	Local Area Data
RDVIP	Voice Information Processing
RDWAD	Wide Area Data

Best Practices Groups

EBP	Enterprise Best Practices
IBP	Interactive Best Practices
BPG2	Best Practices Groups-2
BPG4	Best Practices Groups-4
BP4AD	Applications Development and Support
BP4ADS	Advanced Development Solutions

BP4AM	Asset Management
BP4ANET	Intranets
BP4CC	Call Center
BP4C/S	Client/Server
BP4DM	Database Management
BP4HD	Help Desk
BP4IEC	Internet and Electronic Commerce
BP4IF	Infrastructure Forum
BP4ISOS	IS Organization Strategies
BP4LRN	Learning for Enhanced Productivity
BP4N	Networking
BP4OM	Outsourcing Management
BP4OPS	IT Operations and Support
BP4SAP-P'95	SAP R/3 Systems-Production 1995
BP4SAP-P'96	SAP R/3 Systems-Production 1996
BP4SAP-P'L96	SAP R/3 Systems-Production Late 1996
BP4VIT	Value of IT
BP42000-G	Year 2000-Government

Best Practices Groups Europe

BP4E-AD	Applications Development and Support
BP4E-CC	Call Centre
BP4E-I	Infrastructure
BP4E-SAP	SAP R/3 Systems-Production 1996
BP4E-VIT	Value of IT

Management of Technology

BPR	Business Process Re-engineering
DD	Decision Drivers
EAM	Equipment Asset Management

EAME	Equipment Asset Management Europe
ESP	External Services Providers
ESPE	External Services Providers Europe
ESPG	External Services Providers Government
MDC	Managing Distributed Computing
MSD	Management Strategies & Directions
NBM	Network Business Management
SAM	Software Asset Management
TS	Transition Strategies

Executive Programs

ETEP	European IT Executive Program
ITEP	IT Executive Program
ITEP-A	IT Executive Program-Australia
ITEP-G	IT Executive Program-Government

*Service offerings subject to change.

Gartner Group
Business Background

Gartner Group is the worldwide leader among IT advisory service companies. Providing research, analysis and advice on IT strategies for users, purchasers and vendors of IT products and services, Gartner Group has more than 28,000 individual clients, representing over 7,400 organizations worldwide.

Founded in 1979, Gartner Group went public in 1986 and was acquired in 1988 by the world-wide advertising firm of Saatchi & Saatchi. In 1990, Gartner Group management, in conjunction with Information Partners Capital Fund, bought the company back. In October 1993, 2.7 million shares of public stock were reissued.

Gartner Group has experienced explosive growth with the acquisition of several enterprises. By combining the strengths of these enterprises, IT and business professionals benefit from a broad geographical presence, expanded capabilities using electronic media, and the research expertise of more than 430 analysts in over 75 worldwide locations.

Gartner Group Family of Companies
Through its worldwide presence, Gartner Group is able to provide superior value to its expanding client base.

- CJ Singer
- MZ Projekte
- Dataquest
- NOMOS Ricerca
- Decision Drivers, Inc.
- Real Decisions
- Gartner Group Learning

Worldwide Locations
More than 75 offices around the world.

Gartner Group Key Offices
- **Corporate Headquarters**

  56 Top Gallant Road
  Stamford, CT 06904-2212
  U.S.A.
  Phone 1-203-964-0096
  Fax 1-203-316-1100

- **West Coast**

  251 River Oaks Parkway
  San Jose, California 95134
  U.S.A.
  Phone 1-408-468-8000
  Fax 1-408-954-1780

- **Europe**

  Tamesis, The Glanty
  Egham, Surrey TW20 9AW
  United Kingdom
  Phone (44) 1784-431611
  Fax (44) 1784-488980

- **Japan**

  Aobadai Hills, 4F
  7-7, Aobadai, 4-chome
  Meguro-ku, Tokyo 153
  Japan
  Phone (81) 3-3481-3670
  Fax (81) 3-3481-3671

  Suite 5904-7, Central Plaza
  18 Harbour Road
  Wanchai
  Hong Kong
  Phone (852) 2-824-6165
  Fax (852) 2-824-6138

- **Pacific**

  424 Upper Roma Street, 3rd Fl.
  Brisbane, QLD 4006
  Australia
  Phone (61) 73-405-2525
  Fax (61) 73-405-2503

Visit Gartner Group on the World Wide Web
at http://www.gartner.com

Case Studies: How Gartner Group Advisory Services Work

Real Decisions Shows Large Financial Services Company How to Save $5 Million in Data Center Costs

A benchmark analysis for a large multinational financial services company showed DASD capacity significantly exceeding the peer group average. Cost-performance metrics identified significant unutilized DASD. As part of the recommendations and Strategies for Improved Performance, Real Decisions showed the client how to reduce excess capacity and increase utilization to reach peer-group levels. By implementing the recommendations and reducing DASD storage, the enterprise realized a $5 million savings.

Gartner Group Helps Client Prepare for Best-In-Class Lease Deal

A major research hospital in the United States investigated leasing its midrange platform equipment, including midrange servers and administrative systems. The client worked closely with Gartner Group to develop a best-in-class lease deal. Through an eight-step process, Gartner Group helped the client create its own money-saving master lease. The client was able to publish the lease and send it out with a request for proposal to selected lessors and enjoy substantial savings.

Client Saves More Than $500,000 on Storage System

By helping a client focus on what was important to its particular storage situation, Gartner Group was able to turn a confusing morass of vendor proposals into a stack that could be analyzed systematically. The company was able to choose a vendor proposal that not only delivered substantial cost savings, but also did not lock the company into a particular technical direction. By clearly defining its storage objectives, the client was able to save more than $500,000 on its storage system.

Dataquest Helps Start-up Grow By 45 Percent in One Year

Growing a small communications company from start-up to a major industry force doesn't happen by chance — it requires insightful understanding of market trends and dynamics. Dataquest worked with a client to provide the market data and competitive advice needed to develop new products that meet customers' needs. This focus enabled the company to grow by 45 percent in one year, dramatically enhancing its position prior to a highly successful initial public offering. This company has since grown to become one of the leaders in the communications field. Dataquest serves as a long-term partner to companies large and small, all over the world, helping them to formulate product plans, evaluate competition, assess market position, and define future marketing strategies.

Client Avoids $1 Million in Software Costs

Hardware savings usually grab the headlines during data-center consolidations, but unless a company is careful, software upgrade fees and licensing charges can quickly overwhelm the hardware savings. Gartner Group helped a large multinational company sift through software issues affecting the success of a massive consolidation of international data centers. The result? A potential $1 million charge was successfully avoided.

GartnerGroup

IT Glosssary *plus* 14 Executive Reports on One CD-ROM
The World's Best IT Research is Now Even Better!

Gartner Group Executive Report Library

Gartner Group Executive Summary Reports
— *A Resource Unique in the Industry*

- **Distilled from the world's best IT research...** Report contents extracted from Gartner Group Conference Notes, Research Notes and Strategic Analysis Reports

  - **Spotlight Key Issues that will need IT management attention...** A look into the future, not the past

    - **Written with the busy executive in mind...** Easily read — rich in charts, graphs and tables to save you time

      - **A comprehensive view of the industry...** Strategic research covers technologies, products, vendors and directions.

The Gartner Group Executive Report Library on CD-ROM

For Windows and Mac

Keyword **SEARCH** on entire contents of each report

Direct **HYPERLINKs** from report Table of Contents to desired sections

PRINT selected sections, one page or an entire report

FREE COPY of Adobe Acrobat Reader for Windows 3.1, Windows 95, Windows NT and Mac included on disk

---

Gartner Group
Executive Report Library

Reports are available for purchase individually or as an entire library

GartnerGroup
Your Personal Information Technology Advisor

Entire contents © Copyright 1997 Gartner Group, Inc. 56 Top Gallant Road Stamford, CT 06904-2212

All rights reserved

IT Glossary plus 14 Executive Reports on one CD-ROM

This disk contains:
14 Executive Reports plus the new Gartner Group IT Glossary (for Windows and Mac)

Plus:
- Overview of all available Executive Reports
- Sample pages
- Tables of contents
- Adobe Acrobat Reader for Windows and Mac
- Reference web site

Order code 5492

Reports 5302, 5306, 5307, 5309, 5310, 5311, 5400, 5401, 5402, 5403, 5405, 5407, 5413, 5414 plus the ITGlossary 5404

Published and distributed by: Gartner Group Direct Products
Two Stamford Landing, Stamford, CT 06902, U.S.A.
Telephone: 1-888-544-7337
E-Mail: jwhitney@info-edge.com

Order your IT Glossary on CD-ROM directly by
calling 1-888-544-7337 NOW!

ITGCD14

Save 25% off the list price of any of these Executive Reports when you purchase the new Gartner Group IT Glossary on on CD-ROM for $50

Here are the 14 Executive Summary Reports on the current CD-ROM Executive Report Library — a comprehensive management overview of the entire IT industry.

✔ for sample pages

☐ **Electronic Document Management: Selecting Successful Strategies, Systems and Products**
   Report # 5414   170 Pages   List Price $495

☐ **The RFP: A Strategic Tool for It Management**
   Report # 5413   270 Pages   List Price $995

☐ **Windows NT: Can Microsoft Capture the Enterprise Server Market?**
   Report # 5407   250 Pages   List Price $1295

☐ **Integrated Office Systems: Beyond Notes and E-Mail**
   Report # 5405   189 Pages   List Price $795

☐ **The New Applications Development Environment: Exploiting the Potential of Client/Server and Internet Technologies**
   Report # 5403   195 Pages   List Price $795

☐ **Managing Software Selection: From the Mainframe to the Internet and Everything in Between**
   Report # 5402   230 Pages   List Price $1295

☐ **IT in the Midsize Enterprise: Less Volume, But Not Fewer Challenges**
   Report # 5401   240 Pages   List Price $995

☐ **The New Data Center: Emergence of the Enterprise Operations Center**
   Report #5400   224 Pages   List Price $1295

☐ **Wide-Area Networks: The Electronic Road to the Global Enterprise**
   Report # 5311   229 Pages   List Price $595

☐ **Local-Area Networks: Managing Your First Link to the Rest of the World**
   Report # 5310   200 Pages   List Price $595

☐ **Information Technology Meets the Year 2000: Preparing for the Inevitable**
   Report # 5309   83 Pages   List Price $495

☐ **IT Services and Outsourcing: IS Replacement or IS Partner?**
   Report # 5307   180 Pages   List Price $795

☐ **End-User Computing: Finding Value on the Desktop**
   Report # 5306   213 Pages   List Price $995

☐ **The Internet and Electronic Commerce: Creating a New Business Model for the 21st Century**
   Report # 5302   306 Pages   List Price $1295

Order the IT Glossary *plus* individual reports *or* the entire library on CD-ROM from Gartner Group Direct Products

Call, Fax or E-Mail your order NOW!

Tel: 888-544-7337 or 1-203-363-7150
Fax: 800-760-9956 or 1-203-363-7155
E-mail: jwhitney@gartner.com

TO ORDER BY MAIL:

Jill Whitney, Gartner Group Direct Products,
Two Stamford Landing, Stamford, CT 06902, U.S.A.

YOUR ORDER:

Title	Code	Qty	US$ Price	Total
Glossary on CD-ROM	5404CD		$50	
Printed Glossary	5400		$50	

Shipping & Handling:
U.S. shipments add 5% of subtotal. International shipments add 20% of subtotal for documentation, duty and air express shipping via: DHL WORLDWIDE EXPRESS

SUBTOTAL: _____
Shipping & Handling: _____
CT only add 6% sales tax: _____
FINAL TOTAL US$: _____

Yes! I am interested. Please fax me sample pages from the report(s) ✔ checked.

Buy with confidence
Every report on CD-ROM comes with our 15-day money-back guarantee.

DELIVERY ADDRESS:

Name/Title: _____
Company: _____
Address: _____
_____
Postcode: _____ Country: _____
Tel: _____ Fax: _____
E-Mail Address: _____

PAYMENT: (Signature REQUIRED for ALL orders)

☐ Check made payable to **InfoEdge** in US$
Credit Card: ☐ Visa   ☐ Mastercard   ☐ AMEX
☐ Diners Club

Card No. _____ Exp. _____
Signature_____

ITGCD1

You Bought a Copy for the *Top of Your Desk* —
Would You Like a Copy on Your Desktop Too?

GartnerGroup

Put a Copy on Every Desktop...

hank you for purchasing the
artner Group Glossary of Information
echnology Acronyms and Terms.

e're sure that you will find this glossary a
luable addition to your Information
chnology reference sources. To bring the
formation provided by the *Gartner Group IT
ossary* immediately to you as you work, it is
o **available on CD-ROM** for both the
indows and the Mac environment for the
me low price of $50.

ere's even better news —
e CD-ROM on which the *IT Glossary* is deliv-
ed also contains more than a dozen Executive
ports based upon research from the world's
remost IT analysis company, Gartner Group.
y the *IT Glossary* and you will save **25% off**
e list price of any report that is purchased
m this CD-ROM. Just call the Gartner Direct
oducts Customer Service staff with your credit
rd information and you can have immediate
cess to one or all of these insightful reports.

make your decision easier, the CD-ROM also
ntains descriptions, tables of contents and
mple pages for the reports contained on it.

olume discounts and our multiple user
enses now make it possible to put the information con-
tained in the
Gartner Group IT
Glossary at the
fingertips of your
entire organiza-
tion at prices **as
low as $3.00
per user**. Call
now for more
information.

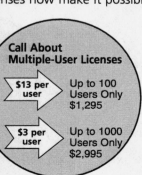

**Call About
Multiple-User Licenses**

$13 per user → Up to 100 Users Only $1,295

$3 per user → Up to 1000 Users Only $2,995

To Order:

 By fax: Jill Whitney, at (800) 760-9956 or
1-203-363-7155 from outside the U.S.A.

 By mail: Jill Whitney, Gartner Direct Products,
Two Stamford Landing, Stamford, CT 06902, U.S.A.
E-mail: jwhitney@info-edge.com

By phone: Call Jill Whitney, at (800) 544-7337
or 1-203-363-7150 from outside the U.S.A.

❏ **I Would Like To Order:**

___ Copies of IT Glossary #5404 (__ Copies of Book, __ CD-ROM)
@ _____ price per copy (*See table below*)   _____

Shipping & Handling: _____

CT only add 6% sales tax: _____

FINAL TOTAL U.S.$:   _____

Shipping & Handling:
U.S. shipments add 5%
of subtotal. International
shipments add 20% of
subtotal for documenta-
tion, duty and air
express shipping via:

DHL WORLDWIDE EXPRESS

Buy with confidence:
Every report on CD-ROM
comes with our 15-day
money-back guarantee.

Price Schedule for IT Glossaries
(Total quantity of books & CD-ROMs
apply to discount level)

Quantity	Price
1 - 4	$50 each
5 - 9	$45 each
10 - 49	$40 each
50 - 100	$30 each
Over -100	$20 each

Delivery Address:

Name/Title: _____

Company: _____

Address: _____

_____

Postcode: _____ Country: _____

Tel: _____ Fax: _____

Payment: (*Signature required for all orders*)

❏ Check payable in U.S.$ to **InfoEdge**

❏ Visa ❏ Mastercard ❏ AMEX ❏ Diners Club

Card No. _____ Exp. _____

Signature _____

ITGCD